D1129182

The Immigrant years

The Immigrant Years

FROM EUROPE
TO CANADA
1945-1967

Barry Broadfoot

Douglas & McIntyre
Vancouver/Toronto

Copyright © 1986 by Barry Broadfoot

86 87 88 89 90   5 4 3 2 1

All rights reserved. No part of this book may be reproduced or transcribed in any form by any means without permission in writing from the publisher, except by a reviewer, who may quote brief passages in a review.

Douglas & McIntyre Ltd., 1615 Venables Street
Vancouver, British Columbia V5L 2H1

Canadian Cataloguing in Publication Data
Broadfoot, Barry, 1926-
    The immigrant years

    ISBN 0-88894-519-1
    1. Canada - Emigration and immigration -
Biography. 2. Canada - Social conditions -
1945-1971.* I. Title.
FC608.I4B76 1986   971.06'092'2   C86-091221-3
F1034.2.B76 1986

Typeset by The Typeworks
Printed and bound in Canada by Imprimerie Gagné Ltée.

Photo Credits
Endpapers: Canadian Pacific
Frontispiece: Canadian National/X 32168
Chapter openings: (1) Canadian National/47417-5; (2) Lt. C.H. Richer photograph, Dept. of National Defence Collection, Public Archives of Canada/PA 128179; (3) Svarre/Cantlon Photographers Ltd., Dept. of Manpower and Immigration Collection, Public Archives of Canada/PA 124956; (4) Gilbert A. Milne Ltd. photograph, Dept. of Citizenship and Immigration Collection, Public Archives of Canada/PA 127043; (5) Victor Aziz photograph, Dept. of Citizenship and Immigration, Public Archives of Canada/ PA 124829; (6) Canadian National/X 32436; (7) Victor Aziz photograph, Dept. of Manpower and Immigration Collection, Public Archives of Canada/PA 124818; (8) Sudbury Daily Star photograph, Dept. of Citizenship and Immigration Collection, Public Archives of Canada/ C 45087

To LORI
always the right girl

Contents

Preface

Looking back now on those years following the Second World War, I realize that I was not really conscious of what was going on. Few Canadians then were aware that a major change was beginning to take place in Canada, because it was happening slowly, quietly, and did not disrupt our smug lives in any material way.

In 1946, an army veteran friend introduced me to his war bride, a strange term as they already had two children born in England. The swamper on the coal truck, lugging hundred-pound sacks into our basement in Winnipeg, spoke no English. The local fruit and vegetable peddler introduced his new helper, a nephew from Italy. Later reporting assignments in Vancouver took me to an interview with a Hungarian professor at the University of British Columbia, the arrival of several large Dutch families at a new farm colony, the murder of a Finnish logger in False Creek, and so on.

New people were coming into the country, starting with the arrival in 1945 and 1946 of 48 000 British and European women who had married Canadian servicemen, accompanied by their 22 000 children. While not true immigrants, these women found Canadian customs, manners and habits just as strange as the 2 500 000 immigrants from

Britain and twenty-seven other European countries who arrived in Canada between 1945 and 1967.

I should explain at this point that this book deals with only British and European immigrants. Although another 600 000 people from other places also came to Canada during those years—including 240 000 Americans—their reasons for coming and their aims and backgrounds are so diverse that there is no real focus to bind them together. In short, they did not come to Canada to escape the aftermath of the Second World War.

The influx of European immigrants had an ebb and flow—125 000 came in 1948, 250 000 in 1957, 194 000 in 1966—and while the yearly figures were not significant in relation to the growing Canadian population, the newcomers were to have a noticeable impact on the very identity and social and cultural face of the nation. Half of all immigrants settled in Ontario. The ethnic mix of many cities, especially Toronto, was changed by these immigrants—called "New Canadians," a government term that never caught on.

Since 1930, Canada had had virtually no overseas immigration because of the Depression of the Thirties and the Second World War. The first huge wave of immigrants who had arrived early in the century and in the Twenties had already been absorbed, so there was considerable consternation among Canadians at the prospect of more immigration. Citizens feared that vast hordes of newcomers would have a negative effect on their small population, which by the end of the war in 1945 was only 11 500 000. Moreover, that population was polarized between those of French and British backgrounds; only twenty per cent of Canadians were of other national heritage.

But it was more than racism that caused forty-six per cent of Canadians to declare in a 1946 Gallup Poll that they did not want British immigrants. Sixty-one per cent did not want immigrants from Europe. Despite the euphoria of the war's end, basking in the pride of Canada's huge industrial strides and its astonishing military effort, Canadians were thinking about economics and, specifically, employment. Jobs.

About 950 000 service personnel were being discharged to re-enter civilian life, and Canadians remembered vividly the deep recession that had followed the First World War. Where would all these ex-service people find jobs? What about the million men and women who had been working in war production? What would they do if there was a recession or if plants closed down or were slow in converting to peacetime production? Such fears were valid.

And what would Canada do with these immigrants, the British weary of war, tired of rationing and facing massive unemployment and looking to Canada, a land with British ideas and values and speech, as a place where they could go to get a fresh start? What would Canada do with the tens of thousands of refugees from Germany, Poland and eastern Europe, their homes and cities destroyed, despairing and without hope, fearful of the Russian armies on the frontiers, penniless and seeking a totally new life?

Fortunately, the naysayers were wrong and the economists were right. Canada did not fall into a recession. War industries were rapidly converting to make other products, creating peacetime jobs to fill. And now that women who had worked in war factories were returning to the home, a baby boom arrived. Businesses were expanding. Canada and Canadians became affluent.

There was no shortage of good jobs for Canadians. But there were other jobs, many thousands of them, that were less desirable but had to be filled. Construction, road building, railroad repair, logging, mining and fishing—often these were jobs that the now pocketbook-healthy Canadians just did not want. They were dirty jobs, usually low paying and often dangerous, in isolated areas. In the cities were the menial jobs in restaurants, laundries and garment sweatshops.

Agriculture was another major sector that needed workers. Throughout the war, the nation's farmers had been crying for help, despite the more than fifteen thousand German prisoners of war and about thirteen thousand Canadian conscientious objectors who had been used as cheap labour. These men were no longer available and had to be replaced.

Overseas, there was a vast labour pool of more than a million Displaced Persons, or DPs as they came to be called—a term that immigrants came to detest, as its use was usually accompanied by a sneer. International relief organizations were keeping these people alive, barely, in the refugee camps of Europe. They were the first to emigrate to Canada, moving in masses on ships to Halifax and Montreal, then onto trains to destinations—farms, cities, logging camps, mines—chosen for them by immigration officials. The Displaced Persons filled the dirty jobs, but they were free. That was all that mattered to them, though the problems most of them faced were enormous. Usually, they spoke no English, had little or no money and no marketable skills; the few skilled ones found that the unions shut them off from the good jobs and had to settle for the jobs that Canadians did not want. The professions also shut them out, creating sad situations where a brain surgeon from Czechoslovakia could be washing dishes in a cheap Montreal café; the reason given for excluding them was that European standards did not measure up to those of Canada. Immigrant workers were exploited, of course. Tales of horror emerged of whole families indentured to one or two years of farm work under slave labour conditions for almost no wages.

Most of those who came to Canada from Europe had a hard time of it. Alone, or in a family alone, without funds, lodged in cramped quarters, not speaking English and unfamiliar with Canadian ways, their plight was often desperate. Federal agencies did, however, provide some help, and school boards set up English classes. The churches pitched in to aid them in any way they could, and ethnic organizations, well established in most cities, helped their own people. Some newcomers found friends, Canadians willing to reach out a hand and show some kindness.

The flow of skilled immigrants began, too, highlighted by the plan of Ontario Premier George Drew, who airlifted about seven thousand Britons and their families to work in his province's factories. The cautious Liberal government of Prime Minister Mackenzie King decreed that Britons would be given first priority, along with Scandinavians and the Dutch. The French were later added to this category. All the rest were considered second priority.

Canada was competing with the United States, Argentina, Brazil and Australia for skilled immigrants, but they wanted only the best. Extensive advertising was carried out in Britain and selected European cities, and a point system was used for admission. At least fifty points were needed: occupational skills counted for fifteen points; a good education, twenty points; being a healthy young male, ten points, and so on.

Even today, immigrants complain that through zeal or lack of information about their own country, some Canadian immigration officials painted far too rosy a picture of conditions. After all, a poster showing a cool, beautiful mountain lake at Banff hardly compares with sweating it out for thirteen hours a day picking sugar beets in Picture Butte, Alberta.

British immigrants had it made in some senses. They spoke English and often had some money. They also usually had some factory or office skills and had good educations. They might even have relatives or friends to take them in, find them a place to live, steer them to a good job; hard labour at low wages and long hours was not for them. They headed mainly for the big cities. Almost a million Britons came to Canada between 1945 and 1967.

In the 1950s, more and more immigrants began arriving by air rather than by ship, a reflection of the growing wealth and sophistication of the newcomers. The number of managerial and professional immigrants rose from four per cent in 1950 to eleven per cent in 1957, and those with manufacturing and construction skills rose from eleven to twenty-four per cent. Year by year these proportions grew higher, and in 1967 the percentage of professional, managerial and skilled immigrants was about eighty per cent; labourers and agricultural workers were a mere six per cent. Many of these people spoke some English and found much greater acceptance from employers and ordinary Canadians.

Canada's cultural life has been greatly enriched by the contributions that European immigrants have made because of the enthusiastic way most of them entered into the mainstream of society. The evidence is everywhere, not so much in themselves, perhaps, but in the deeds and accomplishments of their children. Few became millionaires; the thirty-five-room mansion is a rarity and so is the yacht, but the comfortable, paid-for home and a runabout are the rule rather than the exception. Most did well and some helped bring more immigrants to Canada, especially the Italians in Toronto.

All they wanted was to make a new life and prosper: a job first, then a home and an education for their kids. They worked hard, terribly hard, to reach their goals. They asked only the chance to take fair advantage of the opportunities offered, and they knew that in order to make it they would have to do it all themselves.

For each one of them, there was the experience of coming to an alien and often hostile land. This book deals with the funny, cruel and heartbreaking stories of the first hour, often, or the first day, month or year; their wry impressions; the culture shock; the hardships and the first small victory that meant so much.

I can assure you that the great majority of immigrants are success stories—small, perhaps, in terms of wealth, but large in happiness, satisfaction and their contributions to Canada, their deep and true love of this nation. But the success of their children is what gives them their greatest feeling of pride.

Barry Broadfoot

1 FREEDOM AND A NEW LIFE

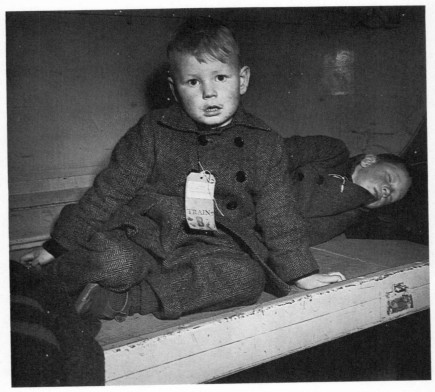

1 FREEDOM AND A NEW LIFE

After the war, people came to Canada for a hundred reasons that actually all zeroed down to one—a better life. To make a new life and prosper and to have their children grow up in a free country and without the threat of war.

Britain was sick, exhausted by war; much of Europe was finished, devastated. The Russian menace on the borders was too much to contemplate. Millions of people were homeless, penniless, full of despair and without hope.

Canada beckoned. Untouched by the long struggle, Canada was wide and open and clean, free of old animosities, a country that in European minds was still part of the frontier.

So the immigrants came, hesitant, perhaps fearful of what they might find, but with the hope that they would have a chance to make a new start. A chance to prove themselves. A chance to fulfill their dreams.

Canada certainly gave them that chance, but it was up to them to seize it. Of the 2 500 000 immigrants who came between 1945 and 1967, over a third were from Britain and, in the main, they expected to find a country not unlike their own. They were right and wrong. The tens of thousands of

Displaced Persons who came in the late Forties had nothing left in their own countries; they found a land of plenty beyond their dreams and were willing to work hard for every bit of recognition. They were the most grateful, and today they still are.

Later, other immigrants came because they had friends or relatives in Canada or had been excited by letters home praising the new land. How many came because of American movies, and how many left for the United States once they had become "Americanized" in Canada will never be known. But the vast majority put down their roots and stayed.

People came to Canada for all the right reasons and all the predictable ones: to get a good job, to find a good life for themselves and their families. But they still love their homelands and keep some of the old ways, the customs and traditions, the feasts, the food, the language in the home; and I think that is good, for it adds to the depth and vigour that makes Canada a cosmopolitan nations.

TIME TO GET OUT

It was 1944, and my father said it was time to get out. We had to get out of Latvia. He said he could see terrible times ahead with the Russians.

This was the time when the fishermen were taking people out. They demanded pure gold in payment. Money was worth nothing. Nobody knew what the value of money was, so they wanted gold. They always took more people than they could on their boats. I mean they'd take gold from eighty people, but their boat could only handle forty people. That was the kind of people they were. The rest were out of luck.

One day my father was walking along the dock and he saw the boat was getting ready to go, so he came back, and my mother packed one small suitcase, and at night we went down to the dock and we got on. Next morning they landed people on the island of Gotland, at a town there, and the Swedes took us in. Sweden was pretty socialist, and we thought we should go to Canada.

We went on the *Gripsholm*, which was a famous Red Cross ship during the war, and they landed us at Halifax and sent us to Ajax in Ontario, where there was a big replacement camp. My father had had to sign a paper saying we would work for a suger beet farmer at Lethbridge but, thank God, we didn't have to go to Lethbridge. Oh, what

I've heard of those sugar beet farms! But I came down with measles, and so we did not have to go on the train to Lethbridge with all the other families.

So they sent us to Niagara Falls. We worked in the orchard there, working for a family. My mother and father and me, we all worked, and I was just a little kid. About six years old. Sure, I picked fruit too. We had to to live. I remember clearly, one week, I made three dollars.

I don't know how much we made. I know that three dollars I got for that week, that to us was a lot of money in those days. I don't know, oh, when you're that age you don't worry about things like that. But my mother and father were picking, and so was my grandfather who had come over with us. He had been the minister of railways for the Latvian government before the war, so he maybe had some money to help us out, and my father, being university trained, he spoke English.

But there was a lot of cultural shock. A lot.

FREEDOM AND BEEF STEW

To be free. To be free in a country that is free. That is why we came to Canada. No other reason at first. Just freedom.

I don't know how. I didn't read about it. I didn't know any Canadians or about Canada. I just knew it would be a free country, and when I said to my wife, "This camp is no good, we'll be here forever, so we're going to Canada," she said, "Good. It will be free, a place where we can have our children being free."

In the camp where we were interviewed, the Canadian official said Winnipeg would be a good place to go. I didn't care. I didn't know where Winnipeg was. It sounded like it might have been an Indian word. He said, "There are a lot of Jewish people and they will look after you. They have organizations and things like that and if you want, they will find you a place to stay and a place to work."

That's the way it was. We were met at the station by the hotel which is torn down, the Royal Alexandra, and there was a big bunch of refugees. We were called Displaced Persons. No home, no money. Nothing. Just ourselves and our kids, and saying we want to be free.

First they put us into a hall over there on Selkirk, but just for about four days and then, how they did it, I don't know. I knew there was a big shortage of places, but these Jewish ladies . . . I call them Jewish because I'm not. Only Sarah is. It didn't matter. They found this old house on Cathedral away out and there were two other families with us. That didn't matter. We all spoke German and Czechoslovakian and some English, and we got along and they gave us money for food. That was the first time I saw a supermarket. Not like the ones now. This was a tiny one. I remember the name. Piggly Wiggly. You don't see them any more. Gone, gone.

The food. Look, mister, in the camps there was no food, and this was in October of 1946 when we left, some of the first ones to come to Canada. You got a bowl of soup. You might find a bit of meat in it. Tiny, like this. No bigger than this, my thumbnail. Bread at first was terrible, so we baked our own bread and then it got better. A few potatoes. Turnips. You know, not much vitamins, I think.

So the food. Jesus Christ! I never even saw so much food in any store in Prague, even before the Germans came. That was the Putsch. Remember? That started the world war. Not Hitler going into Poland. Nah! Nah! It was Hitler pushing around little Czechoslovakia.

Then the government people, the employment office, they said we'd have to work. We should have been going to farms, but it was coming winter, so they said, "You, Jacob, you, Josef, and so on, you'll go here and you'll go there." I went to work for the paint company, Sherwin Williams. Labour work, but not bad. I got good pay.

Then we felt we couldn't live in the house anymore. Too many people, you see. The committee said, okay, Jacob, it was going to be hard, but they went around and found a little apartment on Ellice Avenue, and it was tiny, but who cares. We were together, Sarah, the two girls, me, we didn't care. We had pots and pans and blankets and I bought a little radio in a secondhand store and a bed and a table and some chairs, and we did okay. We listened to the radio all the time, and the girls learned English that way. So did Sarah and me. We learned better from listening to the guys on the radio.

Oh, sure, there was a lot more. We went for walks when I could buy better clothing, boots, you know. Warm underwear. We went to the park, they called it City Park. Assiniboine Park. You know it? We'd go on Sundays and nobody would be there, and all this snow on the ground, and we'd run around. Even me. Laughing, saying we're free. This is a free country. We're in it. Look at the trees. Hear the train whistle way over there. There might be a rabbit we could chase. And nobody there. Eight hundred acres, maybe more. Ours. The girls would run and jump and play in the snow, and we would walk about three miles home, and I'd think, why don't Canadians go to their wonderful park? See, nobody was there.

Then we'd walk home. There would be the big stew and dumplings ready—just turn on the electric range and it would start bubbling. The dumplings. And we'd have ice cream after. Hot tea and ice cream.

When Christmas came, people from the committee came with a huge box. Presents. For Sarah, Julie, Pippi, for me, and we didn't ask for them. They'd come, say "Merry Christmas," and I'd say, "Thank you, we are very happy. You are so nice. What kindness you are showing us."

That was Christmas of 1946. We didn't have a turkey. I don't think there was any way to cook it. We had stew and dumplings again, but it was the best in the world. Then we prayed before we ate, and I said, "Remember, children, a year ago we were in the camp and what we had to eat. Remember?" They said yes.

That Christmas was the best we ever had. I wish I could write a poem about it. I'm no good at that stuff, but I had it in my heart what I would say. I'd say, "Canada, all you people in it, excuse my bad English, but my wife and babies and me, we thank you. We thank you so much." I could cry.

HER WEDDING RING WAS ALL WE HAD

We had been what they call upper-middle-class, and the war hadn't touched us, no bombs, no fighting—but when the fighting got close and the Russians were coming from the east and the Americans from the west, we hid in the forest and we couldn't take a thing. It happened very fast as the war was ending. We panicked. We ran. We didn't think at all.

The Russians got to our town and they took over our house, and a week later when our food ran out we walked back, and these animals had smashed up our house. They took everything, smashed everything up. The only thing they didn't do was burn it down, so we could live in it.

All we had was my wife's wedding ring, which had been her mother's, too, and her grandmother's, and it was very valuable by now.

Now I won't tell you about the next five years because it was too awful, too terrible to tell, but finally we were given the right to come to Canada. We had lived in camps, in fields, in towns where we had to work hard for nothing but food and a place to sleep, and we thought it would never end. Never. But it did. We got permission to come to Canada. Just the two of us. Not her father or my mother. They won't come. Just me and my wife. Then I was fifty-three. She was fifty-two. Too old, you'd think.

When we got to Toronto, the relief people came to the station and took us to a place to sleep. They fed us and looked after us and found us a room to stay. Bathurst Street. It was small, but it was fine. I worked washing dishes for six weeks or about that, and then I got on working on the subway. It was dirty and hard work, but the wages were good.

We thought, what will we do now? We had money, and my wife was working on Queen Street East sewing in a factory. We had about seventy dollars together a week, and I said, "The lady who owns this house wants to sell it. We should buy it." We had $1,100 saved in the eight months I had been working on the subway. She was now a cook at a café.

This was 1951 now. I told her if we took the thousand and sold the wedding ring, we should have three thousand dollars, because that ring was very valuable. She burst into crying. She cried and cried, and then she told me that when she was washing dishes she had been wearing the ring. I stopped her and said that was a stupid thing to do. Then more crying. She said it had slipped off her finger through the slipperiness of the soap, and she had lost it down the drain. She's afraid to tell me, see? She thought it had gone down the drain and into the pipes and was now in the lake. She didn't know that much about plumbing and thought, you can see, that plumbing was like we had in the Old Country.

This was a Sunday, and I phoned a friend of mine, this Austrian who was a plumber's helper on the subway. He brought some tools over to the café. There he was twisting with his wrenches and swearing, my wife started to cry again, and then he got out the U-pipe, and after shaking and pouring water in and poking, ha ha, out comes the ring. Nothing wrong with it. We all danced around a little and then Joe got a big kiss on the schnozzle from my wife, and I gave him one too, and he put the things back and that was it. We had a bottle of rye whisky, and the three of us had a party. That was a good time.

We sold the ring. I took it to a jewellery store and I said, "I know this ring is worth five thousand dollars but if you give me three thousand for it I will sell it." The man looked at it for a long time and said to come back in two days. When we went back, he said he would give us $2,500, and that's what we took.

We knew he knew we were immigrants, so he could take advantage of us. That is why I said it was worth five thousand dollars and that I wanted three thousand. You see, two thousand is what we wanted for it. That ring would be worth maybe sixty thousand right now. That's over with. We needed two thousand and got $2,500. Oh boy, that was good.

Then he wrote us a cheque, and my wife said now she didn't have a wedding ring and what would people think. The jeweller, this little guy with a beard, he reached onto a shelf and brought down a tray of rings. He said to take her pick, make a choice of one. She looked and finally picked one. "This one," she said. He said, "On the house." It was maybe a $20 ring, but it looked good.

With the savings and the ring money we put a three thousand dollar payment on the house and took it over that week. The lawyer just rushed it through as if our money would go away. In two years we paid off the other three thousand and we owned the house, and that was the start of being a success in Canada.

It was so easy those days. You just had to have imagination and move fast and work very hard and that was it. It all came to you. Oh, yes, of course. You are right. You had to have a wife with a diamond wedding ring. A big one like she had. A big, big one.

WE FEARED THE GROWLING
RUSSIAN BEAR

The Germans, we would suffer. The Russian Bear was only thirty miles away in East Prussia, and we knew that their tanks would go right through to the French Atlantic coast very quickly. Then all Europe would be Communist.

That's why I brought my wife and three children to Canada. They wanted us because we had money and I was director of a company. I had skills. We didn't come in a leaky old boat like the first people did after the war. We flew in a British airliner and although it was a long trip to Toronto, it was pleasant. We were not your poverty people.

Tired of life. Scared of living. We were well dressed and well fed. We had lots of money because we had sold our house and possessions and our two cars.

When we got to Toronto, we moved into an apartment. My wife's cousin found it for us. We both spoke English and the children did, too. At school they had learned it. I needed it in business. My wife was a teacher.

I got a job in a month with General Electric, and my wife got a job teaching in a private school. She taught German. Our children went to a nice school and were well behaved and got good marks. We, well, it was as if we decided to visit Canada on a vacation and decided to stay because we like it. Do you understand this?

It was not because we did not like our homeland any more. It was because of the Russian war menace and the childish way the Americans were acting, and we had to get out. Canada was there. So big. Quiet and peaceful. That's why we chose Canada. We love it here, but we didn't come for the ordinary reasons. A lot of Europeans were just like us.

We thought the Russian Bear was too close, and growling.

JUST A REFUGEE, A DP

This was in 1952. Yugoslavia was put back together again. I mean Tito the Communist was in full control, and I was a student, and there was nothing I liked about the way he was doing things. It may be the least harsh now of the Communist states, but it still is one, believe me. It was a very harsh place then.

On consideration, I suppose I could be put down as a traitor. I'll tell you why. I was a student at the university, and we had to sign a declaration that when we graduated in engineering, you became an engineer in Yugoslavia wherever they wanted to send you. I signed. Everyone signed. If you didn't, you were sent into the army and, my God, nobody wanted that. Treat people like cattle, and poor cattle at that. Or you went on work gangs.

I graduated, and we got married the week after, and I was to be sent on a dam-building job, no wives allowed, but we had made our plans. We had to have a honeymoon, and we decided we would tell the police—because you couldn't leave your political district otherwise—that we were going to Porec. That's a little village on the coast.

I said I had an uncle who owned an inn there. I didn't have an uncle, but Porec was just a hop, step and jump from Trieste and Trieste was freedom. We made it. We stole a motor launch one night and just putted across, and that's how I headed ourselves to Canada.

It was so easy. I hear people talk about how hard it was. Not for us. We were blessed by the stars that night. I was an engineer and Marta was a teacher, and we could have gone to the United States. In fact, she wanted to go there. I thought, America is too crowded. But Canada is not. Canada, will you take us? "Sure," the immigration officer said. "When do you want to go?" "Now." "Okay, sign here and there's a ship leaving Naples for Montreal in a week. Do you want to be on it?" "Sure," and off we go with our two little bags of clothing and necessities and not a cent to our name. They gave us twenty-five dollars, the limit. When we got to Montreal, I had the grand total of eleven dollars, and that got us to Toronto.

On the ship, one of the officers I got to know said that if we did get to Toronto and needed help, there was plenty. There was a booth in the station, but if you want the right kind of help, do this. He handed me a piece of paper, and he'd written "Kensington Market" on it. Just that. He said to go there and we'd find friends. It was an ethnic market. It still is, of course. You can go down there any day and buy a lot of produce and things you won't find anywhere else. It is also a grab bag, a big junk store, and a lot of it is rip-off now. Yes, very much so, but that's the Canadian way of life. Not then. It was different and it was Canadians and Italians and Greeks and Ukrainians and the odd Chinese guy and, well, all nations.

The first day we went there and asked a few questions, and in five minutes we were sitting in the back of a shop run by a family of Croats. Now, Croats and Slovenes never did get along too well at home, but they wanted to know everything that was happening in Yugoslavia. An artificial country then, before and now, but it works, I'd say. People forget old feuds.

We went home to stay with them that night, and there was a big party, and we told the Kropics and their friends who came in, drinking wine and eating cakes, all about how we got out and how it was at home. I'll just pass over that part of it, but I will say this. We got our start from those people. They'd been in Canada for twenty years or so, right in Toronto, and I got a job in a laundry plant and Marta got a job in the Royal York Hotel. In each place there was one of these people. They worked there, and they told the boss, "These are good people and they should get a break. They are fleeing Communism." In those days that would do it every time. The iron curtain. Czechoslovakia. Stalin. Flaming words.

I should tell you this. I never heard it happening where a refugee, people like us, they ever got a job like me becoming an engineer or Marta becoming a teacher. Maybe later. I was lucky. Marta never did become a real teacher. She taught, but in ethnic schools and where ethnic people met. It just did not happen. You had fairly good English and a good education and I could design a bridge, but a refugee never—and I mean never—got a job right off the whistle. It took time. It was so Canadian.

Refugees, landed immigrants as we were, we were expected to do jobs that Canadians did not want. Working in a laundry at the sorting bins was no picnic. Washing walls in the hotel, making beds, that was no picnic, either.

You had to get over the stigma of being a refugee. The term DP was a dirty word. "Oh, he's just a damned DP. He'll work for nothing because he has to." There was no other work.

You had to accept this attitude. I know doctors and accountants and men who had been directors of companies, and they did what they could get to do. If you accepted it, then it was okay. Then you worked your fingers to the bone and saved money. No overtime. Just straight pay. You lived in poor apartments and ate frugally and when you had enough money, you busted out. Got your real freedom in Canada. That's it! Your real freedom!

Canada would let you in, but they wouldn't exactly help you. "Work hard like me and you'll be a success," and this was the foreman of our shift at the laundry, that was him talking. Who ever said a foreman of a bunch of DPs was a success? That was another thing about Canadians I could never figure out. It just didn't make sense.

Then spring came and I got on as a draftsman at Bright's, an engineering company. A small outfit, and I spent the next winter in the designing department at much better pay. I think I was up to $1.50 an hour by then, and that was fine. Food was cheap. Lodging was cheap. The Toronto Symphony was about one dollar a ticket. Transportation—you didn't need a car.

They were building the Trans-Canada Highway then, and I was sent out to supervise bridges. After all, they were my designs. That was $2.75 an hour, and we were doing well. We had lots of friends we could talk with in our own language and lots of Canadian friends who didn't think we were just DPs. That summer and fall I was out in the bush putting in these new bridges, and we saved a lot of money. I had no expenses, and Marta had two jobs because she had nothing else to do around the apartment. We saved a lot of money, and in 1955 we started this little drafting company with two helpers and Marta working in the office, and we were a success right from the start.

You see, I saw an opportunity. All these small companies. Why should they have their own drafting sections when we could do it for them? They brought in their work until we had to hire two University of Toronto fellows that summer, too. The small engineering and construction companies saved a lot, and we made quite a bit of money. It was something that wasn't done much. They'd never thought of it.

Okay, there you have it, briefly. In five years we were sitting pretty. A cock and a hen sitting on a lot of eggs that hatched money.

WHAT I'VE BEEN THROUGH

I was from Yugoslavia. I won't go into the reasons why some Croatians were in the German army, but I'll tell you this, right here and now—most of us didn't want to be, but it was do that or die and have our families killed too.

So, these hundreds of thousands of people, and most of them innocent, when they were captured by the British and Americans, they were turned over to the Russians, and most of the soldiers were executed or died in Russian labour camps in Siberia.

I knew what was happening, and before we were to be marched back to Yugoslavia, I escaped the camp I was in. I had a black passport. That means I had no passport and I would sneak across borders at night. I wore civilian clothes and I scrounged, and there were tens of thousands of other scroungers like me, so nobody would know me from another guy.

In 1947 I had a chance to go to Canada because I was in a refugee camp in Germany and, believe me, talk to anybody who was in those camps and you'll find out how tough that was. The food was getting better, but it was still very poor. Soup would be potatoes and cabbage and maybe a bit of meat, a scrap, and a slice of black bread. That was it. It kept you alive, and after what I'd been through, okay, it was enough to live on.

You got a medical, and I got through that, although I'm not sure how. I had a talk, with an interpreter, see, with the immigration guy, and they tried to find out if you had been a criminal and why you wanted to go to Canada. The damned fool! Then a man from the Department of Labour, I think, he talked to you and he'd say, "Well, would you be willing to work on a farm in Canada?" What he was saying was if you want to go to Canada, you will have to work on a farm for a year. They had complete control of our lives and our futures.

GOOD-BY, CONTRACT!

If you wanted to work for a farmer, then the Canadian government would pay your passage, and your contract was for a year, and you paid the government back at so much a month. If you were a person who didn't want to work on a farm under contract, then there was much more red tape, and you had to have a certain amount of money to carry you for two months until you got a job, and you had to pay your own way.

Nodody earned much money in Britain in 1950—if you had a job. At times I wondered if Britain would ever recover from the war. It showed no signs of doing so, and there was great disillusionment everywhere, and the returned men were definitely not getting a fair shake.

That's why I left, and on the *Empress of England* there were, oh, maybe two hundred emigrants, and from what I could gather, they were all bound for farms under contract in Ontario. I thought, bound to the land like a serf for a year! My God! But they slept in the same staterooms as I did and ate the same meals, and jolly good they were, and they all seemed in good spirits.

In Montreal off we went to Toronto on the train, and then I saw why they were so jovial a lot of jolly Britons. If I saw one, I saw ten of those men tear up their contract papers and let them flutter away in little pieces. Good-by, contract! And when they got off at Union Station, they just disappeared into the crowds of Toronto, and there went the farmer's chances, but no sympathy for him. No. They paid dreadfully low wages. But there went the contract to pay the passage, and they didn't give a hoot! Not a dribble of a hoot! They'd done someone else in. Ha ha!

ALONG FOR THE FREE RIDE

On the boat there were enough people who had got letters from their relatives who had gone to these farm jobs, and I spoke some German and that helped, so I would hear these people talking and understand.

A lot of these people were just using the free ride thing. A free passage and food and guidance, and when they got to Canada they did not intend to undergo the conditions their relatives and friends had described. I don't blame them. Those letters, they did not make it sound very good.

That was when I made up my mind. When we got to Toronto and some would be sent to London and Chatham and Thamesville and Delhi and places where we were to go, I would just slip away, and that's just what I did. I kept my papers, you know, but as we said it then, we tore up our tickets, and if you had a bit of money, maybe thirty dollars, Toronto was such a big place you could just slip away and never be heard of for a long time. That's what I did. Hundreds did it.

The government didn't seem to care. I never saw anything in the papers about immigrants being caught, sent back home. Punished. Told they had to go and work for some farmer. Nothing. We just quit, we vanished.

THE POLICE WERE GOOD GUYS

I don't know why, but they wouldn't let us in the dining car they had. This I couldn't understand, and there was nobody to look after us. We were from the camps, although this was 1948, so you can see that I had been in the camp a long time, though it wasn't too bad. There was food, soup and things like that, bread, meat, and if you worked, you could get more. This was why, when I heard that the Canadians would let us come to Canada, that's when I said I would go. The Russians were in Poland and I couldn't go back there because I would have been shot. Yes, shot.

I had been taken out by the Germans when I was thirteen to work in Germany on a farm, so they said I would be shot as a traitor to Poland. If I went back, the Russians would have shot me. They just did things like that. I don't know. It was a crazy thing, that war, wasn't it?

I will tell you, there are a lot of people from Poland in this country will not even talk about those times, because it makes them cry. Still makes them cry.

I remember the day they let us off the train. It was May fifteenth and it was a Sunday. In the morning. I didn't speak English. Just about ten words. I had a little cloth bag and that was all I had. Everything. I had four dollars and my cousin Janz, who was with me, he had three dollars, and I don't think anybody had any more money.

I couldn't see any way why we should stay around the station. There was nobody to help us, so we started walking and we came to this park after a while and we lay down for a sleep. We had been sitting in this old railway car for four days and we were tired. Then we see two men coming to us and Janz said it was the police. They asked us something and I knew about police. I handed them my card, the one I wore around my neck, my name and where I was going. Then my papers. The one older guy, he looked at them and went like this, with his thumb, and they put us in the police car. That was the best thing that happened to us in Canada.

The police were good guys, and they took us to the police station, and soon another policeman came, and he started talking to us in our language. He wanted to know everything. Then he went away and came back with two cups of coffee and told us that he was doing something. "Just you wait here," he said. Run from a police station? I would have to be crazy. He was a nice guy, this guy who spoke Polish. He knew we had no money. He was trying to help.

Then he came back and talked some more, asking about how things were in the Old Country. I said I didn't know, but I thought everybody had been killed by the Germans and the Russians. He wanted to know how we had escaped, and I said how I had and Janz said how he did. This took some time, and he asked if we wanted to work on a farm. I said I thought we were supposed to, the paper we had signed, but nobody had been at the station to help us, so we had left.

He said he had an uncle at Hazelridge, which is near Winnipeg. He said there were lots of our people living there and they would take us. We could work on the farms, and we said okay, and this guy, I remember he smiled, and he said he had already arranged it. This policeman said we didn't have much choice, but it was nicer that we said we would go. Like we had made the choice.

That was my first day really in Canada, in Winnipeg. This Sunday, May fifteenth. The policeman said the station was on Rupert Street and we could walk around for a while but be back at five o'clock. Be sure. Five o'clock. He said, "Here, I'll give you a piece of paper," and he wrote "Police Station, Rupert Street" on it, and I still have it. He said to show it to somebody if we got lost.

Today, I know where we went. Along Portage Avenue and back the other side and down Main Street to the station and the park where the little Fort Garry is, and then we had coffee in a café. A man in the next booth came around and he started talking Polish to us. He worked for the railroad. He said Winnipeg was the best place for a Polish immigrant to be because so many people were Polish. He said there were social clubs, card clubs, dances, everything, and churches and stores with newspapers in Polish and books. He said it was the North End, a Polish, Ukrainian, Jewish town, and you could get Polish food, Ukrainian food, everything you wanted, and people all spoke Polish. I thought, this is fine. It was, too.

Then he said, "You hungry?" We said yes, and he said he'd give us a Canadian meal, and he called over the girl and that's how I got to know about the hamburger. The potato chips. The vinegar on them and the salt and ketchup. Honest, I had never seen any one of those things. And the ketchup. Like blood. I didn't want to use it, but we did and it was good. You should have seen us later when we'd go to a café! Ketchup over everything. The pie, even that. We were crazy guys.

This man said we seemed like good young men, and he wrote his name down and when we came to Winnipeg, phone him. We'd go to his place for a big Polish meal. He said he'd have other Polish people there. He said he had to go, but he said, "Learn English. Learn it the best you can. Don't wait. Now. It is important!" That's what he said. You can see, my English still isn't that good, not Canadian English, but it is good enough to make a good living in business. With furniture. New, secondhand, buy and sell, time payments. You know.

We go back to the police station and it is nearly five, and the police Polish guy is waiting there, and he's got his uncle. You'd call him an Old Country Polish guy. Big moustache. Blue eyes. White hair. Wide but short. He would have been one tough guy when he was young. We talk and then he says, "Okay, boys, into the car," and

away we went to the farm. We worked there for twenty-five dollars a
month for June and July and fifty dollars a month for harvest until the
end of September. Hazelridge, Dugald, Oakbank, around there, over
to Beausejour, and every chance I'm learning English.

There it is, kiddo. My first day in Canada, really. In Winnipeg. I
meet guys—three policemen, the guy in the café, the old man farmer,
and it was just the first day, but it was a very good day.

NO MONEY, NO FRIENDS, NOTHING

They said, okay, guys, here's your chance to go to Canada.
That is fine, we thought. I thought, I knew there were a lot of Polish
people in Canada. I'd see some of them and they'd help.

We were the Polish Division. All that fighting in Italy, and there
were a lot of us in France and the rest of the way to the end of the war.
In the north, with the British. Always with the British, but the Canadians were with the British too, and I'd met them and I thought they
were a hell of a good bunch of guys. Just like us.

I don't know how many of us said we'd go to Canada. Just about
everyone, I think, except the guys who were dead. And the ones who
wanted to go to England. Poland? Let me tell you, we couldn't go
back to Poland. We would have been killed. There was nothing there
for us. I would have loved to go home, to my father's farm at Poznan,
a good farm, and all those nice girls. But I figured they were all dead
now, killed by the Germans. I didn't even know what happened to my
father and my brother.

Most of the guys were the same, so we all came to Canada. All in a
bunch. In railway cars, they took us across from the east to the
prairies, and we worked on farms. That's when we found out that the
jobs we had with these farmers were the jobs that German prisoners of
war had been doing. Now, that was one awful surprise.

That is what Canada offered us. A job for us, but it was only to re-
place these bloody Germans, the kind we'd been killing in Europe.
You know, that's something to think about. I've thought about it a lot
and I was mad at first and for a long time, but I'm not mad anymore.
I'm a good citizen and I work hard and make good money, and what
good is it to get mad? Be a good Canadian, I say, and be happy and
forget the bad things the government did to us after the war.

THAT'S WHEN I MADE MY DECISION

I think it was 1951 when the Canadian government said, okay, we've got all the DPs we can handle. They were the people who had fled from their countries, or more likely, they had been scooped up by Germany and made to work in our war factories, and when the British won, these people had no place to go.

So, when they had been settled, or the free countries had done with them what they wanted, brought to Canada, the U.S., Rhodesia, Brazil, Argentina, then it was our turn.

I mean the Germans of Germany who wanted a new home, and I was one of them. I had put my name on a list about 1948. They called us Reiches. That meant we could emigrate to another country.

I was desperate to go. I had a wife and a job in Hamburg, but I did not like the idea of living there. Russia was so close. The Berlin blockade showed us all a thing or two. It showed there would be no mercy from the Communists.

I knew there would be another war, this time with Russia with the rest of the world—meaning the United States—doing the fighting. England was finished. Anyone could see that.

Canada, I thought. I had fought against the Canadians when they were in the Scheldt. That was the toughest fighting of the war for anybody. I thought, these are ordinary men like me, these Canadians, but when I saw what they could do, how they could fight, how they could die, that's when I said to myself—and I remembered it always—if a country can produce men like this, soldiers willing to die for freedom in the mud and slime, the Scheldt, then that is the country I would like to live in.

That's when I made my decision. Years before in that campaign against the Canadians.

HE WASN'T A WILD WEST TRAPPER

It was like a fairy tale. Nobody could believe it. Dutch people are hard-headed. This was something they couldn't believe. My family were shocked that I would do this thing. My Oma, who was sort of the head of the family anyway, she wanted to go to the police to stop it. That's the way these old people thought.

I got the letter in January of 1948, and I though the writing looked familiar. It was from Allan, and he said he didn't know if I was married, but he'd take a chance and write. He said he was still in love with me and if I was in love with him, would I come out to Canada and marry him? Would I marry him? I had never forgotten him.

I should say he was a Canadian soldier in the artillery, and he had stayed with our family in the winter of 1944, when there were no battles going on in Holland. He was stationed in a camp near and we saw a lot of each other. That's when I think we fell in love, but then the battles began and he moved with his regiment. I only saw him once again. After the armistice he came back once and, somehow, with all the family around and that business, nothing seemed to work again.

Then this letter. I wrote back and said I would come to Canada to marry him, and I waited a couple of days, and then told my mother and father. They told my grandmother and that's when old Oma went a little crazy. It just wasn't done. It was crazy. I think she sat up nights thinking of ways of how crazy it was.

Allan had said in his letter he worked in a little town in British Columbia called Ocean Falls, and he drew a map of British Columbia and marked Vancouver on it and put a dot where Ocean Falls was. It was so far away, up in the north. He said he had a good job in the paper mill and made good money, and he said they were building a hotel and we could get an apartment until he got a house for us. He said it was on the ocean, the town, and there were lots of women and kids there and the scenery was beautiful. Mountains all around. There were things he didn't say, things he couldn't say, but I found out later that you had to get in by a passenger boat. There were no roads.

In a month, I think it was, his letter came back. It was a parcel, you'd say, and there were all kinds of instructions and maps and pictures and things I had to sign at our city hall in Hilversum, papers the government had to sign. He told me the first thing I was to do was go to Amsterdam and see the Canadian immigration but, wait a week, he said, because it would take time for them to know about me. Oh, dear me, what a time, because here I was with my family running around like chickens with their heads off, and me, just a clerk in a tobacconist's shop, not knowing anything and having to go to Amsterdam and see these Canadian people.

I forgot to say, I was nineteen and Allan was twenty-four, and all the Lussiers, my family, were saying, "You don't know anything about him. He might be one of these Wild West trappers. Look where he comes from." I said, "You know him, he's eaten right at this table many times." I should have said that a lot of times he brought the food we ate. I said, "Does he look like a Wild West trapper?"

I went to Amsterdam with my brother, who was a schoolteacher, and we saw the Canadian immigration man, a nice man, very kind, and he said he had a file on me and did I have the money for the steamship to Canada and things like that.

I took out the money order Allan had sent me for four hundred dollars, and he said that would be enough. When it was settled we went back to Hilversum that night on the train and, well, I won't go into the next two months, but it was crazy. My family wouldn't let up on me. You know how stubborn a Dutchman can be. I was so upset, I think for the first week I could only eat soup, but then they got over it a bit and started planning what I would take. That sort of thing. Parties too, and people giving me gifts, mostly clothes, and that was good. A friend would unravel two of her precious sweaters and knit me a thick one so I wouldn't freeze to death in the Canadian sixty-below winter. Soon it was just a week before the boat for Canada, everybody was very kind, and Oma gave me some jewellery she had hidden from the Germans during the war. She said she hoped I would have a happy life in Canada and for me to remember her. We both cried then.

We got married in Vancouver and he took me to a place called Harrison Hot Springs for a little honeymoon. He said, "At home we've got mountains three times higher than this." I thought the mountains there were high, but they were just hills.

My husband, because that's what he was now, had telegraphed ahead, and a lot of his friends were at the dock when the boat came in. I never wanted that boat trip to end, so beautiful. Oh, the scenery, I never wanted it to end, never, never, never. I was in love with Ocean Falls before I even got there, but then I knew we would have to find a place to live. They were still building the St. Martin's Hotel then, so we couldn't stay there. Allan's friends put us in their house for a week while they went out to Vancouver, and the company held a party for us, everybody there in the school, and that was when I got the big surprise.

The manager stood up and said that the present they were going to give us was a house. We had to rent it, sure, but it was a real gift because others were wanting it, but he said because Allan was such a good worker and Louise, that's me, was from so far away, we could have the house. Everybody cheered, and next morning we went to the little house in the subdivision and hey, you know what? It was mostly furnished, cups and saucers, chairs and cushions, even bath towels. Everybody had known of the gift, and the people in the town had furnished it and kept it a secret the week we stayed at Allan's friends until they got it just right.

I thought how much I loved Canada and those awfully nice people at Ocean Falls, way up there, so far from everything, but working and bringing up their kids and, oh, it is hard to tell this way.

We stayed there seven years and then we decided our first child, maybe it would be best if she went to a city school, and the little girl would be going to school in two years, so we moved. I'll never forget the scenery and the narrow streets and picking up the mail and talking to people every day and, yes, the rain. It rained and rained and rained and rained, but I didn't mind it. When it cleared you could see the mountains. There were three of them, right up there. You could almost touch them.

WE FLED FROM OUR MEMORIES

A lot of people you will talk to will tell you they came to Canada because it was the Land of Promise. That it was paradise. Perhaps they had always dreamed of coming to Canada.

I would suggest you take these things with a liberal dose of salts. I would suggest many of these people from these European countries have convinced themselves this is so, but I do not believe it. I can speak from personal experience.

We came to Canada to forget what we had done to each other in the war. War is terrible, and it is also a great equalizer, and it reduces every person to the lowest common denominator. It means that it was a method of reducing every man and woman to the lowest common denominator, in that they only thought of themselves and then their loved ones. Everyone else in the country, the city, the village was their enemy, because they were all fighting to get that one thing, food. First, food, any food, food you wouldn't feed your worst dog today, food no government would allow to be sold or even fed to the poor.

So in Holland, that I know of personally, but also in Belgium, France, Germany after the war, all countries, I suppose, all of these countries the quest for food overwhelmed the common decencies each of us carry around in our genes. We fought for it. Lied for it. Stole for it. I suppose some killed for food. City man against city man. City man against townspeople, villagers and, naturally, everybody against the farmer, who did have some food and who profited mightily if he could sell it. No, barter it, five pounds of potatoes he'd hidden for our family heirloom. These things went on all the time.

People joined the Resistance, the Underground, not because they wanted to fight the German army and help liberate Holland. No, the Resistance had arms and organization and they knew how to get food and, if you risked your life, you were risking it for the food. To stay alive. A few potatoes. A bit of meat. The Resistance had access to food because they would act against the Germans, get food and arms, but their acts caused retaliation by the Germans against the ordinary people.

Look, I am not talking about Holland alone. This happened in France and other countries. It happened where people were starving.

Now we'll look at the end of the war. You've seen those pictures of Dutch girls being brought up before the Resistance committee in the village square and having their heads shaved because they had consorted, danced with, prostituted for the German troops. Fine, they were punished. But there were a lot of others who were not. Those women were just the highly visible ones.

So, for many, so very many, Holland was a land of bad memories. They did these things. They saw things being done they should have stopped. They . . . well, I'm sure a lot of them said, "I don't think I want to live in this country anymore."

Juliana had lived in Canada and everyone knew it. A princess had been born there in Ottawa on a piece of ground proclaimed to be Dutch soil. Canadians had liberated Holland. So why not Canada? Why not?

It is a wonderful country, they'd say. Everybody says so. I don't know anything about it, but they want us and we want to get away from this country, from our memories, from the bad things we saw and maybe did, and, besides, what kind of a future does Holland have? Or more like it, what kind of a future do I have in Holland?

The answer, you must agree, was that nobody knew. Maybe we wouldn't know for ten years. Maybe it would take that long. It didn't, but people didn't know. About 1947 there were the advertisements in the newspapers, on the radio, the signs, all saying Canada wants us. Come, we welcome you. Jobs for everyone. Come and live the Canadian way. That was a strong inducement, I might add.

I am only trying to make this one point. A lot of landed immigrants, and not only Dutch people but all nations, I say a lot, came because they had guilt feelings about what had gone on during the war. I have only touched the surface on these. I've left out a few of the more despicable things and I will not be cross-examined on them. Perhaps you can guess.

But we were human. We were starving. We had no electricity. No wood to cook the little bit of food we managed to find or buy or steal. We were a desperate people those last few months of the war. We knew the British and Canadians were coming to liberate us, but we didn't know when. That is when the Germans got very desperate themselves, and that is when a lot of us lost hope.

So it is a simple matter. A lot, some, how many nobody will ever know, but a lot of the people who came to Canada, in my opinion—in my opinion, mind you—came because of guilty feelings and thinking, oh, Canada will be the place to go. There I will forget the bad things. A new life, a new country. A new job. Free from all that from the past. But you won't hear people talk about this side of it. Do you know why? Because it is the dark side of people.

THE FREEDOM TO GET AHEAD

You ask any of them, and I don't care how they tell it to you, right down at the bottom of it all, the reason they came to Canada was to escape the class system of England, Britain and Europe.

That is something that had been there for centuries, and I've talked to a great many of these people. Hell, it has been part of my job. That's why I'm firm in saying this, that they had to get out and although, mind you, they didn't know a great deal about Canada and its ways, somehow, somewhere down deep in every one of them was the idea that Canada was without a class system.

None of this business of being born of a certain mother and father, say a blacksmith, maybe a foundry worker, and that was what you were going to be doing for the rest of your life too. Working in a foundry or an auto plant or a factory making stoves.

They'll say they came for other reasons. Not the refugees just after the war—the Displaced Persons—no, not them. We all knew why they came.

But the rest, freedom from being what your father was. Freedom from the whole business of not looking up to somebody, the upper class, and not having too darn many people to look down upon.

I'm not saying Canada is not a classless society. It sure as hell is. But it also gives a man the freedom to move up, to improve himself, to become a foreman, a manager, a shop owner, a boss, a capitalist, if you want to think of it that way.

The freedom to get ahead. I did it. An awful lot did it.

A LONG TRIP FOR A GOOD MEAL

My old uncle in Exbury had died and left each of us £2,300, and that was a fortune then. For me, anyway and I didn't know what to do with it. You couldn't get a decent meal. All the good restaurants were jammed with those bloody war profiteers and discharged generals and Americans from all those international relief agencies, and even with a packet in my pocket I didn't feel like paying those prices, even if I could have got in.

One day I had a couple of whiskies with an old shipmate in the Six Bells over in Chelsea and we're talking and he suggested why didn't I just spend my packet foolishly, take a passage to Canada first class on one of the Cunards, take a trip across Canada by train and live it up. We'd been talking about not being able to get so much as a decent dinner, and he said I'd live like a king first class. Go across to Canada and then out to Vancouver and home again and I'd have plenty of money left and I'd have had some decent meals. It sounded like a lot of common sense. I'd be spending the uncle's generosity anyway, in London, and nothing to show for it. What a jolly good idea, I thought.

I trotted off to the shipping company and snaffled off one of their staterooms. Deuced if I can remember its name, but it did have a bunch of war bride lassies on it, but we weren't allowed to mingle with them. Second or third class, I suppose, and a hundred squalling brats.

The trip was marvellous. The service was excellent and the food was superb. Everything one couldn't get at home they had in more than abundance. Just first class all the way. The trip to Halifax seemed too short, but there were a lot of Canadians on the ship and I talked with a lot of them. Everyone assumed I was emigrating, and to this day I'll remember the sales talk I'd get from them. A person from Calgary would say that Calgary was the best place in Canada to settle and so on, Toronto, Fort William, Winnipeg, Vancouver. That sort of thing. Then I'd tell them I was really travelling first class to get a decent meal, and they could hardly believe me.

Then we all got on the train, and that opened my eyes. After we got into Montreal next morning, I walked around. I'd bought one of those tickets where you could stop off. A day here, two days there. They said I could only take forty pounds Canadian money, all Labour would let you take out of Britain, but I'd brought the whole bundle. They couldn't stop you from doing that. Hiding it away.

There was no problem whatsoever cashing pounds to dollars. Such a stupid rule and if emigrants had known it, they wouldn't have suffered so many hardships because they had no money. Pounds were just as good as dollars. Walk into any bank. I just said I was an English officer travelling home in mufti, and pounds is what I was paid in. Simple as falling off a log, you know.

The trip across Canada, Toronto two days, Winnipeg, Regina, Calgary, and in those days the CPR knew how to run a decent train. It was absolutely marvellous. The dining car, absolutely first-rate. Words cannot describe it, and now look what you get. Slop. Terrible service. Then, I had a lower berth and a porter who could get you anything. It was on that trip that I learned what a mickey was. The porter seemed to have an endless supply of whiskey and he did a brisk trade. A jolly black fellow who seemed to function without sleep.

The bonus was the Canadians. I must have talked to a hundred, the people travelling with me. Suddenly, there was one sitting beside you, wanting to know where you were going, who you were, what you did for a living, and when I turned out be be an eccentric English sailor, they were all the more fascinated. I think I could have spent half a year just travelling across the country and staying with friends I made on the CPR.

Calgary did attract me a bit, I admit. I spent three days there, but in the end I thought it was too small, too small-townish. Nothing to do, really. Pretty girls, though. Very beautiful.

I wanted to see the mountains, the Rockies, and I saw more mountains that day than I needed for a long time. I'll remember we came into Vancouver about nine o'clock in the morning and I thought, this is it. Something about the city, the train coming in along the harbour, the downtown and the bustle, everything about it I thought was just grand. Just a couple of days and a trip to Victoria on the boat and I was sold. Like that. I just stayed, hung around the yacht club with a chap I'd met on the train, and in a few days a job fell into my lap, and you could say that was it. No hardship. No what-am-I-going-to-do? All very easy. The right contacts and soon the right girl, and I can honestly say I never really thought about London and England much again. With all its troubles, it was just not where I wanted to be.

YES, CANADA WOULD BE NICE

Hey, you are asking me about a long time ago. It was thirty years ago. Things, you know, they weren't too good in Holland. We had terrible times through the war. I think it did something to us as a country. The people were different after it. Not as nice. If you asked a friend to help you, he'd ask why. Not like before the war. If you asked a friend to lend you a few guilders, he'd say he wanted interest. That was not like before.

It was the Germans. What they did to us. There is that saying: every man for himself. I didn't like that.

I thought, maybe there is a better place to go. I was a mechanic, cars. Give me a piece of wire, some solder, a wrench, pliers, I'll fix your cars. My wife a secretary for a big Dutch insurance company. We weren't making money and we couldn't find an apartment. I was thirty-three. She was twenty-four, a little Dutch girl from Appledoorn. Nice girls come from there.

We said, Canada. Canada liberated Amsterdam. They passed out the food and showed the little kids pictures of their own little kids. I remember that. Big men, tough. Goddamned tough. Good, though. I thought I'd like to live away from Holland and in a country where these kind of men came from. Killing Nazis one day, giving chocolate to little children in The Dam the next.

That's why my wife and I went. America? No. Too big, too violent. Look at it now. Where else? We didn't even talk about it. Not once. I said Canada, and my wife, she said that would be nice.

Just like a woman, you know. That would be nice. Leaving homeland, family, friends to be with her husband, a new big land, knowing nothing about it. She said that would be nice.

THIS MUST BE SOME COUNTRY!

Expo, that did it for me. I know other guys that did it the same way. See Expo and you'd want to stay. This was in 1967, remember?

We knew a lot of families from our town in Greece, a little town between Trikata and Larisa where there is some farming but mountains all around, we knew families from around who had gone to Canada. The father first to make money, and then the rest would sell the farm or the shop and they'd get on a ship and away they'd go.

I knew nothing about Canada. My ship never went there, because we were in the Mediterranean trade and up to Britain and the Baltic, but this time we signed on for Montreal and it was the time of Expo. It was something coming up the St. Lawrence and our ship, a ten-thousand tonner, small the way they are now, but coming up the river—that was a real sight. No other country had anything like that, and then there was Montreal and we had six days' turnaround so I saw the fair. About four times. The other sailors would be in the bars getting drunk and finding girls, but I'd go to Expo '67.

They had all those pavilions there, the Russian, the U.S., Britain, Australia, Sweden, you know. Every country. They were good, but the most wonderful pavilion of all was the fair, Expo itself. I thought, if a little country like Canada can do this, then it is some country. This country can do a lot of things. This is big stuff! There was just a good feeling about the fair and the good way the Canadians felt about the fair. Like my kids would say: Hey! Neat!

I got talking to a Greek guy I met at the fair and he said, "Sure, there are a lot of us here, we all came over and we're doing good, real good. Why don't you come? You can get a job. I'll get you one. No problem," he said.

So I went back home and signed on for Canada as a landed immigrant. It was easy. As simple as that. So I'm here.

2 WE WERE WAR BRIDES

2 WE WERE WAR BRIDES

The war brides—they were all young, all excited, yet probably somewhat apprehensive of what they would find in this new land as their special trains rolled through the night, through a vastness that astonished them.

The 48 000 women who arrived in 1945 and 1946 were not immigrants in the strict sense of the word, and not brides either, as most had been married for years and were bringing 22 000 children "home" to their Canadian servicemen husbands.

Forty-six thousand women came from Britain, and two thousand from Holland and other countries where Canadians had been stationed. When the special train halted in a small town, a woman and child would be dropped off to be met by a man standing alone on a deserted station platform. In a major city, the arrival often turned into a public spectacle as husbands and wives greeted each other amid the confusion.

Women from Britain enjoyed the major advantage of speaking their own version of "Canadian," but they were still lonely and tended to seek out each other, forming friendships that have lasted to this day. They wondered at the breeziness of Canadians and at the profusion of goods and foods in the stores, and they marvelled at the spaciousness of houses and apartments and the good things contained therein—an electric hot water heater, for instance. They wondered if Canadians knew there had been a war on, for it was obvious there had not been much rationing or wartime restrictions.

City girls became farmwives, and village girls had to learn big city ways. Many war brides found resentment directed at them, especially in small towns. After all, they had married some of the eligible bachelors.

No one will ever know how many homesick wives took the "Thousand-Dollar Cure," the return home by air to see Mom and Dad. Once there, however, the contrast between Britain and Canada struck home. Britain was so depressed and depressing, still war weary, still struggling to return to a normal life. The women could not wait to return home to Canada. It was a wise husband who allowed his wife to take the cure, even though the amount of money then was enormous.

Undoubtedly, the war brides were often a catalyst for more immigration, as their letters home described wonderful new experiences in the new country where their future lay.

HOME—MILES FROM ANYWHERE!

The train would stop and there would be this station in the middle of Saskatchewan, and you'd see the porter take the bags down and then this girl would get off, and it would be Margie or Jane or Dora, one of the girls you'd got to know so well on the ship and on the train coming across.

These little towns, and if it was at night, and we did cross Saskatchewan at night, there wouldn't be anybody on the platform but a man waiting or just a few people, and the wind would be blowing and the snow everywhere and it was so cold, and you'd think, oh God, what is she letting herself in for?

We were war brides. Funny term, don't you think? Some had been married for two or three years. Some had kiddies. Usually one, and here they were being dumped off this special train into the middle of nowhere.

I thought, at least I'm going to Vancouver, and the place is big enough that I've seen pictures of it in books home in England. But here, this particular town might be only five hundred people. Maybe a thousand. You know how it was in those days. Just after the war. And there she was, meeting a stranger who was her husband and getting into a truck and going to some place miles from anywhere.

I've often thought those girls had more guts than I would ever have. I think I would have got back on that train.

Surprisingly, when you attend the reunions and read the books, very few of us got divorced. Those marriages, they seemed to last.

YOU'RE ONE OF THE FAMILY ALREADY

It was all pretty unbelievable, that here was a carload of British war brides travelling across Canada, and some with kids and the odd one eight months pregnant, and they didn't know what they were coming to.

I know I didn't. I can tell you that. Oh, I was a stupid young girl. I married Charles, a small wedding because there was so little time. I'd met him at a dance at the station, and then we were married just five days before his ship sailed from Liverpool. Now the train was going across Canada, and la de dah dah, I was happy I'd be seeing him and, great sigh, I didn't know anything about him.

Now I won't say I was the only one. There were lots. That was one of the things we'd talk about, what was ahead for us, and we'd see these little stations as we went across the country, just a few lights in the towns and then they were gone, all so dark, and we'd wonder, oh my God! Is this really happening to me? What are Mum and Dad doing now? Sitting in the local having a pint and watching the darts and thinking, where is our wandering Sheila tonight?

Girls would be crying, and some would just be staring out the window, and the kiddies, their mothers trying to keep them from bothering the rest of us, and the Red Cross ladies trying to help. Oh, they were so wonderful.

Then it was my turn and I had to get off at Swift Current, and it was in the middle of the night and the last fifteen minutes . . . Oh, I remember this. I spent the time saying good-by to my new friends, and you could see them thinking, oh, I wish it was my turn.

Charles was waiting at the station, and when I got off he came running down the platform, and I'll remember this, he had this awful dog running behind him. Tag. That was his name. I'm kissing Charles and there is thumping on the windows, the girls were thumping from the train and this dog is barking. People are watching and thinking, or so I thought, oh, another one. You could see it in their faces when you met them in town later, like: How did a little thing like you snag such a nice fellow?

I'd never seen a pickup truck before, but off we went to the ranch, and the stars were out and it was cold, it was February. All I wanted was to be in a nice warm bed and not bouncing around on mud and gravel roads in a truck and that damn dog squirming around my feet, and I guess I wondered: Why? I mean, why am I doing this, in my mauve wool wedding dress and this man beside me jabbering away a mile a minute? He wasn't nervous. I was the one. I loved him, I thought, but does it have to be like this?

You know the prairie at night? There is something about it, something calming, something that reminded me of home, the black night and the bright stars, and I thought, the stars, where is the Big Dipper? And where is Orion and the three stars in his belt? Mind you, I put this down in my diary after, so I am not making this up, because I read it not too long ago.

Each time we went through a little town I'd ask, "Is that where we're going to do the shopping?" Oh, stupid questions like that, and he'd say, "No, farther on," and that's what our talk was about.

Oh, why am I blathering like this? The truth was I was so scared, and it was such a huge country and this man driving that truck, I didn't know him. And there he was in his farm clothes and fiddling with the damned radio trying to get Great Falls, Montana, or some other station, and I thought, lady, ain't this a mess?

Then we got to the ranch, and his kid sisters were out waving and shouting and here it is, about four in the morning, and his dad and mom, and Charlie yelling, "She's here, she's here, my sweet Virginia bride," which I didn't know then but it was part of some cowboy song, and we're all in the house and having coffee and talking a mile a minute and I thought, what a nice kitchen. I think that was the best thought I'd had in the last two hours. The big room and the stove warming up every corner of it and the deer heads on the walls and the pictures, all this I put in my diary, and I began to feel happy, and then I thought, oh, oh. Oh, oh! Here it comes. They're waiting for Charlie and I to go upstairs to the bedroom and, well, I thought they were thinking, those two teenage sisters, they were thinking, what are they going to do?

But then I was reprieved. The general wasn't shot at dawn. His mother reprieved me, the embarrassment, and she told Dodie to take my bags up to the room and she got me a big basin of hot water from the reservoir and she told me to go and freshen up and breakfast would be ready in a short while.

I knew farm people got up early, but to have breakfast at 5:30 in the morning in winter, that was ridiculous. Not in that family! Charlie and his dad went out to the barn to do something, and when I came down I got a big wink and a hug from my new mother-in-law, Mrs. Williams, such a dear woman, and she said something like, "Oh, my dear, don't worry. Everything is going to be just fine. You're one of the family already."

I started to cry and she hugged me again, and Dodie and Shannon staring big-eyed, and I just said thank you, and it was as if all the tension just drained away. Just drained away and left me kind of weak, and I could only hug her like I would my own dearest mother, and she gave a few big sobs, and then it was over, and I felt so good.

We had a wonderful breakfast and I watched the dawn come up and, well, they talk about life being hard on a ranch in southwest Saskatchewan and it is, but we had this wonderful mom and dad to back us up. No matter how hard it was, and how much we hated to finally leave and go to Calgary, the first years were the best in my life, just getting to know and love my new country.

A BIG PARTY AND A PIPER!

I made this wee list here, with all the things I wanted to say, but I got about half down this page and I wanted to cry and cry I did. Remembering all the wonderful things.

It all happened so fast, Alan back from Holland and coming up to Glasgow and telling us and saying, "Let's have a wedding now," and that shocked my family, but we did have a wedding. Oh, the fussing and rushing about, but in three days we had a wedding and a two-day honeymoon to a hotel in the Trossachs, and then my dear Alan was away to Liverpool and on the ship to Canada. That put me down at the bottom of the war bride list to go to Canada, and I didn't get there until May fourteenth, 1946, when the train came into Saskatoon.

They were all at the station, all his family, brothers and sisters and everybody, and smiling and kissing me and hugging, hardly leaving me any time at all to hug Alan, and his uncle was a piper. There he was. A big man dressed up again in his full kilt, and he piped us through the station, and everybody clapping and laughing and oh, it was a bonny time.

There was such a party and such a big house, and his parents were not rich at all, just ordinary, but this big house and the big dinner and the party after. I just could not believe it. All for us, Alan and his wee Scottish bride, Jennie. I thought, are all Canadians this way or is it just the Macdonalds? But I was right. It was all Canadians, and there we were far into the night with neighbours and friends coming in and out and the men yelling, "Where's Jennie? She's got to have a big welcome," and there would be more hugging and kissing, and these big Canadian men would drink down a glass of spirits to toast us, and oh, you can see how my words are tumbling out and why I started crying when I wrote my wee list. It was like living that day all over again.

I hope I'm not being an old fool about all this, if that's what you're thinking, but it was the happiest day a bride ever had, and when we left in a taxi to go to our apartment, there was his old uncle, as drunk as Sandy McTavish, piping us down the walk and, oh, it was a wonderful day.

I could hear my mother saying, "Now, Jennie, you must not expect too much in Canada, for they may be a rough lot. And you must write straight off and tell us what Saskatoon is like. Such a name."

My poor mother. It took her three or four weeks maybe to get my letter, because I didn't write it straight away because of the excitement but, when I did, I said Saskatoon was the most wonderful place to be and I wanted to be in no other place. I told her I felt right at home, because then it was the dearest place in the world to me.

THE NIGHT SHE BLASTED HIS FRIENDS

You Canadians knew so little about the war. It was something that your soldiers and airmen fought overseas and you sent food parcels to them and that was what it seemed to be all about.

I came to Brandon in November of '45, and my husband was apprenticing in a farm equipment repairs depot and doing some long-distance trucking for MacArthur, and he'd been back since June, so we had a little house at the far end of town, on a little street off Rosser.

He met me in Winnipeg and we stayed two nights in the Marlborough Hotel, which was a nice hotel in those days, and we had a wonderful reunion and then to our wee home, Jamie with his Scottish bride and all the folks waiting.

To be perfectly frank with you, it was a pain. You would have thought I had married the only son of the town's multimillionaire. All these people saying, "Oh, my dear, you're so lucky to have gotten Jimmie. He was such a prize, you know." Oh, sure I figured it out. They were saying I had stolen him away from the ten girls in Brandon who wanted him, but he was in England and I was working in London and he was lonely and he married the first little bit of quiff he saw. It infuriated me, but I held my tongue, and Jamie, when I told him, he would laugh and say not to mind those old biddies.

Then in about two weeks there was a shower. I don't know where the thing started, but I had never heard of a shower before. Oh, yes, it did come in handy. Pots and pans and serviettes and towels and everything nice, that's what little girls' showers are made for.

It was a double thing. The shower in the afternoon and then all the husbands and boyfriends brought over the casseroles and cakes and pies and everybody had dinner, and then it became a triple thing because it seemed everybody had brought a jug too.

Well, I only had been in Brandon maybe three weeks and I did know that Canadian men drank a lot and drove in a very reckless fashion, but I didn't know they drank like this. Rye and water and more rye and water and the ladies, if they wanted to be fancy, they asked for rye and ginger. Even today I cannot think of a more tasteless drink. Rye whiskey!

Jamie, well, we always bought scotch, which was what I was used to when I drank with him, and here was this party raging around me and people drinking hard and dancing, with the chairs and table pushed back, and by this time, that's when the men started pulling the dirty jokes out of their back pockets. They still do it. Why? One fellow told a joke and it seemed each person felt he had to tell a dirtier one, and here are all these friends of Jamie and his family, all nearly falling off their chairs because they are laughing so hard.

Even today I remember it, and it was disgusting, and then somebody said, "Hey, Kathy, tell us a real Scotch joke." A "Scotch" joke, mind you!

Oh, I suppose it was because I'd had one more than my limit of two, or Jamie had been pouring them heavier, but I told them. Oh, God, when I think of it, I told them the best Scottish joke I knew was about a bunch of dirty-minded Canadians. They thought that was going to be a funny one, as if it happened during the war, until they realized I was sounding off on the lot of them about their dirty jokes in front of decent women, and on and on, and on and on. And on!

They sat there with stunned looks on their faces, and I went on, and I guess it was all the frustrations of being a bride but not having a husband for a year and then coming five thousand miles away to this dump of a town on the prairies where everybody thought a grain elevator was gracious architecture.

I told them about the war, what it was like to live on rations and no new clothes for five years, and no fresh fruit and one egg a week and The Blitz and then the V-2 raids, and here they were in Canada, selling everything they could grow and good jobs and big money and talking about how the Americans were a bunch of no-goods and, oh, it went on.

I suppose I cut loose at them for twenty minutes, and then Jamie stood up and he did not say, I'm sorry, friends, Kathy's tired, or Kathy's had a bit too much. He just said, "Thank you for coming, and we'll see you all soon."

They just picked up and left, and when they were gone I sat down and had a good cry. I thought I had earned it. Jamie held me close, and I loved him more than ever, and now that he's gone I realize what a wonderful man he was, even more wonderful than I knew him to be. Well, enough of that.

That was Saturday night, and next afternoon we got in his dad's car and loaded all these hats and coats into the car—these were what our guests had piled up on the bed in our bedroom and hadn't taken when I'd driven them out into the night. Jamie's mother had come over after breakfast and not a word of what happened. What a dear, sweet woman she was! And she said, "This coat is so-and-so's," and so on. She'd arranged the shower at our place, so she knew.

Jamie and I delivered all those coats and stuff, and at each place we went in and had a nice chat, and nothing was said. I got to know them better just that afternoon. And as far as I know, nobody ever mentioned my tirade, my bomb-blasting of them. I thought much better of them for that. It did a lot to change my opinions.

EVERYBODY UNDERSTOOD

I married a gunner in the Royal Canadian Artillery, and they were stationed near my village in Suffolk. He was French-Canadian and his English—he'd learned it in the army—it was quite good. It was kind of romantic the way he spoke, mispronouncing words of three syllables or so. Giving it, these words, a little ripple, so you knew what he was saying, but it was different. It was kind of quaint to our ears.

I didn't get to Canada until November of 1945, and by this time he was home, in La Durantaye, and it was a small farming village and nobody spoke English. I was amazed. He hadn't really told me this. I guess he did, maybe saying I'd have to learn French, and I thought my school French would get me by. Oh, no! Oh, no, again!

You're sure to have heard stories of war brides who were told by the priests that if they didn't become Catholics like their husbands were, then their children, mine, say, they would be bastards. That didn't happen to me, although it did happen, I know. They are not just stories. They didn't happen to me because we didn't have any children, but there was plenty of pressure for me to turn. I wouldn't. Why should I? Marc's mother would say to him that I should join the church, and he'd tell me, and I'd say no, I was an Anglican, I had my own religion and if his mother and his family and the priest and the lawyer—the priest, the lawyer and the storekeeper, they ran the town—if they didn't like it, then that was just too bad.

I wasn't put into purgatory. I wasn't spat upon in the street. Nothing like that. I was Marc's wife and I was respected, but there it was, I was the English woman. All the time I spent there I was L'Anglais. Marc's family lived in the village, but they were farmers. A big family. I think there had been about thirteen of them, but only nine or ten had lived, but still a huge, perfectly huge family by standards I had been brought up with.

It finally got to me, you know. It was like this. You were in a small village like La Durantaye and it was like a big family. It had its own ways and there were feuds, but everything revolved around the church. The priest was quite old but he was broad-minded, and he allowed dancing. Parties. Some village priests didn't. But what he said went. If he said they couldn't do something, then it was not done. Not even if it was a good idea. He had his own ideas of what was right and what was wrong, and it was the worst thing a person could do, to cross him. Nobody disobeyed.

I thought, surely there must be somebody who will tell this man that there is a whole new world out there, and in Montreal and Quebec they are doing things differently. But no, even the men who were wise would just say, "Oh, Père knows. We will let him decide."

The language was another thing. My French was totally useless. I could go into the store and buy. That was simple. You could recognize labels. Sugar was sugar. Salt was salt. You walked around and took things or you pointed, but to try and order, well, that was okay. They could understand my simple English French. But to understand their French-Canadian French, absolutely impossible. They tried, but it was just not the French I knew. Maybe two hundred years of not speaking real French and using their own, with their made-up words, maybe that was it, too.

Finally, and don't get me wrong, Marc's family was good to me, nice, helpful, they tried, but finally I just decided I could not live in this kind of isolation. It wasn't like a prison cell, but in a way it was.

I was very unhappy. It showed, I guess. The family knew I was so unhappy. I knew I could not spend another six months in that village. Not the rest of my life. I was twenty-three, I was pretty and I had been a private secretary to a company director at home, and this was exile.

Of course I still loved Marc. He was still my handsome Canadian soldier man, but I told him finally. I said I loved him but this life in the village was becoming hell for me. Maybe I was responsible. Maybe it was because there was no entertainment, no movies, nothing, and well, I had lived in a village too, but then in 1943 after Marc and I were married, I had gone to London and worked and done well and there was absolutely . . .

Look, this is hard for me to say, but I wrote my father and I asked him to send me the money to go home. I explained. My letters before had told him enough, I'm sure. I wanted to go home. He sent me the money. I don't know how he did it, currency restrictions, but he did. It was £150. Maybe five hundred dollars in Canadian.

Marc understood, and he took me to Montreal after I had sent for my ticket. He understood. He was a wonderful man. So was his family. I can honestly say that. Everybody understood. I love them still for that. There was nothing messy or mean about my going. The parting. It was adult, and that helped.

I went to England, back to London, and in a few years I got a divorce in England. In 1950 I wrote Marc I had it, that he was free.

The next year, and to this day I can't tell you why, but I came back to Canada. Just something about it. I married again.

HOMESICKNESS WAS A DISEASE

I can't really recall what my husband told me about his life before he enlisted, what he had done in Canada, although he did talk about his father having a farm. I suppose I just thought, oh, it's like an English farm, lots of cattle and sheep, and my father going off to the dog trials and the weekly sales in the town.

Boy, did I ever get a shock! The boat ride was fine, just great, wonderful, in fact, and, because it was a Canadian Pacific boat, it had Canadian officers and crew, and a lot of the girls talked to them, and one officer, a Mr. Malone, had a few books on Canada and he loaned them to us.

But you can't find out about your new home from a book—not that much, anyway. How big it was, and oh my goodness, it certainly seemed big. Then the train ride across from Montreal, and we found out just how big it really was. Days and nights, nights and days, and girls getting off along the way. Little stations, little towns, and in the night, just a couple of lights here and there.

And then Saskatoon and then my man. Ah, yes, my man, in all his splendour. This was a sight for my poor eyes to behold! He was dressed like a farmer, and that's when I realized this man with the denim jacket and the pants and boots and the woolly hat, this is not the dashing sergeant in the artillery I married. No, not a bit. He was always a fashion plate in his uniform, but now, on the great occasion of our lives, here he is, standing there, and he is a farmer. Would you believe it was a real shock to me?

I suppose we kissed. I don't remember, but stations are so crowded with people staring, and I remember it was quite early in the morning. We walked around to the Bessborough, such a huge and fine hotel, like a castle, and we went towards the dining room for breakfast. I said, "Bob, you can't go in there looking like that. They won't serve us." Oh, he laughed, and that was the laugh I remembered so well, and he said they certainly would, and when we got in I saw that half the men inside were dressed like him. Farmers! Nobody thought anything about it. Such was my entry into Canadian society. Ha, ha. Denim jacket society.

I remember the ride to the farm. I wanted to say, "Bob, tell me about the farm," until I realized he was telling me about it. Not how wide and vast it was but where we would live on it. A trailer. I had a vague idea what a trailer was, but I was so fascinated by Canadian roads that went straight instead of winding and twisting like at home, I just forgot about the trailer.

It was a trailer. It was eleven feet long and eight feet wide, and at first I thought it was just a box he stored things in, tools. Nope, nope, that was our home and, of course, his parents had a big house and a big barn and a big implement shed and, why, the place they kept their pigs, while not as clean as the box, was ten or fifteen times as big. I'll tell you, the little shed with the gasoline pump for the well, why, that was bigger than our first home.

Oh, why am I complaining? It was just a place to sleep, really. Because we ate with his parents and brothers and sisters and, besides, it really was for the best. If you considered it a place to sleep, to be alone in together, then it was better than in a crowded house.

I suppose I was lucky. I had a husband I loved and we weren't going to stay on the farm forever. There was a summer course starting at the agricultural school and in June we'd be moving into Saskatoon, and it would give me a chance to learn about Canada. There wasn't much to learn, actually. Very little.

Canada was a very simple place in those days. Everybody kept to themselves all week and then they went into Rosthern on Saturday afternoon for dinner and a show and shopping or into North Battleford. Church on Sunday and, well, that winter the men went curling and hunting and they were hauling hay from the marsh. The rest of the time they played cribbage, ate cookies and drank coffee at ten o'clock, listened to the CBC news, checked the thermometer and went to bed, and up again at six when it was still dark.

I did learn about Canadian cooking, or maybe you'd call it prairie cooking, and how to operate the Delco and ring up a neighbour, and memorize the ring system on the party line, and drive the truck, and then I had eleven hours left in the day to think. My mother-in-law was wonderful, but I was what they called an English war bride, like in, oh, Margaret's an English war bride, meaning Margaret is from England so she doesn't know anything. Poor Margaret.

Yes, I thought a lot. I was almost physically sick from homesickness. I wasn't going to mention this part, but it goes with it. I would go to our little trailer and cry, and then I'd spend an hour patting my eyes with ice water trying to get the swelling down. I don't think I fooled anybody. I'd say to myself, Margaret, you've got to stop thinking about this, but it was April and there seemed to be no end of winter. Snow everywhere still, and I'd think, back in England the fields would be green and the flowers blooming and the earth warm and the farmers planting and here we are, still in the deep freeze.

If we had been in Victoria or Vancouver or even Saskatoon, where there were things to do, movies, a play sometimes, a restaurant to visit on Saturday night, and even shopping, though we were poor as church mice. . . . Well, you can see. My first Canadian winter.

There were times I used to dream that we were driving to Saskatoon and I had a ticket in my purse that would get me on the train and then on a ship and in two weeks I would be home again. It is the truth. I loved Bob, but it still was the truth.

Homesickness, I figure, is a disease. If you don't treat it, then it takes hold of you and becomes a cancer and it eats you up. That is why some girls my age—and thank God I had no children then—girls my age who came over, they just let it destroy them, and I know most stayed. But that first winter on the prairies, I'm sure it had a very serious effect on the way they saw Canada from then on. It was like it was a battle you had to fight to win.

It's been near forty years, and I'm a happy Canadian now, but certainly not then.

YES, GLAD TO BE HOME AGAIN!

It was a farmhouse, and we had to live with his parents and his younger sister until we got settled, but that took about three months, and what a year! I won't go into that. Don had done something right, anyway. He had bought two quarters of land and he had a house started for us and it finally got finished that fall, and his Veterans' Affairs loan had come through and the payments were small. What with good heavy rains that year and using his dad's equipment, working for his dad, driving a school bus, working a bit in town and odds and ends, we wound up the year in good shape, and after moving into our house it wasn't too bad. Not too bad, except every time I looked out the windows I got homesick for the chimney pots of Putney. Now Putney isn't your high-class London, but you could get on the tube and be in Piccadilly in fifteen minutes. Davidson had two or three stores, a theatre and a beer parlour, and that was about it, and Regina, well, when you got to Regina for some big shopping, Regina was still Regina. The Regina Roughriders, that was a big event. Go down on Saturday for an afternoon game after you did your shopping and had a lunch. That wasn't exactly London.

I was dreadfully homesick by 1949. This was three years later. I was so homesick I would cry for hours, just thinking of Mum and Dad, and one day in August I told my husband I wanted to go back. I meant going back for good, but I just told him I wanted a holiday, to see Mum and Dad. I'll say this for him, he didn't say boo. Okay, when? I said after harvest was in, and he said he'd get the tickets, and that was a lot of money. I forget how much. Maybe eight hundred dollars.

November was the very worst time to go. London was cold and dreary that year and somehow nothing looked the same. I remember we took the bus from Heathrow to the London air terminal, and the seats were all slashed by hoodlums and nothing had been done to fix them. That was just one thing. I can remember the first morning, about six, I heard Mum downstairs with the coal scuttle, and I thought, good God, she's starting up that goddamned little stove so we can all have some hot water. Even on the farm in my new house we didn't do that, and we were in the wilds. Everything was wrong. There was still some rationing and the stories in the *Daily Telegraph* about the jobless and the dole and the strikes, and you know the *Telegraph*, always railing about labour, big bad labour, and the Labour government. My father putting a bad light on everything. My mum trying to make do with what she had. My friends all pushing prams with their fourth kid in it and mooning after the milkman and all that bloody nonsense. England was just different. I hated it. It rained. It rained and rained. Everything was so damned soggy and I thought, well, fellows, you won the war for the rest of the world and this is the can of worms they hand you, strikes and rationing and, oh, you know. It was a mess. I wanted to get home to my husband and the chickens and the dog and the cats and go bouncing down the road in the pickup. Go into one of the crummy stores in Davidson and have people say, "Margaret, you're back! How glad to see you, welcome home. And how was London? Same as ever?"

And I'd say, "Worse and getting worser and if you want rain, I could have brought you back eighteen billion tons of the rotten stuff."

Much weeping at the airport, you know. My Mum. You're leaving so soon, and all that. You're darn right I was leaving. I wanted to get back to my cheery kitchen and my boiling hot water and to see my husband out watering the stock. Going off to curling in town, those sunrises and the sunsets and all that jazz, as we used to say. Some jazz, eh?

I wanted something more than a snarl when I asked for some toilet soap, and saying no, we haven't got it, and everybody blaming everything on everybody else and on the Americans too, although to this day I still don't understand that.

Anyway, I love England. I still do. I always will. But the England I knew, I'm afraid it was gone. It was exciting during the war. Everyone doing his bloody bit and hating the damned Germans and then it was all over. We had to get back to what England and Britain was really like.

Canada! I could have kissed the mayor of Regina when the plane landed, and the kiddies were so happy, and we were dead tired, but Bob was there. There was snow on the fields on the way home. So white. London grimy, dead, dull, mean, gone to hell, and twenty hours later all those fields of white snow and then the little towns, the elevators. I can see it all now. And my little house, Bob's mother and father waiting at the door with a turkey in the oven ready for us, a bottle of scotch, and talk, talk, talk. Good to be home, I'll say. Never again. Yeah, Riders!

THE THOUSAND-DOLLAR CURE

I'm not sure why it wasn't our husbands, but always us who took the Thousand-Dollar Cure. That's what we called it in those days. You'd have come over from England maybe two years before, maybe eight months, who knows? But it would hit you one day when you were doing those everlasting dishes that you just had to get home to England and see your old mum.

In my case, it was a winter day in February and I was down in the laundry room of this apartment building we were living in at Scarborough. Please, don't ever ask me about Scarborough. God, it and its Golden Mile and those god-awful little boxy new houses, miles of them, and the factories moving in, and shopping in that Golden Mile

and people saying, oh, wasn't it exciting to be part of a new develop-
ment! Why, we're opening a new city.

I was too polite to tell these silly little housewives in their curlers
where to stuff their shabby but new Scarborough, but, anyway, this
day I'm third in line. Can you believe it? There is only one washing
machine for the twelve families in that block and everyone wants to
wash on Monday morning. Me too, of course. I must have been brain-
washed on that one. For some eternal reason, Canadian wives washed
their bloody clothes and sheets on that day. No, no other day would
do. Monday or nothing, and ironing Wednesday. Carved in stone,
that was.

I'm two to go before I get my whack at the machine and if I so much
as step out of line, I lose my place. Those little housewives were fierce
on that one. Step out of line, even to go to the biff, and try and get
back in, then it's shotguns at ten paces.

I thought, did my man bring me all the way, on a poky old boat that
leaked and stank, did he bring me out to Toronto from lovely Cornwall, Helston, for this, standing in line like a Shaftesbury frump? Not
likely, I say, there and then, and I told him that night I was sick of
Canada and I was going to take a trip home.

I didn't know what they called it in those days, but he knew. A lot
of the lads at work had gone through it. Okay, he says, it's no car this
year, and here he was car-pooling out to Oshawa and General Motors
plant, and we can't afford a car, and at his good wages for that time.

It cost a thousand dollars. You flew Air Canada from Malton and
that, if I remember, was about seven hundred, and you had to have
money for home, maybe taking the folks up to London for a day and
night and oh, you know, the things. Then you had to have time to
think of what you were going to do, whether you could stand Canada,
whether you could go into another of those dreadful supermarkets
again, so much to buy and nobody to help you. So unfriendly. The
people in Scarborough so unfriendly. The whole experience in Canada just a bit of a big twit.

Now you must remember, back in those days, a thousand dollars
was an awful lot of money. Today, people will go shopping for
groceries on a Saturday afternoon and before they know what happened, they've bought a Jenn-Air for twice that much. Back then,
wages were low. Prices weren't, though, and George had to borrow
three hundred dollars and promise his right arm and leg to the bank.
But that week we talked about it, I was becoming so homesick for my

old Mum and Da that I actually became sick. Then we got the ticket and I was to be off in April, about six weeks away.

Oh, it's such an old story that you know it, but George would look after little George. He'd stay days with a neighbour, and I'd only be gone three weeks, and so I flew away on Air Canada and I'd say maybe twenty of that planeload were girls like me.

Mum came to meet me and we stayed in London that night, and oh, it was dirty and crowded and I didn't much like what I saw, I can tell you that. We took the Penzance train next morning and there we were, and I was a bit of a shocked person when I saw Helston again. I'd been away only two years, but I didn't remember it being such a silly and stupid little town. I'll say this, you don't find much written about it in the tourist guide books, but it was my home and I now didn't much like it. We went to teas and to the pub, and prices were so high in the stores, and here it was spring, and everybody was so downhearted. Crabbing. Bitching. England, she weren't like she use'ter be, you might say.

I saw Mum's kitchen with all the drudgery and grudgery about it and the wee house and Da going off every morning with a heavy heart to the works. Okay, I'll make it short and sweet for you. What happened to the England I knew? The fun was gone out of it, and there wasn't too much laughter in the hearts of the people. They were dead, you might say, and I was asked once, then I was asked twenty times. What is Canada like? What do you think of Toronto? I'd tell them what my three-bedroom apartment was like, and the central heat with the thermostat, and even about the washing machine in the laundry room, and they'd ooh and ah and say, "Lovely. Isn't that nice!" And so on. And here's me thinking I'm bitching and they, the girls I'd gone to school with, my Mum's friends, all think I'm living like Her Majesty the Queen.

Here I am, back home and supposed to be happy after being away in dreadful old Canada where I'd been weeping and wailing and making things miserable for dear George, and all these women thinking oh, such a lucky she. Wouldn't it be lovely to live there!

When my time was up, I had had it. I missed George and little George dreadfully and my homesickness for England was gone. I thought, I guess, well, I had to do it, or otherwise I'd have made my own life and their lives some sort of hell. It cost a lot, but when we came over the coast, coming home, and the pilot said that Labrador was down there, I looked and there were those huge waves smashing on that grey coast. Huge waves and great clouds of white spray. I thought that was the loveliest sight I'd ever seen.

I'm sure a lot of other women can describe it better, but that was the Thousand-Dollar Cure. I'm glad I took it when I did. It was money well spent. Money we couldn't afford to throw away, but it was worth every cent of it. I'm still homesick for England in the spring, but it is the Cornwall and England I remembered as a schoolgirl, and I think that makes all the difference in the world.

3 NOBODY TOLD US WHAT IT WOULD BE LIKE

3 NOBODY TOLD US WHAT IT WOULD BE LIKE

One question I asked of everyone was: Did you experience culture shock?

I am not sure that the phrase had even been coined when these immigrants began pouring into Canada, but the question was always met with an explosive exclamation, a giggle or a laugh. It always set off a string of memories.

Yes, they did experience culture shock, even the British. For those who did not speak English, the shock was even more traumatic. After all, centuries-old Edinburgh was not upstart Prince George, and London, Ontario, was quite a change from the scratch-and-starve farm plots around the hill towns of southern Italy. The dignity and grandeur of old Vienna were a far cry from the boomtown rawness of Kitimat.

Most newcomers knew very little about Canada, and what they had been told by harassed Canadian immigration officials in the refugee camps of Europe was largely inadequate. But they dug in to learn Canadian ways, realizing that it was the only way to survive the first few years and prosper in the later ones. Some people, however, managed to keep the old ways of Europe and prosper too. It was all a matter of attitudes and adjustments;

often the children of newcomers learned quickly and became the teachers of their elders.

Loneliness was a major problem. Not only were there no friendly faces to be seen but there was the frustration of not being able to talk with others in one's own language. And there was also the feeling, especially among young Displaced Persons, that they were not wanted in Canada.

Immigrants had come to Canada with the highest hopes and long-held dreams, but found themselves alone in an alien land. They learned that Canadians did not much care what happened to them, and this probably was a major aspect of culture shock. By their very indifference, Canadians indicated to immigrants that they were on their own.

Canada and Canadians were different, too, and newcomers needed a measure of common sense and a sense of humour to get used to it all. Getting acclimatized was not something people could learn in a night school English course. It came through work —and how they worked! —and experience and the realization that there was no going back, ever.

I LOVED THE CULTURE SHOCK

You'd hear people talking, oh, we're going to Canada because it is English and part of the British Empire, and what they were saying was, you'll be just going from England to Canada and it will be just the same.

I didn't want Canada to be the same as my homeland. That is the last thing you wanted! If you'd lived through the depression in the Midlands and then the war, six long and bloody years of it, then the last thing you wanted was a little bit of old England again.

I wanted a place where it was different. Not this confinement. Not this awful socialism going hand in hand with the old class system, which I knew would never go away, and it hasn't.

I'm sure these people looking for what they had in England were in the minority. People just can't be that stupid! Didn't they notice the conduct of the Canadian troops in England? I'll say this, their conduct was not that of men from a race brought up under circumstances we had in England. Not a bit!

We all wanted something different, and I'm talking now about Germans too, and the Dutch, the Belgians, the Ukrainians, the Italians and all the rest. We wanted freedom! We wanted the chance to get a job and earn money and not give it all back to the government. We wanted a house of our own, and not some crummy row house with a biffy out in the brick yard and lighting the stove every morning to get water to wash, and that's what a lot of us had. Even though we had the money to live better, there just wasn't anything available.

And, imagine, rationing two years after the war!

No, we didn't want to see the South Downs or the lanes of the Cotswolds, although that certainly would have been nice in Manitoba or Saskatchewan. Not every bloody Brit is enamoured of Saturday afternoon football games and cheering for Manchester United and, frankly, the mandatory cup of tea and a biscuit before going to bed never turned me on. Tea has caffeine and caffeine keeps you awake, but it was a tradition and, blimey and gor blast, we had to do it!

Of course Canada was a culture shock! Was it ever! I don't think I'm over it. But I love this country. I loved it from the moment our ship steamed up the St. Lawrence, and those little villages all painted white, and the blue skies and Montreal. The trip across Lake Superior, my God, that was awesome, but it was only a preparation of what was to come. The prairies. Not flat, like we'd been told. Rolling. Small hills. Sloughs beside the tracks and filled with ducks. We saw two coyotes outside of Medicine Hat, and then those fields just becoming green, and the miles of it. I thought, I wish I was a writer. I wish I was a poet. You didn't have any then of either category as I found out, and I thought, I should get this down with pen on paper.

But it was the freedom. The taxi driver in Calgary was free. He felt free. I could have been the Queen of England and he would not have treated me any differently. I think it was only a twenty-minute taxi ride from the station to my cousin's house, and by that time I knew everything there was to know about Calgary.

Not much, really. This was in 1947, and it was a small place.

I had been a nurse during the war, but I didn't want to nurse in Calgary. I'd rather be on a bread wagon and talk to all my customers every day. I didn't want to be confined. I wanted to get on all the buses and streetcars in Calgary and see all the places and visit the parks, and I did. That is how I spent the first week, spending some of the pitiful few dollars they let us take out on riding around seeing Calgary.

It had no galleries and no museums, and the stores were pitifully poky and old-fashioned. There was scarcely a tall building in the downtown, and I wondered about all the dust and that wind that seemed to blow all the time, but it was so different. There was no place in Britain like it and no place in Canada, for that matter.

I even liked the name. Calgary. I'd ask people, what does Calgary mean? They'd say, oh, Sarcee, I guess. Or Blackfoot. Or Sioux. One day I went to the library and I asked, and a woman said it was a town in Scotland. Well, imagine that!

The people were so friendly. So generous. Offering to drive you hither and yon, down into the valley, over the hill. Parties. I was invited to so many. Big men, drinks in their hands, laughing loud, but good, decent and wonderful fellows, and all so mannerly, so gentlemanly, not an ounce of phoniness in them. The women? The same. So eager to please, to help, and they sincerely meant it.

I thought, what a wonderful country.

When it came time to get a job, I had lots of offers, from friends of my cousin, and they were so sincere you felt you'd be hurting their feelings by not taking their jobs. But they didn't mind. I went to work for the city, which got me outdoors a good deal, and I just loved, just loved the culture shock I went through.

WE ASKED ABOUT THE WEATHER

Prince George at forty below! That's what I think of when someone today asks me what my first thoughts were when we moved to Canada. Prince George at forty below!

Nobody at Canada House had told us what it would be like. They told my husband and myself: you'll find good housing, you'll find good jobs and you'll find Canada a very friendly place to live.

To this very day I know there are people who came out from England and Scotland who curse those people at Canada House. I am convinced they were told: just get the right kind of emigrant, a man with skills, a good wife and a couple of nice kids, and make sure they get on that boat before they find out what Canada is really like.

Can you imagine any Canadian sitting across from you at a desk in downtown London not knowing what a Canadian winter was like? No, of course not. Why, the rat may even have come from Prince George or Dawson Creek or Saskatoon, but even if he comes from Ontario, the winters in Toronto are nothing to smile at.

We asked about the weather. What should we take? Was it cold? Brisk, cold but brisk and very healthy. That's what he said.

And Prince George. Business was booming. Jobs for everyone. The streets were paved with gold, you know. Friendly Canadians would welcome you into their homes. Nothing too good for a British emigrant and his nice family. Horse feathers! If I wasn't a lady I would use a different word.

Well, I'll tell you. Prince George in 1952 was a dump. A small city tucked up there miles from anywhere. Nothing to it. No suitable houses to rent, but you could get shacks at reasonable rents, like seventy-five or eighty dollars, which was highway robbery. No decent stores. They even boasted they still had whorehouses. Fine, let them have whorehouses, but don't boast about it. On Friday and Saturday afternoons and nights, a woman couldn't walk along some streets downtown. Drunken loggers and bums and Indians everywhere.

All that winter my husband worked out in that cold, frightful cold, working on heavy logging and road-making machinery, and you know what this little 95-pound English lady did? She stoked the fire in the living room of this $75-a-month shack with green fir and poplar, trying to keep the house warm so our two kiddies wouldn't freeze to death.

In the spring, when people kept telling us things would be so much better and that we should stay, we packed the few things we had and got on a bus. We rode over the bumpiest roads in Canada down through Quesnel and Williams Lake and we stayed in an old motel at Cache Creek. The road to Calgary went one way and the road to Vancouver went the other. The bus was coming through next morning and my husband said, "Tails east, heads west." I said, "Heads," and it came up heads and we got the bus to Vancouver. You had to make decisions like that in those days.

Vancouver was another world. This was in the spring of 1953. It was not England, but it was the next best thing, and though we had very little money, we soon began to prosper.

B.C.'S LAST FRONTIER

When my fiancé wrote and said he was working in a place called Prince George and that he was liking it, I went to the library and looked it up on the atlas and it was about fifty-three degrees, and I figured it out, that is just about the latitude of Manchester, where we lived.

That wasn't so bad, nice weather most of the time and, oh, I don't have to tell you. I knew nothing about Canada. None of us did. All we knew was what Canadian soldiers had told us.

In about a month he finally got around to asking me to come to Canada and marry him. If I had married him when he was stationed in England, I would have been a war bride as they called them, but I wasn't.

I came over on a Lancaster bomber which had been converted into passenger seats. I think it was one of a couple that fellow had who has the big airline now. Anyway, it was an absolutely awful flight, sheer terror all the way, but the fare was cheap.

Then I got the train to Edmonton and something was wrong on the line, a train wreck, so I waited in Edmonton for two days and then we went on to Prince George, and the next day was the wedding. Nothing fancy. How could it be? It was supposed to have been two days earlier and I guess everybody had said, oh, she's not coming, and they stood around and drank all the booze and that was that. So, just the minister and my husband's boss and his wife were witnesses, and then we went to a restaurant in this crummy hotel, the King Edward. I should have known. It was food, yes, but to call it a wedding feast would be very generous. To call it a meal would even be generous.

Prince George then? Oh, maybe five thousand people. Say eight thousand if you counted the people who lived in shacks, the Indians and the stray dogs on the main street. It was pretty awful. The streets were dusty, gravelly, and my husband hadn't been able to find any place for us to live. How we lived! A shack down on the Fraser, where the fancy apartments and homes are now, overlooking the river, but this was 1946. That's a long time ago in the life of a Canadian city in the north.

There was nothing, and coming from Manchester which had a very good cultural life, that was my culture shock. Was it ever! Was it ever!

Never a dull moment! Friday and Saturday night they fought the Battle of the Bulge in the streets. It was a mill town. Railroading. Logging. The provincial police were in charge then and they couldn't handle a dogfight at high noon. Not shootings. No, I don't mean that. This wasn't the Wild West. This was just the Drunken Canadian West!

You couldn't buy anything you'd see in the stores of, say, Vancouver or Edmonton. I guess nobody ever asked for them. You got so you dressed for the summer or the winter, the heat or the cold, and the effect at a party was devastating. Some women in finery, and the wife of a local lawyer in jeans. I couldn't get over it.

But it was fun. The people were so friendly. Everybody was in the same boat. Everybody drank rye and beer. No such thing as wine. When the booze ran out at a party, you just phoned the taxi office. Every taxi driver was a bootlegger. But people were kind and good and they worked hard and they played hard, and at any one time half of the girls in our group were preggers. That's the way it was. Have a baby, lay off if you could for six months, and have another.

We had our coffee parties and the men worked, my husband in an office which had about a dozen of these tiny sawmills scattered out in the bush. He'd take me out to them in his jeep, and that was quite an experience. It was a raw country, and they were hacking it down for lumber as fast as they could. You can see the awful results now when you fly over it. But that's the way it was done in those days. Get it, cut clear, get out and to hell with it all. I never heard the word *environment* used up there, not in all those five years we stayed there.

You could get out to Kamloops and Vancouver by plane, one of the ones that flapped its wings. There was a road of sorts to Kamloops which was not in much better shape than we were. I mean by that it was hardly civilized, either. Williams Lake was worse. I've seen men wearing guns there. No kidding. In Vancouver there wasn't much. This was the late Forties. I always thought B.C. was the Last Frontier.

But you know what? I'm saying this honestly. For the terrible cold, for the terrible heat in summer and the mosquitoes and the raw nature of it all, and Prince George squatting there in all its glory, I wouldn't have missed it for the world. Not ever! It was an experience, and the only way you could fail to enjoy it, enjoy it all immensely, was if you didn't have a sense of humour. God, that was the one thing you needed! If you didn't have it, you would go stir crazy in a month.

A barrel of laughs, and when we go back today for a visit and see that big city, it has a lot of things going for it, and I think of saying to the people, you just don't know what you missed.

WE FOUND PARADISE

I arrived in Winnipeg in early August, if I remember. Winnipeg was a culture shock, believe me.

Two weeks later, Crystal City, Manitoba. Population six hundred.

I don't know how they could ever call it *city* but they did. No water, except what we drew from the one and only pump in this place. No electricity. Only oil lamps.

After Brighton, my home town, God, what a cultural shock!

There was more to come. For some reason we moved to a cabin at Rock Lake, still in southern Manitoba, but much smaller. The population was four. Us and another couple.

I had to melt snow for water, and do you know how much water there really is in snow? About one-tenth. My husband killed wildlife for food. We were visited twice by a Mountie that winter and once by a trapper. Our social life was, as you can see, one mad whirl.

But it was a wonderful experience. Believe me, it was. Cultural shock, yes, but nice cultural shock once I got used to it.

In June we packed up and headed for a home in B.C. but it took us until 1952 to get there. Six years to go a couple of thousand miles. Things just kept getting in the way. Stopping to work in one place, and then moving on. Two children born along the way.

When we got to Chilliwack in the Fraser Valley, we knew we'd found paradise, and we've been here ever since. Very happy.

TEACHER VERSUS THE DEVILS

Culture shock! I could write a book about it. Just give me that tape recorder of yours and stand back.

There I was, a little Scottish lass, a schoolteacher. Lured to big old Wild West Canada by the Alberta government, who promised me the world. That meant a school of my own. You know what that means?

It meant a schoolhouse west of Nanton in the foothills of the Rockies. The recruiting man said it was in the shadow of the Rockies. He was right. On every other point he was wrong. It was a one-room school. It should have had three rooms. The other two being a toilet for the boys and another for the girls and myself. No, it had biffies at the back. Right beside the log stable where the children used to tether their horses.

Nothing in the school. Have you read John Charyk? He's a former teacher who writes about one-room schools. He's good, but he never ran across this one. It is gone now. We drove by there a few years ago and there was nothing. I guess it is being used by some farmer for a granary.

That first day. The farmer I boarded with drove me to the school. Two miles away. Think of that when it would be minus twenty below and a wind blowing. Just think of it! It was September and I was wearing a smart mauve and brown suit. The finest Scottish wool, and made by a dressmaker. It was for curtseying to the Queen. Not for your first day in a one-room version of hell on earth.

Those children. First graders. Sixth graders. And all hell and its devils in between. They yelled, they fought, they cried. They had curse words I'd never heard of and others I never dreamed children knew. They fought, they bit, they tore at each other.

The farmer just turned into that yard and plowed through them and there they were, scattering like quail. He was a wonderful old rancher, an older man and the son of a pioneer around High River, and he knew everyone in the country. His family made my life worthwhile for that first year. Parties, dances and just good evenings before his big log fireplace.

But the kids! All this roaring around was show. They were putting on a show for the new teacher on her first day. After that they calmed down. Instead of being hellions they became devils. A big difference.

Old Mr. Campbell, he just laid down the law. He said there would be no monkey business. He had everyone in their seats, the five rows six deep, and there were seventeen children, ones to sixes. He told them, "Look, the teacher lives with us and every night she's going to report who has been kicking up a fuss, and next morning I am going to come here and beat the shit"—and please excuse that word, but that is exactly what he said—he said he was going to beat the shit out of every bad one.

Well, as you can see, that put it squarely on the kids, and me. If John Tugwell misbehaved badly, then I would have to tell Mr. Campbell about it, and next morning he would come and beat the you-know-what out of Johnny. If I didn't tell on Johnny, Mr. Campbell wouldn't come and Johnny would know how far he could go. How much he could get away with. And that day, Johnny and his two pals would go even farther. It was one of those situations.

By good grace, Johnny, who was the tough guy in class, he didn't push his luck. He behaved, so thank God I never had to have Mr. Campbell come and whale the daylights out of him. But I had to be firm, very firm and make sure they would know I'd snitch on them.

This system worked very well, and I saw Johnny at a reunion in Calgary a few years ago and he was quite a man now, a businessman with a nice wife, and we laughed about it.

But he almost broke my heart when he said, "We didn't want to raise hell with you because you looked so young and so pretty and we thought you might start to cry and we didn't want to see you crying."

Lovely. Wasn't that lovely?

Oh, it all ended nicely. The autumn we had together, we'd take walks and they'd teach me about the country, and I'd work in lessons that way and we all got along. Shared lunches. Helped with the coal stove. Did the Christmas concert, and it was the best they'd seen in the district. I learned a lot, a great deal about Canada and Canadians from those children, and I taught them a lot about the world and Britain that wasn't in the Canadian textbooks.

I stayed a year. I hated it and I loved it. I hated the winter and I loved the autumn and spring. I loved the people, but I hated what that cold and lonely land did to some of the women. I learned to ride western style, and shoot gophers with .22s, and eat barbecue beef, and sing, and build a fire, and cook the way Mrs. Campbell did.

I was sorry to leave, but my fiancé was coming over from Kilmarnock and we were to be married at his aunt's home in Calgary. I had got a job in Calgary and he would teach too, but that one year was a wonderful experience.

HOW I CURED THE KIDS' TV MANIA

I think back, now I can see it. It takes many thousands of dollars and a lot of time to make one TV commercial to sell a $1.99 toy for children, so they make those TV commercials pretty good, pretty nice, and my kids just wanted everything.

That first Christmas, about ten months after we got to Toronto, it was worse. Buy this, buy this, buy this, said the TV. Gimme, gimme, gimme, that was my kids.

I felt it was distorting my kids' sense of values, and maybe it was doing that to me too. I know it was to my wife. She'd look around that little kitchen and say, "Why can't we buy this?" A machine to make batter, or something like that. All those pretty young women on the TV showing how easy it was.

Nobody has to tell anyone how much those TV ads were powerful, even though they were in black and white, and I could see it was having something to do with the way my kids looked at things. From nothing in Yugoslavia, there was this kid their age on the screen saying you can have this. No trouble. No problem. Just go and buy this wonderful toy or bike at your nearest store.

I thought about it, and then I said, "Josef, you have to do something," and the next night when the kids were in bed, I took off the back and undid some screws and loosened wires and next day, no TV. The boys got stupid and yelled at me and I clouted the older one and I said, "No more TV. You can watch it when I get money to fix it," but it was a year before I somehow found the money to open it up and tighten the wires again. Hah!

THAT IMPOSSIBLE SCHOOL IN THE BUSH

The gist of it was, we were accepted for the 1950 school year, which they told us began in September, and by the end of July we were ready and on the way to Liverpool, where our ship would leave. It was a large boat and a good crossing and good food and interesting people, all like us. All going to Canada and a new world and a new life. You know how it is when you are twenty-seven and twenty-six. Full of beans, but a little unhappy that we were leaving our loved ones. Especially my mom.

The train took us to Winnipeg and another to Swan River which is a small town in northern Manitoba, and that's when the fun began. A man came up to us on the station platform and asked if we were Mr. and Mrs. Berton. Well, that was us, and without a word he picked up two of our bags and went around behind the station. We followed him, and without further ado, we were off. In a wagon with two horses, and Harry and myself up on the seat with this man who was not Mr. Etzinger, who we were told would meet us. This was a man named Mr. Slovoba.

It took us seven hours to get to the district, way north and west of Swan River, and there was no stop for lunch because there wasn't any. Just a few drinks out of an old water jug and all my thoughts of a happy life on the prairie and happy and red-cheeked Canadian youngsters so eager for education seemed to be vanishing. I couldn't ask my husband his thoughts because Mr. Slovoba was right there, silent as a sphinx and besides, by this time, Harry was walking most of the time, because his bottom was sore from the bouncing on this wooden seat.

Finally we arrived, and there was the Slovoba home. We had been told we would be living with a farmer in the district, and I guess I imagined a large home with a lawn and fruit trees. I didn't go so far as a peacock or two on the lawn. What we saw shocked me. At first I thought it must have been some stopping place and this was the stable, but it was the Slovoba mansion. The only bright sign was a couple of geranium pots blooming in the two windows. I thought, at least there is a woman here. The house was long and low and had white plaster walls.

We went in and there was one very large room, a huge stove, a huge table, some cupboards, and I remember two guns hanging on the wall. It was the first time I had seen guns in a kitchen. The floor was wood and the whole place was clean, but you wouldn't have found a house like this anywhere in England. His wife was there, a big woman. She was shy but very nice, as far as I could tell, but she hardly spoke a word of English, and the both of them rattled on with each other and finally he said, "Wife show you room. Cooom."

The bedroom was at the end of the house, down a hall. Our room was small, a large bed and a dresser and a board with nails in it, and I knew this was our wardrobe. It was so primitive, but it was clean, but I knew it would be very cold in the winter. There was a black tin pipe across the ceiling, and if that was our heating, I knew we were doomed.

They had three children and one of them, a boy about twelve, started lugging our suitcases into the bedroom, and he would be one of our students. A nice kid, but he was as talky as his father. He smiled but he didn't say a word and when I talked to him he still kept his lip shut. How old was he? He thought he was twelve. How did he like school? Okay, he figured. What grade was he in? Three, sometimes four. He should have been about sixth grade by that time, and I couldn't figure that out. Then he lugged in the other two bags and was gone, and that was the last I ever saw of him.

It was about four o'clock and the farmer said, "School down road," and he pointed. We decided to look at it, and there it was, painted white. It was wood and had a bell on it, and I thought it might be used for a church too. The door was open, and it was one room. A big one with a big black stove, long like a barrel, in the centre. There were six rows across and eight seats deep, and my husband looked at me with amazement and said there was only one room. I must have said something like that fact appeared obvious, and we had a fight right there and then. Our nerves were frayed. We were tired. We were hungry and we were thoroughly pissed off, if I may use a polite expression.

The worst school in the wilds of Wales in the nineteenth century could not have been as bad as this. There was nothing. It was an insult to us and an insult to the children we would have to teach, and we had been betrayed. Yes, I used that word. Betrayed. Lured out from England to this, and I wondered how many other teaching couples had fallen into this trap. There were several dozen of us on the boat coming over, and they were all going to Manitoba and Saskatchewan. I have never felt so sick in my life, before or since. You just can't imagine this feeling. I was a dedicated teacher and I wanted to teach as best I could. Here in this district and in the boarding quarters and in this school, it would be a very large struggle just to keep alive.

We went back to the house a mile away and we were a very subdued couple of people. The meal didn't help. Oh, I suppose it was good by their standard. My husband said it was like sludge. Heavy, greasy, thick with potatoes and onions. Whole onions, mind you, and a greasy gravy which was the soup. Black bread which was several days old and sour, and milk. No coffee or tea. Nothing. That was dinner and we each ate from a bowl, and the farmer reached under the table and took out a bottle and poured about a cupful of white whiskey into his bowl. He didn't even offer my husband any, not that he'd have taken the damn stuff. We ate, practically gagging the food down, but we were hungry and I admit it was filling. It had to be.

All the time the farmer and his wife talked, rattling on in this heavy Slav language. Russian, maybe. Ukrainian, I don't know. Not a word to us and the two little girls, they just sipped and sipped and stared and stared and giggled and giggled until I thought I would go completely stark and staring bonkers. I was glad to get out of there.

My husband said, "We'll take a walk," and about five minutes down the road we met a man on horseback. He stopped and said we must be the new teachers. He said his name was Etzinger and he was chairman of the school board. What did we think?

Harry isn't what you'd call a strong man, but I was so proud of him when he said, "Mr. Etzinger, you will have to get other people or teachers. Children cannot be taught in that school by two teachers, and teachers cannot live in the conditions in that house or eat that food. You will just have to get another set of teachers. This is not what we were expecting and what we were told we would face, and I tell you that in no uncertain terms." I was proud of him for that. I remember it all.

This man Etzinger got down from his horse and said it was not as bad as all that, and I piped up in my little English soprano and I said it was worse and we were leaving. I said it was disgraceful that we should be lured, that word again, from our home to this and that it was just impossible.

He gave in. Just like that. He took off his big hat and sort of sighed and said, "Well," he said, "I guess it is better you told us now than jumping ship in October when school is in." He turned out to be quite a nice man. He said this was called Gillie country and almost all of the farmers were like the Slovobas and they couldn't get teachers, and he knew how we felt.

There is not much more to say. We got back to Swan River after dark and next day we took the bus down to Kamsack and the train to Saskatoon.

There is no use worrying over spilled milk, but I wonder to this day if they ever got a teacher that year for that impossible school up in the bush. It was such a handicap for the children, but if the Slovobas were any example, they didn't seem to care. That supper seemed designed deliberately to drive us away. All this has been totally rectified by now with big schools and school buses, but I wonder. I'll always wonder how many children missed wonderful opportunities to become useful citizens instead of staying up there in the bush forever.

KINDNESS FROM A STRANGER

I got off the train, straight out from England, straight off the boat, straight off the train, straight into Vancouver at about nine on a Sunday morning, and there I was. I had this fine English woollen suit on and it was already a hot day, it was in July, 1949, and I had exactly two dollars in my pocket.

I walked and walked and walked, the sun getting hotter, and I hoped I'd run across one of those shops where they had jobs listed in the window. They didn't. I was green as grass so I didn't know that. And I was hot. I didn't dare take off my suit coat. I mean, in England you just didn't do that.

I can remember it so well. I thought, at least I could find a policeman who could give me some advice. Where I could cash a cheque, maybe, and then I thought, oh God, I'm in Canada now and there isn't a Lloyd's around the corner. I mean, I really got panicky. Lord, I couldn't sleep in the park. Besides, what was I going to do tomorrow?

To this very day I can remember it. I was standing in front of a little shop on Pender Street and it had medals and coins and stamps, stuff like that for sale. A poky little shop. Then I heard this voice say to me, "You all right?" I turned and there was this gentleman, well dressed, about fifty, I should judge, and I said, yes, I thought so. Why did he ask? He said, "Well, young man, you've been staring in that window for at least five minutes and there's nothing I can see of all that interest in it, and I just wondered." He just wondered! The truth of it all was, I guess I was in some sort of a trance.

I decided to take a chance. Yes, I did. I told him I had just got off the train three hours ago and I didn't know Vancouver, had no friends and didn't know what to do with myself.

I remember even now, he said, "Eat'n?" Lord, I thought he meant had I gone to Eton, the English school. I said no, I'd been educated in Bristol and now he got a funny look on his face but we had a bit of a laugh when that was straightened out. He had asked me if I had eaten. I said no, not lunch, and he said to come along with him. We'd have a bite to eat. A bite to eat? Now, that was a Canadian expression I'd have to use again. A bite to eat. When you think of it, isn't it silly? Oh, most expressions are.

For two hours we talked and talked. He asked the questions and I answered and then he gave me advice, enough to fill an encyclopedia. I was taking it all in, smoking his cigarettes, drinking his coffee after our lunch, and I remember this because it was my first real contact with a Canadian in his own country. Everything else had been on the train, hardly a way to get acquainted when people were getting on and off all the time, but this was different.

One thing he did, he went to the phone and came back and wrote on a piece of paper and said this was to be given to the clerk at the Dufferin Hotel. It would give me a room for four nights, and I could send the ten dollars to him when I earned some money. He also gave me ten dollars for food. I didn't ask for these things. How could I? Straight from England? He was just a very kind man who took an interest in young people, and I guess he could read character. I hope he could. I paid him from my first month's cheque. He, oh, by the way, his name was Sandwell. R. Sandwell and he worked on the railway. He was a big man, a rough man from what I saw of him, but you know, to this day, I never forgot him. He made me feel good about Canada. I've always felt good about Canada ever since that Sunday. I never saw this Mr. Sandwell again. Never heard of him again, and I guess he'd be dead now.

I POINTED BETWEEN MY LEGS

There is one story that will make you laugh.

It was 1948 and we were still living in a refugee place, and my mother said she would write her cousin in Moose Jaw and ask him if he would sponsor me and look after me for a while. I was eighteen and it took until I was nineteen before everything was arranged, and I got on the ship at Hamburg and came to Canada and then on the train. I didn't speak English, but there were people in the government and the Red Cross who helped you.

I got off the train at Moose Jaw and nobody was there to meet me. No cousin, I guess. I took my suitcase and sat in the station, and all these people around, not seeing me at all, and then the train left and the people left and no cousin, and I became very afraid, and I had to go to the bathroom badly. I had to go badly, and I think it was because of fear, and I didn't know which door to go into, and there was a policeman watching me.

I started to cry and I thought I would have to do it down my leg, right there with the policeman by the door, and then he came over and said something. I guess he was saying, "Why are you crying?" I was hysterical with fear, think of it now, and I pointed between my legs.

This man he took my arm and led me to the door of the bathroom and pushed me in, kind of roughly, as if he thought I would do it there on the floor.

When I came out I wasn't crying any more, and I had washed my face, and there was a man talking to the policeman and looking at me, and he came over and spoke to me in Polish. It was my cousin.

MRS. CARSON HAD HER OWN IDEAS

I got off at the CN station in Vancouver, and it was a Sunday, and I checked my luggage, and there I was, an Englishman in a strange town and I didn't have a penny in my pocket, but I had the address of a friend of my father.

I went over to the black porter and I showed him the address, out in Kerrisdale as it happened, and I asked him how far it was to walk there. He grinned and said too far, just too far in the heat, and he said phone him from the phone over there. I said I didn't have a penny to my name.

I think that shook him up. A well-dressed white man without a nickel for a pay phone. I told him I had lost my wallet somewhere on the train from Edmonton. He took me over to the phone booth and looked up the number, and he said if I couldn't get through, he was off work in two hours, and if I couldn't find this family friend, I could go home with him and eat with his family and they would fix me up with a bed.

I just couldn't believe it! He hadn't known me more than two minutes. He didn't know me at all. I could have been Jack the Ripper. But here was this lowly black porter—and that is what they were, lowly in pay and status—and he's offering this quite proper young Englishman a meal and a bed.

Well, as it happened, Dr. Carson and his wife were in and they had the letter saying I was coming. They came and picked me up and I thanked my new friend profusely, very profusely, when he put my bags in their car.

On the way to their house I told them about the porter. How he had been so kind to me. They were absolutely horrified that I would think of doing such a thing, going home with a black man and staying with his family for the night. But they were even more horrified that he would offer to help me. What, a black man! I never heard of such an unlikely thing before, and I can hear Mrs. Carson saying it. A Negro, just imagine!

I caught myself before I said anything which would offend them, but I certainly was offended. I was quite annoyed at them. This man had kindly gone out of his way to help me, and they thought he had committed some sort of a crime. I thought, well, I've learned something the first day in Vancouver.

I wasn't going to let their attitude upset me, certainly not. The wallet showed up soon enough. Somebody had found it on the train and taken the money and turned it in to the station, but I had money because in the letter to the Carsons my father had enclosed four £50 notes. You could only take $250 worth of Canadian money out of Britain at that time, so this was the way to get around it. You cashed the pounds at the bank. When I went around to pick up the wallet, I hunted down my friend and gave him ten dollars. I guess he thought he was just doing me a favour, and although he didn't, I understood, and this was my way to give it back.

I just hope he wasn't thinking, oh, this is his way. Here's a young Englishman and I'm a black porter, and this is his way of establishing the difference again between us. I hope he never thought that. I wouldn't have thought of it either, but when I told the Carsons what I'd done, it was Mrs. Carson who put that idea in my mind.

GOD BLESS THE SALLY ANN

If I had to do it all over again, and God forbid that, I would tell everyone who came over to Canada: be a Canadian, talk Canadian, work Canadian and play Canadian, but do not throw away your connections with your own people.

I did that, and whether it was because I was too young, seventeen, or too proud or too scared or what, or just because I was a stubborn Hollander, I cannot put them together and give an answer, but I went through a special kind of hell and every minute of it was my own fault.

Honestly, I did not know until later that there was nothing wrong with asking for help. I did not know there were lots of people out there who were more than happy to help this tired and scared young kid who came off a farm and didn't speak a word of English. I was too sap-dumb to even show a stranger a card they gave us, which was printed in English, which asked for help.

I know now if I had asked, it would have been given. That people, Canadians, would have taken me into their hearts and fed me. Not just because I was Dutch and our Queen had spent the war in Ottawa. No, not that. But because Canadians have huge hearts. They have a great gift for helping.

When we got off at Union Station, I had no Canadian money and I went out on the street, right away, with my suitcase, and I started walking and I didn't know what I was supposed to do. I would tremble when I saw a policeman because I thought all police were like the Germans. I remember how it was when a drunken German soldier staggered into our farmyard and suffocated on his own puke when he passed out. When we found him next morning, we buried him in the manure pile, and when the dogs found him and were barking, a German patrol came along and they shot my father.

I couldn't ever forget that, in Toronto, all alone, scared, and I walked all day. I walked all day and slept at night under a loading dock behind a warehouse, and two policemen came down the lane with flashlights and they found me. I had heard them coming. So I got up and ran and they chased me. I was weak as a child. They thought I was a burglar and I was taken in a car to the station, and then they found out who I was. A constable had been hidden by the Dutch Underground after an air battle and he knew some Dutch. So they knew I wasn't a burglar and they called the Salvation Army.

That is when I found out about Canada. How good the people were. I still give what I can afford to the Salvation Army kettles at Christmas. Five dollars. Ten. I couldn't count the amount I've put into the kettles over the years. Maybe five hundred dollars, I'd say.

They gave me a place to stay, a place to eat, and the Dutch Reformed Church took me in and got me a place to stay with some Dutch people, and they got me a job greasing machines. It was in a cloth factory. An awful place to work, but it was only for a few months, and I studied English at night school.

You see, all my troubles would have been nothing if I had just gone to the authorities, the people in the booths in Union Station, shown them my card. They were there to help people like me. They had their arms out for me and I didn't know, and all the time I walked the streets I felt like a rat in a corner.

That was not the way it should have been, but that's the way I let it be. You can say he's a stubborn Dutchman.

THAT DARLING MRS. URBANIK

Because my husband was a mechanic in a factory and his family was all around, we would have been tied to them. To their life. The family dinner on Sunday. The drinking Saturday night and every night when anyone had a spare pound. And the football! Surely there had to be more to life than association football on Saturday afternoon and the fights after it? Bloody noses. Teeth knocked out. Oh!

It was me who decided we'd come to Canada. My husband, Ralph, said no. This was his home. Well, I told him it was my home too, but it was not going to be home for our children, and we had two then. George and James. There had to be, I said, there had to be a better life for this part of the McGregor clan, and it would be Canada. And I said to tell the boss and pick up his tools at the works and we're going to Canada. I didn't know where. It was just to be going, to get away from all that.

You'll notice I don't have my accent. Only Webster on the television has it. They say it's good for his business. Websterrrr! I even managed to get rid of that brogue, as they called it. I had it when we first came to Kamloops. Oh, naturally. It was part of what they called culture shock for people to say, "Oh, I just love your Scottish brogue. Say something else."

Oh, I didn't mind it. In fact, in a way, I guess I did like it and anyway, it only happened a few times. Kamloops, not being Calgary or Vancouver, didn't get too many of us, I'd say, but so many things were culture shock.

The size of the pay packet, for one thing. My husband got a job in a place repairing automobiles. He'd always monkeyed around with ones his friends had. We could not afford one, although he was a mechanic. The pay packet . . . I mean the wages, were at least twice as much as he got at home. More. For the first few months I'd just lay the money out on the kitchen table and count it three or four times and then I'd say, "Two hundred dollars!"

And the food. The meat. The freshies. The vegetables, I mean. The fruit. I just could not believe it. The supermarket just a way down the wee street from our big apartment. Why, a little city like this, and here there are two of these great big supermarkets in it, the shopping centres with stores everywhere.

The apartment. That first apartment. Before we bought a house two years later. Two bedrooms, one for the boys and a bigger one for ourselves. When the superintendent showed it to us, I couldn't believe it. Ah, yes, yes, I'd seen the pictures of places like this. All the magazines, but that was for apartments in London. Stove. A fridge. Get up in the morning and it's freezing outside and what do you do? You walk over and twist, up goes the heat. Go to the sink, twist, and there's your darling hot water. No lighting fires. Not even a fireplace. Do you think I missed one? Not on your life. And here was the superintendent, that kind Mr. Baker, and he's kind of apologizing for the apartment not having a fireplace. At first I thought the man was daft. He'd showed us the little knob and you turned it. Oh, don't think I was simple. I knew what it was. The heat. He was just showing. But I thought, if you have a big boiler down in the basement making heat, why would you want a fireplace? I laugh about it now. Oh, it was gleeful. We've had fireplaces in both our houses and we use them all the time in winter. Fireplaces are for looking at. To make a room happy. It doesn't make it warm. The little thermostat knob, that's what makes it warm and snug and cozy. Oh, I'm going on like I was daft too, aren't I?

You asked at the start how I liked Canada. The neighbours. The people. That's what I liked. The lady next door, for instance. We moved in with no furniture. Just suitcases. Ralph went out to buy some beds and things. There was a secondhand store. We'd call it a junk shop then.

Oh, yes, the door knocks that afternoon. Ralph has hired a truck and we've got two beds and two dressers and a table and four chairs and not a dish or pot in the house yet, and we're wondering how we're going to get on. I should say that the government had somehow arranged this job for him, and he was going to start next morning, I think, but we're wondering how we're ever going to pay for things we needed. We didn't have much money. About three hundred dollars or something like that, and there would be a time before we got the first wages.

The door knocks, about four in the afternoon. I go and there are these two ladies. Standing in the hall. And they smile and say welcome to Kamloops and in they march, both of them into that bare apartment. On the table they plunk two dishes. Each. Four dishes. A stew. Buns. Potatoes and a cake.

The little one, the old, old one, she says, "You eat?" Or "You eat!" Like she was commanding us to eat. We, well, I knew she was foreign and I thought, now this is a real lark, isn't it? We come to an English country and here is our first visitor and she looks Russian and doesn't speak English very well. Oh, she was a darling, that Mrs. Urbanik. Of course, we found out, she was some farmer's wife, a widow, who had moved out from Saskatchewan to be near her son and her grand-

children. The other woman was visiting her from this place in Saskatchewan. They were like the Welcome Wagon, I guess. But a two-
woman Welcome Lady. We laughed, and I said we had no plates and
cutlery, and scurry, scurry, scurry, out the door they go and back they
come with plates, mugs, knives, forks and spoons and yes, they even
had salt and pepper. God help us, they even had a bottle of tomato
ketchup and some paper towels.

I remember that day so well. It was January. It was cold, and the
hills had snow on them and the boys came in. They had been out
walking around and they had a thousand things to tell. That's where
we got our first lesson on Canada. People had said to try and be like
Canadians. Canadians don't like to be criticized. They are sensitive.
We sat with those two old Ukrainian ladies for two hours and we
talked. I mean, we asked questions and they were bright as buttons.
What to do. All about credit at the stores.

We needed everything, and the next day we went hog wild, the
boys and myself. Buying for the apartment. All on credit. Yes, it was
$286.25 in credit. I remember the amount exactly. I thought, how
will we pay? But the stores were so good. They said, your husband
works? Yes. You have an apartment? Yes. Boys in school? On Monday, I said. Okay, Mrs. McGregor, the store's yours, or something like
that.

But back to the little ladies. Time didn't matter to them. They had
no husbands to feed, so they just sat and told us what we wanted to
know. Now, you've got to picture it. Ralph and I, just off the plane
from Scotland. Church mouse poor, in a way. An apartment the second day after that night in the Plaza Hotel. All snug, clothes hung in
the cupboards, a job for Ralph, and the kids starting school soon and
these two little old ladies, both from farms and telling us all about the
big city and its wicked ways. It wasn't wicked, and it wasn't big. It was
nice. It was beautiful with the snow on the hills. Friendly. You never
saw such a friendly place. Ah me, bless me, but I get a little choked up
when I think of it, and that was twenty years ago.

Oh, yes, the medal. I've often thought about it. If she was alive,
Mrs. Urbanik, I would have made one up for her. Or bought one.

It would have read something like this—Thank you, Mrs. Urbanik,
and your friend too, for the stew and the potatoes and the knives and
forks. Something silly like that. And then I would have added—
Thank you for telling us all about Canada.

THOSE BLOODY NICE CANADIANS

I thought, oh, I have sold the house, our home, and all my lovely furniture and all I've got are my three children and we're on this awful train and is it ever going to end, this train ride through this bush and prairie?

I felt that. On the way to Regina after leaving Winnipeg, those long hours were the worst I have ever spent.

I was thinking, I have left my lovely England and it is spring there and the snow is not off the ground here and I have no home and what is Regina to me? It was where my husband had found work with an oil company, and I couldn't reach him when we were in Montreal. Those cursed pay phones in Canada. Again I couldn't reach him when we stopped over in Winnipeg, and I was desperate.

But there he was waiting at the station, big smiling Jeremy, and after we had kissed and hugged, I asked him why he was dressed like that. He looked down and said, "Why, Monica, everyone dresses like this." I thought, Oh God! He was dressed in a leather windbreaker and an old hat, heavy work pants and boots, and I thought, everybody goes to parties, shops, goes visiting dressed like that? Then I found out these were his working clothes. What a relief! You can imagine. The Wild West and all that.

We got in his station wagon, but all our things seemed to have been lost, and they did come on another train, but that is another story. He drove us to this subdivision, out on the east side, and I can tell you as I've told one hundred people, my impression of Regina that afternoon was something else again. Mud everywhere. Bit of snow. No lawn. Just gravel and bits of boards lying around. And the house. The house!

Here a room, there a room, everywhere a little room, and Jeremy saying, "This is our bedroom, and the girls will sleep here and Rupert will sleep in this one." My, but they looked like the cupboards in our house in Evesham. I don't know why I just didn't sit down and cry. No clothes, no nothing, and a house with barely a stick of furniture, although I must admit, the sight of that kitchen was something I never forgot. New stove. New fridge. The world's first garburetor, I think. Ooh la la! And a washing machine in the basement.

After we'd had dinner it looked better, and my husband told me we'd go shopping tomorrow. I thought he meant to the greengrocer and the butcher, but he meant to the furniture store. And go shopping we did, and we bought and bought and bought. The salesman following around, positively drooling at the thought of his commission.

Then the bags arrived, and a few days later the barrels with my china and silver and all the precious little things my mother gave me, and with the new furniture. Mind you, it was the only kind of furniture you could buy in Regina, so I was stuck with that but, all in all, the house was quite pleasant and homey. I missed terribly the flowers I'd have had back in England, but I accepted the fact I was in a new and raw land and things would be so different than they had been.

One had to cope. Adjust. Make do. Dismiss so many of the annoying big and little things about Canada, and soon you came to accept them.

After twenty years! Oh Lord, those first few years! Never forget them. In twenty years I got used to it!

But, oh, the neighbours were nice. The people were nice. Jeremy's bosses were nice. The milkman and the breadman were nice.

I used to say to myself, oh, if these Canadians just weren't so bloody nice!

ALL THOSE INTELLECTUAL MINERS

One day a bus comes into the town, Elliot Lake, and these fellows pile out, and this is a Sunday and a bunch of us are hanging around, and a strange lot these fellows are.

First, they don't look like hard-rock miners. I don't know just what a hard-rock miner looks like, but these fellows didn't have the stand of it. They looked like city fellows, and some had little beards and some had glasses, and their clothes looked pretty good. Like, they were well dressed.

One of our guys, a Greek named Peter Something-akilis—that's what we called him, Something-akilis, because we couldn't pronounce his last name—he said he thought they looked like Hungarians. I don't know why. I thought they looked kind of elegant and fussy and stuck-up, but if that is what a Hungarian looks like, then that's what this mob was. He was right. These fellows, they were a bunch of these Freedom Fighters.

I remember thinking, if they all cut and ran for the borders to escape the Rusian tanks, then why do they call themselves Freedom Fighters? Maybe the newspapers called them that.

But that is what they were, from Hungary, and they split them up among the men's quarters. You might get one in your room with you for a time, and you got to know them. A lot I met spoke English okay. They weren't just guys who worked in factories and being masons and carpenters and truck drivers and that sort of thing. These guys were educated. Some of them were professors and a couple of doctors and engineers. They weren't like us, lads from the pits, at sixteen and in the pits until we die. They spoke English with education, and you could see they just weren't your ordinary workingman.

Miners usually be a rough and tough lot, even if they've got their families with them from the Old Country. They drink a lot and they get into fights and they swear and they, well, they're not like these intellectual miners. That's what we called them. Intellectual miners. Soon everybody was calling them that.

Not that we didn't like them. Oh, we did. They were a fine bunch of lads, but when they came they had soft hands. Soft hands means they had done no hard work. All the work was up here, in the old bean. Paperwork guys, like in the mine office. They did their best to fit in, friendly, and always wanting to learn, and a lot of them had a lot to learn about underground. They did it, though. The first two weeks, maybe, that was sore hard for these lads, but they stuck it. Stuck it hard and good, and you didn't hear much complaining from them.

Of course, coming from this Hungary to Steve Roman's Elliot Lake, this was something. Something they'd never seen before—with all their learning and reading—this little town all new and working and clean and wide streets and the homes and the stores and the schools and all. The lakes and river and the bush, this was all new to them. They didn't know what a pool hall was, and the drugstore, they'd go in and just walk around, just gazing, you might say. The theatre, and they would say, "How can this town have two theatres?" The fire department. The library. All the things they had in Hungary, I guess, but in such a different way. I mean, one guy, an immigrant guy like Steve Roman, he comes in and starts a mine a few years back and puts everything in it. Nothing is more than ten years old, you might say, and everything in Hungary might be 250 years old. You understand? They just couldn't believe it. Even from England, we took it all as natural, because Canada and England were much the same, from the same beginnings.

Now, take skating and hockey. Now they must have had skating in their country, but not like here, not in a huge rink and everybody all dressed up and in bright colours and skating, skating. Or the hockey. Little kids, this high, no bigger, playing and trying to be like the NHL. Curling? Now, with all the brains these intellectual miners had, they sure thought that was something.

Maybe Hungary goes back a thousand years in history. Maybe more, don't you think? But here they were in Canada, in the bush, and they were thinking, 'cause I know, if Canada can do this, one man, this Roman fellow who was an immigrant boy from somewhere, Yugoslavia, I think if he can do this, what can we do?

They worked hard and they didn't talk much about what had happened. I know they had a lot of thoughts about their families and what they had run away from, homes and good jobs and things like that, but they knew they couldn't go back. So they had to work hard and get a lot of money.

Working for Denison Mines you could do that. Stay away from the booze. These guys seemed to like wine anyway, and the stuff never makes you drunk. You can't drink enough. So they worked hard and they skated and went for walks and went to the library and got books and went to the dances. A big hit, there. Good dancers. Put us all to shame. And they were all gentlemen as far as I could see.

Then I went back to England to get married, and when we came back, I decided I would stay in the city. I took Hamilton because there was work in the mill there. I don't know how long the Hungarians stayed, and there must have been a hundred of them, but I don't think they would stay too long. They were scholars and they were rings around us in that way.

A company town like Elliot Lake was no place for them. Okay, yes, for a time. To get to know Canadian ways and fix up their language more and decide what they were going to do, with their education and their manners and all that.

I think though, for a year, maybe more, to save money and to get to know Canadian life, it was a good place for them to go. Sort of a breathing time, like a boxer between rounds. Then get on with the fight. I'm positive, yes, positive, that all of these Hungarian fellows I know are doing very well right now. They seemed just that type. Guys that would get ahead in any country.

ALONE IN MY LITTLE ROOM

Those years? Ah, so long ago. So long ago. But you know, I can remember them, the first year, because I was so lonely. A person would think he would be lonely in jail, and I used to say to myself, you fool, if you were in jail you wouldn't be as lonely as you are now in Canada.

I had a job in a factory which made wire rope, cables and things for construction companies and the work, ah, it wasn't so hard, but it was noisy and everybody had their job to do and there was no time for talk. Anyway, Canadians didn't know how to make talk. Good talk. All they could do was talk about fishing, what they caught on the weekend, how many salmon, and how many they were going to catch. The B.C. Lions, how they were going to do at the next big game.

I understood some English, but I couldn't talk to these guys too much and nobody would say, "Hey, what was it like, the Hungarian Revolution?" Things like that. They didn't care about anything, about music, about literature, about politics.

Ah, I know, there were other Hungarians around, but I wasn't like a lot of them guys. I didn't even want to see one of them on the street. A lot of them were pretty tough guys. You've heard. I know you have, about so many of them getting out of the civilian jails and getting on the flights to Canada. Yes, that happened. The good with the bad. I just didn't want to have anything to do with them.

This was in 1957, and do you remember? Vancouver, well, it had the symphony orchestra, and I guess there was some theatre, but not much, and there was nothing to do, and you could walk around Stanley Park and that was nice. But at nights there was my room and books. Books from the library. My only friends.

I wanted friends. I wanted somebody I could talk to. Ah, just sit in a café with some music and talk. Argue a bit. Drink some wine. Listen to some music. Order some more wine. I would have paid fifty dollars for some Wexel Duck. The skin is crunchy, there's no fat and it is wonderful. Even some langos bread. That's what the peasants in the Old Country eat, and it is better than the best bread you could get in this country. Just to have a waiter in an embroidered jacket stop by the table and tell you a joke or talk about football. Soccer, I mean.

There was none of this. Vancouver had no ethnic restaurants then. You can't call Chinese ethnic. They use a lot of rice, but they didn't know how to cook it, fix it up like the Hungarians do, with duck.

Even some goulash would have been wonderful. Ah, but it didn't happen.

There I was, a grown man, twenty-five, and I had a good job, and I'd lie in my little room in the house I lived in and I'd cry. Yes, I'd cry. I was so lonely. If I had had a girl to take to a picture theatre, that would have been nice, but I didn't even know any girls.

Ah, anyway, that was the first year and then I decided, look, fool, this is no good. You've got to go out and meet people. Canadians don't care about your troubles. They've got plenty. Their own. You've got to go out and find friends, and that's what I did. I'd go to public dances, and that way I met girls and things got much better. For me, anyway.

TORONTO'S CULTURAL LIFE, AH ME!

This was about 1950 and I saw the advertisements in the British papers—Come to Canada, Land of Opportunity. That sort of thing. I thought, oh, Canada is just begging for us. I'll just walk down to the office and say who I am and they'll give me the works, shake my hand and thank me for coming and in a couple of weeks I'll be in Toronto and making big money.

Funny, but I was wrong. They wanted people from Britain, and I don't really know, maybe it was because I was from Belfast or what, but we all had to go through a lot of tests. A certificate of health, but that makes sense, doesn't it? Canada didn't want a lot of wrecks coming over, would they now? But I practically had to prove my family had been loyal to the Crown for a thousand years, and I had to have a certain amount of money and be of good character. About the only thing I didn't have to have was the results of an IQ test.

I had done some acting in college and I had the gift of the gab like Irishmen have, so there I was, and now I'm talking about Canada, you understand. So I thought the best way to meet people would be to join a little theatre group. My first job? Why, I had grabbed the first one offered me, and it was shoving crates and boxes around in Eaton's store on College Street. I didn't have much money, so it was just to carry me over until I was offered the presidency of the Canadian Pacific Railway. But joining a theatre group in Toronto was a wise move on my part. It got me in, if I may put it that way.

Canada, or Toronto, surely you must know, was what we'd call a cultural wasteland. Oh my, but it was barren. Ireland and Britain, so rich in culture, and then to come to Toronto. Why, it was what they called culture shock.

Shock in so many ways. A country so big and so rich and so interesting, and it was a backwater, but the shock was, for me anyway, that nobody thought they were living in a cultural desert. People I would talk to, they would look at me as if I was some sort of crazy man when I'd discuss this with them. They couldn't even bother, didn't care in the slightest, not even the least, in casting their eyes down the rails to Montreal where there was French theatre, because, don't you know, those people are French-Canadians. That sort of thing. New York with all its cultural riches just a train ride away, perish the thought. As for London and Paris, anywhere, that was the ends of the earth for them and, as you must know, Canadians had not become the world travellers they came to be, so I suppose all this was understandable.

This theatre group was no more than a United Church group and did stock plays and rehearsed in the badminton court in the church basement and put on the plays in the church hall, and I guess I had more experience than 75 per cent of them. It must have put a strain on the audience imagining this person up there on the stage was a farmer or a doctor with this Irish accent. I couldn't change it, but they seemed to think it was fine, or I hope they did.

But the people were a fine bunch of souls and they welcomed me and we all had a fine time that first winter. Lots of laughs. Lots of fun. It was a great time. We all enjoyed each other.

When all is said and done, I think I enjoyed that first winter in Toronto as much as any time in my life. Oh, yes, I still say it was just a terrible city to live in in those days, but again, what city isn't if you didn't know people? The city itself, I mean, was sterile and cold and dull, dull, dull. But the people I met, while not cosmopolitan, well, how could you expect them to be so?

And I used to tell one or two this, the few at first I thought I could talk to or who asked me that inevitable question. Oh, Lord, that question. How do you like Canada? I'd tell them and they'd say, "Oh, David, you can say these things to me, but you mustn't say them to anyone you don't know." I'd ask why—being me I'd say why can't I? They'd say, "Oh, it will hurt people's feelings." I'd say I thought that was the strangest thing I ever heard, but they said it may be true, so just say nice things. They said I'd get along better.

For the first few months it seemed to me that all the Canadians I had met wanted to get along better rather than get better. Hmm.

But they were a fine lot and some of them are still my friends, and one of them offered me a job driving a goods truck all through southern Ontario five days a week, and I saw that part of the world.

I think of my Toronto experience as a step up, because in 1952 I came to Vancouver, and it was flexing its muscles, and I stepped right in, working in radio and the arts and meeting new people. And the climate here. Ah, yes, the climate. So all in all, I had no experiences worth talking about, no having to learn English, no money problems, no loneliness, no anxieties. I just fit in, I think. No real culture shock in the main, but Toronto in those days, ah me!

TORONTO AND NAPLES: THE DIFFERENCE

There was this newspaper in Toronto which was written in Italian, and I read it every week, and it had lots of stories in it about Italians, and it told us how to do things and what to do. It was very helpful.

It didn't say things like we should be nice to Canadians and be like them and don't criticize them. We knew that. They had told us in Italy in a little pamphlet so we knew that but it told us things that would help us. Where the church was and the places where immigrants could go and get help. This was in 1951, and it had advertising about stores where you could buy papers from our country and the places where you could see movies in Italian and the churches and clubs and if you were in trouble, where to go and people would help you. This was stuff you would call common sense.

The paper was good too, because it was nice to read things in Italian. I was only eighteen, and it was a long way across the Atlantic Ocean and a lot of us were lonely. I had no friends in Toronto at the start. No Italian friends, but soon I got to know people, because there was the Kensington Market near where a lot of Italian immigrants lived. I didn't know any English people for a long time. I think I would have liked to, but I was shy. Besides, I think, they didn't want to know anything about people like me.

I would go into a store. You see, maybe I'd be buying a pair of shoes, and in Naples if you went into a store and bought shoes, you would have a lot of talk before you bought the shoes and after.

Do they fit? No, well, try these. How does it go with you? Fine, and how is your family? They would say fine, good, and you would talk, but in the Toronto stores they just wanted to get your money and get you out of there. They didn't care about your brother being married or your sister getting a medal at school. It was so different.

You'd say to yourself, well, I'll never go in that store again, and next time you'd go to a store owned by an Italian guy. Then it would be like in Naples, back home where you felt good.

You'd read in the newspapers about an Italian store that had shoes, and you'd go to them because you wanted somebody to talk to. They showed that they liked you to come in and buy. Buying a pair of shoes was something important. It just wasn't buying and going out with a box with two shoes in it.

So, the Italian guy, you'd try to help him. Help his family. They could become your friends, and they'd tell you about things going on that you could go to and meet people and maybe a girl. You went to stores with the ads in this paper and you thought, I'm helping them and maybe some day they will help me.

Even if they didn't, these guys were kind to you, and, if their wife was making sausage in the back of the store, she'd come out and give you a piece of pepperoni and ask you, how was it? That made you feel good.

There's a way of selling which I think is Italian, and a way which is Canadian. Buying in an Italian store makes you feel happy. In a Canadian, an English store, you just feel they are selling to you because you are in their store, but they don't want you hanging around, because you are breathing the air in it and not paying for it. That is why I felt so lonely at first in Canada.

LONELINESS, THE WORST THING

The worst thing in the first days was the loneliness. You had nobody to talk to. You talked a bit in the shop, but when the whistle blew everybody went back to their homes and you were left alone.

I had a little room in a house on Carlaw Avenue, and I'd sit on this little bed and listen to the radio I had, and when a song reminded me of some other time, I would cry. I cried a lot.

I guess I didn't cry quietly because one day the landlady knocked on the door and asked what was wrong, and I told her I was lonely. She said that was too bad, but why didn't I catch the streetcar and go down where there were the Ukrainian social clubs, the places where men were and played cards? She said she had seen an advertisement in the paper. I didn't know that, because I didn't know how to read English yet.

Next day when I came home from the shops she handed me a piece of paper and said this was the address of the Ukrainian social club where I could talk to people from my own country. She had phoned the *Free Press* and they had told her the address.

That night I went down there, and I knew when I walked in the door it would be okay. There were men and women playing cards and I could understand every word they said. A man came over and talked to me and then he introduced me to some other people, and from then on it was okay. I was living in Winnipeg in Canada where I wanted to be, but I was with my own people, and that was the most important thing.

HOPING TO HEAR ONE FRIENDLY VOICE

I was lonely. I used to walk downtown for hours because I had a job from midnight to eight in the morning and I'd sleep from six at night to eleven, so I had all this time, and I'd think, I will count off one hundred steps walking down Granville and at the end of those steps I will hear somebody call to me and ask, "What are you doing in Vancouver?" I would walk miles that way, but I never heard anybody, and I knew people were leaving from my district and coming to Canada, and I thought at least one must have come to Vancouver.

Then one day I went to the church and I talked to the priest and he was a young guy and he laughed a lot and he said, "Come here Saturday night and come to church Sunday and you will meet a lot of other people like yourself, tired of being lonely, and we'll go together to a party and drink some wine and have a good time and eat a lot of good food and maybe you'll meet a nice girl who you will marry some day and you'll have babies." He talked this way and, you know, this priest was right, because this is the way it happened to me. And I was thinking all the time, the church is as rotten as the politicians, but this was in Canada, not Greece, and, boy, it was good.

COSMETICS FOR A LASSIE

I just couldn't believe the way Canadian girls dressed. They must have put half their salaries on their backs. Looking for a husband, I guess.

But the cosmetics. The lipsticks, creams, the powders, the everything, and here I was from Scotland, four thousand miles away, and we hadn't had any of this sort of thing for five years, seven years, and I'm looking at this in Eaton's and I'm fair drooling.

I'm working in an insurance office down there by Dundas, and every day at noon I walk up to Eaton's and drool, and I want to buy it all, but I don't have any money for anything, really. And the prices then were, I guess, about one-tenth of what they are today.

About the fourth time I went, there is this really smart shopgirl behind the counter, and she's kind of smiling because she knows me by now, me in my solid brown clothes, my skirt and jacket and blouse, what they call sensible, and my sensible Scottish shoes. She calls me over and asks if I had made up my mind. I'm standing about six feet away, you understand, so it won't look like I'm buying or taking up their time.

I tell her I just haven't the money for these things, and she asks me where I come from, from Scotland, over five months and living alone, that sort of thing, and she says, "Now you listen to me. Tell me exactly what you want. Just point," and I didn't know what was going on but we moved up and down her counter, and I guess I picked fifteen things. Kind of a game, you'd say, and me giggling.

She must have had a sharp mind, because she tells me, "Now, you come back tomorrow and you go to that counter two down and ask for Miss Black's parcel and she'll give it to you. Don't even come near this this counter or me. Straight to that one," she says, and, oh my, the mystery of it all.

The next day I go to the counter I'm told to and there's a lady there and she sees me coming and smiles and hands me a parcel and says it will be two dollars, please. By this time I'm fair bewitched and there goes my lunch and car-fare money for a few days, but I get the parcel and scoot back to the office.

That night I open it out on the bed, and you wouldn't believe it. The box has written on it, "Seconds," and all these wonderful cosmetics and everything I could ever want, if I knew how to put them on, but there they were. Just a grand lot! A grand lot!

These weren't seconds, you know. They were from the expensive counter where this Miss Black worked, but she'd taken them down to the counter where they sold the cheap stuff and worked it that way. I thought, what a kind thing for a Canadian girl to do for a little poor girl all the way from Scotland!

Things were good for me and bad for me in the next few years, aye, but I never forgot that kindness. I never did. It was just, well, I found it just so Canadian.

JUST LIKE AN IRISH PEASANT!

I came back from the Far East in a small draft and I wangled it so I could stay over in Vancouver for four days, and I'd make my way back to England for discharge. The reason—I had a sister who'd come over in '45. A war bride. She'd married Fred, a Canadian soldier.

I thought I'd surprise her, and I had the address, and it was in what is now Surrey. Just mostly bushland there then, but I found their little house on this straggly kind of street, and there was nobody home. No surprise. I went to a neighbour and she said, "Oh, Maureen's digging peat." Peat! Digging peat? "Sure," she said, "over in Burns Bog for a company. They need the money," and I thought, Holy Christ, my sister digging peat!

The woman said she wasn't busy and she'd drive me over there and there was this bunch of men and women, and it was a hot day in July, and there she is in this muck, this goo, this . . . Ah, I can't describe it. I felt sick for her.

We found her and would you know it, my crazy sister. She was cheerful and happy as happy could be to see me, and it didn't seem wrong that she was doing this coolie work. She knocked it off then, of course, and we drove home and had a long chat and she said, oh yes, I remember. She said there was nothing wrong with doing this kind of work. Not if you were working towards building a home. Kids could come later, she said. A house was important, and if she could bring in another five bucks a day, then what was wrong with it?

But my sweet little sister! Miss Fancy Pants as I used to call her. Digging bloody peat like an Irish peasant. I sure as hell didn't tell my mother that when I got home. Not on your life.

A VERY IMPORTANT BOX SOCIAL

One night after work, when we'd finished taking off the last of the wheat, Mrs. Burns said there was a box social at the school and I was coming if they had to drag me by the ears. I didn't know what a box social was. You all go and the women take a big lunch for two people and they make it the best they can, devilled eggs, tuna fish sandwiches, cookies, fruit and everything fancy. A picnic, you see, and one fellow is the auctioneer, and all these boxes—this is the way it worked—they were auctioned, and you didn't know whose box it was. I asked, what if I got an eighty-year-old granny and I had to spend the evening with her? Mrs. Burns said if I did I was to be awfully nice to her, but maybe that wouldn't happen.

We went the next night and I knew most of the men and boys but that was about all. I only knew some of the women from working on their farms or seeing them in town on shopping night. On Saturday. The big classroom had been cleared and the desks put to one side for the dance later, and the men sat along one side and the women the other. This big pile of boxes, maybe thirty, all brightly decorated. You bid, you see, three dollars, four, six, whatever you wanted, because the money went to the athletic fund. Baseball and hockey skates. Balls and pads.

I sat beside Mr. Burns, and about five or six boxes went off, and the lady whose box had been auctioned, when the bidding was over and it was lots of fun, jokes being yelled, a lot of noise, she'd come up, and the man who had bought it, they'd eat together later.

A box came up and Mr. Burns said, "Helmer, you've got to bid. Try for this one. Go on, bid for it," and I said to myself, I hope it doesn't go to ten dollars, because that was two days' wages for me. That was a lot to spend for dinner you didn't even know what you were getting.

I'll tell you, that was a popular box. When it got to nine-fifty, I thought, ten dollars and no more. I put up my hand. Ten bucks. I got it, nobody would bid more, and that was the highest so far, and I stood up and a young lady across the room, she stood up. Everybody cheered and clapped and laughed.

I didn't know who she was. I'd never seen her before, but she was about my age. I thought, she looks about thirty. We met up at the table and she said, "I'm Kathleen," and I said I was Helmer, and she smiled and said, "Yes, Helmer, I know."

It was called a put-up job. She was the new schoolteacher who had started in September, and Mrs. Burns had passed the story around, and I found out this later, that I liked her. I didn't even know her. Mrs. Burns asked people to let me win as I'd told her that ten dollars, that was as high as I'd go. Things went for twenty dollars later on when the bidding got hotter when there were only a few boxes left, but my ten was highest up to then.

Mrs. Burns told me the next day that the schoolteacher had seen me around town a couple of times and she hoped I would buy her dinner, so that's the way Mrs. Burns arranged it. We have a word in German for it, but the Canadian word would be *sly*.

That is how I met my wife. I mean Kathleen became my wife. We were married when the school ended in June, and the wedding feast was in the same schoolhouse in the district. It was a big affair, and everybody came, and that's just about the way it was. I might have met her later and married her but the people thought, oh, that Helmer Holtz, a big German guy like that, a stingy bachelor. Saves all his money. What he needs is a wife.

I got a wife and she got a husband, and after the wedding we went to Drumheller, where she had a job waiting in the town school. I worked for a hardware store and did a lot of other jobs to earn more money, and then two years later we moved to Calgary where we had two kids.

MARRIAGE—AN OCEAN APART

When they started really working on the subway, up Yonge and around there, I went to the hiring place and they hired me and that made my pay so good I couldn't believe it. Nearly three times as much, and I was only a labourer. Most of the labourers were Italian. We worked hard, but we made good money. I still worked for the Italian restaurant at night, for three hours, and that way I got my meals and my bedroom in the storage room. I didn't care.

Now I'll tell you about getting married. I wrote the village mayor and I told him I wanted a girl from the village. He said I'd have to pay her father what was three hundred dollars Canadian then. That was okay. I went to the priest of our church and he signed a paper saying I was not married, and two other men in the church signed them too. Then I sent them and it was arranged. This took six months. All I had was a picture of Anna. We wrote letters, and I thought I might love her when she came. Then a day was arranged. I was married in Toronto at ten o'clock in the morning in our church with the priest and the witnesses, and she was married at ten o'clock in the morning in the village church, and we were married. They call it a proxy marriage.

A year later I get an apartment and a bit of furniture and I meet the train at the Union Station and there she is. Just like her picture. We don't kiss or anything like that, but I take her to the apartment in this old house, and she thinks it is pretty good. That's when we get to know each other the way we should, after a little time. First, we have a party with my friends and Italian food and homemade Italian wine, and then we sing and laugh and joke, and then everybody goes home and then, well, then Anna and me are wife and husband.

It all worked out pretty good.

WATCH, BUT DON'T ASK!

This is something I don't even think I should tell, but I will because you'll see how it was with some of us.

I can't remember how I thought of it, but I got a job with the Parks Department of the University of B.C., and I'd see all these girls, hundreds of them, and I'd been in Canada for six months and I hadn't been out with one single girl. Not one girl.

In Greece, in our town, I'd always had girls. Not one girl, because I wasn't going to get married, but girls. There would be five or six, maybe, of us unmarried guys in the town, and we'd go to the café, and there would be girls there. We'd drink and dance with them and have fun. They'd be with their families, so it wasn't dating like the kids do here, but it was girls and it was fun. If you were getting married to a girl, then you didn't do that.

I'd been working on the lawns, and it was springtime, and I'd been in Vancouver for six months, maybe. This Sunday I got dressed up in my best clothes and I went out to the university, and there was this bus stop. I'd watch and see a girl student coming from the residences and I'd ask her if I could take her out to dinner. I'd smile and say it politely. My English was pretty good. I'd studied very hard at it. I mean, my clothes weren't old things. Better, let me think, yes, better than what most of the students wore. And I'd just ask this girl or that girl if they wanted to go out to dinner with me.

Some smiled at me and said no. Or they'd smile and shake their head. Some would just hurry by. I guess I asked about ten or twelve of these students, and nobody would say yes to me.

No, I can't say how I felt. I guess I didn't feel too good. Yes, of course I knew that what I was doing wasn't the way things were done in Canada in those days. This was in 1960. The spring. I came from Spiros in 1959.

Then, oh, I remember, the bus drove away, and I thought, well, maybe it isn't such a good idea. I'm scaring them off. There had to be another way to do this. Somebody will get the wrong idea, and I sat down and waited for the next bus.

A few minutes later, maybe ten minutes, a police car came up and the Mountie got out and he asked me if I had been talking to the women students. I said yes, and he told me to get into the car. Well, what could I do?

They took me back to the police office and talked to me. No, no, they didn't question me. They just talked to me. Asked me what I was doing. Why I was doing it. I just told them. I said I was a Greek landed immigrant and I had no girlfriend and I wanted to ask one of these girl students for dinner. I had the money. I showed them. Maybe forty dollars, maybe fifty.

"Oh, we believe you, you look fine, but this is not the way to do it and you must not do it again." And this is the older policeman talking. How do I do it then? "Well," he said, "you'll have to do it the best way you can or want to, but you can't do it this way."

Then they let me go, and one of the Mounties drove me to the bus stop and he said, "One of the girls you spoke to, she complained. We had a complaint from the bus driver. She'd complained to him and he'd stopped his bus on Tenth Avenue and used a phone, and that's why we picked you up. Just don't do it again," he said. He was a nice fellow.

I told this to a friend, the only friend I had. He was a fellow named Bryce Cameron and he worked with me on the lawns at UBC, and you know what he said? He said, "You should have asked the cop if he had a sister."

SVICKOVA SOLVED EVERYTHING

You can't say that food is part of culture shock, but when the landed immigrants came to Canada, say Toronto as we did, and then got that bombardment and battering from you Canadians, oh, how can I say it?

I'll say it this way. You are nice people, but you were so damned smug and complacent and stupid in those days. Yes, I'll use those words. You were infuriatingly smug and complacent and stupid, and I know I hated you for it. All of you.

For one thing, you felt that just because we were landed immigrants and poor or penniless, that we had always been that way. I wish I could have shown you my grandmother's house in Prague, or my mother and father's house. Your eyes would have popped, and still you people thought those little boxy-woxy houses out in Scarborough were just great. Shacks! That's what they were.

But we'd been through a terrible war and the terrible things that happened after it, invasions, Russians, purges, killings in the streets, and you had the nerve to look down your noses at us and offer our wives forty dollars a month to cook your dinners and clean up your messes after your parties. It took some getting used to, I can tell you.

In other words, part of the culture shock Czechoslovakians experienced was the shock of the lack of culture of the Canadians.

There was my mother and myself, my sister and her husband and their two children and two boarders, all from the Old Country and living, just getting by in that old house on Gerrard Street we rented and finally wound up buying. We'd talk about this, how we all had had such a good life in Czechoslovakia long ago, before the Germans came, before the war, before we lost everything, and there would be a lot of hard things said about Canada. Not the country, oh no, a wonderful country. The people we had to deal with who considered us no more than DPs.

That hurt. Not even a picture, one single photograph to show them of the mansion we had, the furniture, the barns and horses and the lawns and gardens. Not a single thing. Probably my grandmother's mansion now is a house for prostitutes for the Russian officers. Twenty-seven rooms.

We'd rage. You know how Czechs can rage. We're not like Hungarians, who sniff and snort paprika and then get mad. No, we just would get plain mad at it all, and the Canadians.

Then my mother would say, "Off to bed, don't worry, everything will come right. You will see. God in his wisdom will provide. We'll get some wine for tomorrow night and I'll made svickova." And we'd all cheer and laugh and that would be it.

Svickova? That's beef, and you marinate it and it is cooked in a sauce of sour cream with cloves, and when it's done you serve it with a big dumpling called a knedlicky, and it is the best thing in the world. Nothing better.

That's why these little ethnic restaurants, Hungarian, Polish, Russian, that's why they did well. An emigrant would say, "I'll start a restaurant and we'll serve food from home," and people would hear about it, hey, food from home! They'd go and talk and laugh and dance, and it would be a way to get away from all the culture shock, as you call it. These little restaurants were good for all of us. I'd think they wouldn't make much money, but that wasn't the point. There would be people you could talk to, and maybe they'd have a newspaper from home, or a record, and we'd play it, and it was just talk and eat and have a good time. Forget yesterday.

That's how my mother would always be able to stop one of these big family arguments or fights about how we were treated by people in Toronto. She'd say, "We'll get some beer, some wine, and I'll make a big svickova for all of you, so forget your troubles and we'll have a good time tomorrow night."

DRINKING LAWS AND THE POLICE

I know one thing—my parents, what was a real culture shock to them was the drinking laws.

Like coming from Europe, over there before the war. Of course, everybody worked six days a week and Sunday was the big day, the day of rest, to relax, enjoy themselves. They'd go out to a café and have a nice dinner, a few drinks and then they'd dance and have a good time.

In southern Ontario there was none of that. It was bluestocking, bluenose. WASP. None of that stuff. No enjoying yourself. No way anyone could with the liquor laws. Sunday to my parents was a good day, but people in Ontario, they had it as the worse day of all.

I can remember a neighbour of ours, he lived just four doors down the street. He made his own wine, and one warm Sunday evening he was sitting on his own porch, drinking a glass of his own wine. Somebody phoned and the police came and arrested him.

And such hypocrisy! Farther down the street there was this Bulgarian. He'd come to Canada after the First World War, and he was the town's biggest bootlegger. People could come and take away beer and wine and booze, but mostly they just drank in his house. There would be fights—the knives and axes would come out. One guy died right out on the street.

Somebody would phone and the police would come and stop in front of the house and shine their flashlights on and off at his windows, and then they'd drive around the block and stop for five minutes and then come back. Of course, he'd had lots of time to get rid of the booze and the customers. Then he'd pay them off.

My parents just couldn't understand this kind of hypocrisy.

Everybody had their own bootlegger. Everybody, say they were going to visit friends or relations at Galt or Guelph, then there was this farm where they would stop in and buy wine or beer. Everybody knew they sold it. It was no big, dark secret.

But there were all these stupid laws, and my parents, they didn't want to break the laws. They just couldn't understand why these crazy laws were there in the first place. That was culture shock to them, in a small way.

I think, as the laws loosened up as much as they have, I think it was a lot due to the influence of these European immigrants.

STEAKS! BUTTER! PEACHES!

The meat! The Great Canadian Meat Counter, as I called it. I'll never forget it.

My uncle, Everett Gardner, lived in Winnipeg, and in desperation I wrote him. I'd never met him. I knew nothing about him. My husband said we just had to get out of England and Everett was the only Canadian I had heard of. I said my husband was an aeronautical engineer, a fine job if England happened to be building planes, but they weren't doing that in 1946, and Bristol was a gloomy place, so downcast, and George was working as a janitor. He was lucky. Thousands were on the dole.

We would like to come to Canada and if he would guarantee us, that was all we would ask of him. The dear old soul did. He phoned, of all things, at three o'clock in the morning.

In four months we were in Winnipeg, and there we were in his little house on Jubilee, a lovely day in October and, oh, it was grand. He took us out for dinner that night in his funny old chug-chug of a car. I can see it now, gasping and puffing along and him saying, "One more mile, old dear, one more mile and we're home." It was hilarious, but I think George and I were punch-drunk with fatigue and anything would go over big.

Next morning he gave me a twenty-dollar bill and told us to trot off to the Piggly Wiggly on Osborne. On my word, I thought the poor dear was mad. The Piggly Wiggly. Yes, it was a small supermarket, and he said to freshen up the larder, buy things, as he was a widower and ate most of his meals out. The cupboards were pretty bare, I must say. And off he went to work.

So, hi ho, hi ho and a fiddle-de-diddle, off go George and I and my list reads: meat, vegetables, fruit and dessert, and I emptied out one of our suitcases to carry it. I couldn't find a net bag.

I'll never forget that store. Heavens! Mind you, this was 1946 and somehow I thought, stupidly as I saw shortly, that Canadians were in a pickle the same way we were at home. Rationing, you know. Great shortages, just right and left. Line-ups and the preference system. If you shopped at a certain shop all the time, you'd get preference on the good cuts or the stockings or the lipstick. You know what I mean. The butcher was a powerful man in an English High Street.

Food! Boxes of cookies by the score. Fresh vegetables. Piles of them, all along one wall, with the most lovely fruit. Pears, apples, lemons, more apples, more pears, more peaches, fat and luscious ones.

Nothing had prepared us for this. We'd flown over on that Tiger Airline and it was sandwiches, baloney and cheese, a piece of cake and tea, and I thought my uncle had been going all out on the dinner. I found out it was quite an ordinary dinner.

But the meat! The eggs! One egg a week if you could get it, and then you were lucky. That was Britain, and for four years of that, too. Cream. Whipping cream. Butter. You see, I can remember all this, as it was kind of my own culture shock. But the meat! Roasts galore. Joints, to me then. Bacon, bacon, bacon. Liver. I was a bit shocked by that. We didn't eat liver at home, but there it was, the little sign saying "liver." Ham. Cold cuts. Steaks. Every kind, although I must admit I didn't know Canadian cuts of beef then. Lamb. Pork. You never saw so much pork! Sausages. We'd have killed for two of those sausages on our plate on a Sunday morning at home.

I couldn't believe it, and when I was talking to the butcher, I told him. He said, "Well, lady, it's been no different than it was." Something like that. I asked him about rationing, and he said that hadn't mattered as nobody had gone without meat. I remember asking him what Canadians had gone without, and he held up his hand and made an "O" with his thumb and finger. Even I knew that, dumb emigrant that I was. Nothing. They had not gone without a thing. I asked him about rationing and I remember his answer. He said, "What a laugh!"

In the other stores, the clothing stores, the hardware, the draperies, the . . . well, the everything. There was so much, and I think it was then I realized I was in another world. I had lived with wartime and bombs and even German fighter planes machinegunning the streets where children played. Yes, I am serious. And then to come and find that this, all this wealth and luxury, this had been going on all those years of the bombs and the rationing. You know, I often wondered since why Britain had such an egg shortage. We didn't have a shortage before the war. Why should we have one during the war?

That was my culture shock. Just the incredible abundance. The so much of everything you had in this country, and I won't talk about my new Canadian friends who complained how hard it had been to get gas to go to their cottage at Ponemah or Matlock or Winnipeg Beach during the war.

The meat. I'm sure old Winnie himself would have made goo-goo eyes at that meat counter, and that was just one small supermarket. Not even a supermarket. Just a big grocery store, four times as big as an ordinary one. But my God! The food.

I just loaded up. My husband said I went a little crazy. The whole twenty dollars went, in one store. Enough to feed an army.

When we got to the checkout girl, my husband asked me how he was going to carry all this stuff in one suitcase. I think the girl thought we were a little mad, and so I explained, and she said, "Oh, don't worry, we'll deliver it for you." I thought, I've got an awful lot of learning to do about Canada. This is another country.

4 ANOTHER LAND, ANOTHER LANGUAGE

4 ANOTHER LAND, ANOTHER LANGUAGE

Imagine yourself standing in a hiring shape-up at a construction site in Toronto, the foreman questioning the other men about their skills. You have only a few dollars in your pocket; your wife and children are waiting in a small room in a boarding house, and you cannot explain that you are a skilled carpenter because you have just arrived in Canada and you do not speak a word of English.

The great majority of European immigrants had a big strike against them: no English. Most realized immediately that they had to learn the language in order to survive. Workers often picked up enough English on the job to get by or went to courses provided night or day by government and school boards across the country. Those who had children were fortunate, for the young newcomers picked up English amazingly quickly and spoke it around the kitchen table. Immigrants with a good education became quite fluent in six months, but others never rose above the level of broken English. A few, usually older folk, just did not try to learn and so ghettoized their minds and their lives.

Immigrants from Britain, of course, had no such problems. Customs and attitudes might be a bit different, but the language was the same, and they *were able to step right into good jobs, make friends and take full part in society.*

For all the other immigrants, however, learning the English language was a significant step forward. Without English, they were doomed to poor jobs, and those with skills could not work at them until they became reasonably fluent.

EATON'S CATALOGUE WAS OUR TEACHER

They don't have it any more, but in 1952 they did, and it was the Eaton's catalogue. It was big and smooth and our family just loved it. There was everything in it. It was just like the Eaton's Department Store in Winnipeg, but I think there was even more in it because there was a lot of things for farmers that weren't in the store.

We weren't farmers. It was not any good to us for buying things, but I had been a teacher in Holland and I knew what I would use it for. I spoke English. Most teachers in Holland did, but my husband, his English was very poor, and our five children didn't really speak English.

I used the catalogue as a textbook. It was so easy. There were the pictures and the descriptions, and they could look through that book and say, this is a hoe, and they could identify it with the hoe in Holland. This is a sweater. This is a frying pan. This is a bed. And so on. You see how easy it was.

When we came to Canada, my husband got a job in Edmonton as a janitor, but soon he found out there were a lot of jobs in the oil fields. He got a job with Imperial Oil. He worked on one of their big trucks, and he was away for one and two weeks at a time. The truck would load up at depots and deliver things to the oil rigs and the camps out in the bush, and so our family was without their daddy for periods of time. That is when the children would come home from school, and on Saturdays and Sundays they would each have a section of the Eaton's catalogue and they would learn maybe thirty or forty new words a day. In school they would learn more of the grammar and other words they got from the other children.

You see, when children are like that, six up to twelve, and five of them, they were all as if they were starting out at the same grade in school; they could all learn together. It was quite amazing. I never thought children could learn so quickly. Oh, they did. And it was like a game.

In the school, going downtown with me, in the schoolyard and going to the store, the parks and with the catalogue. I don't know who made up that catalogue. It certainly wasn't done for that reason. It was designed and sent out to help people in the farming country to buy from Eaton's without going into Edmonton.

I talked to a woman once about this and she said that what we were doing was not different. It seemed thousands of children and their parents had used the book to learn English. The words to the pictures which were everyday things, you understand. And they were all things people used every day.

The book was a wonderland. It meant, I guess, what Canada had meant to me when we were dreaming of coming over in 1950 because Holland was poor. The war, and all the terrible things that happened to us. We wanted to get away, forget all that. Dreaming of Canada, we thought of all the good things the Canadian people had. The plenty. The riches. And here, in this thick book which a neighbour gave us to look at, here was everything we dreamed of. Such riches. So much of it. If you had money you could buy everything in it. We couldn't. Not then. We were poor, no money, but it was still a wonderful book.

I guess, to our children, Eaton's catalogue meant Canada. That is funny to say, but when we get together, we can still talk about first opening up that treasure. There it was. Page after page. All the good things of Canada. Turn to any page, and there was what Canada meant to us.

THREE CHEERS FOR MISS HUDSON!

When I started school, I didn't know one word of English. Not a bit of English. We were just off the boat, we'd moved to southern Ontario, and that summer we'd worked in the harvest fields and somehow, and I don't know how, my father had managed to put a down payment on a little house and he was working on a farm as a labourer. That was the way it was in September of 1950. I was seven.

Today, you can't imagine anybody going in cold, in a way of putting it. At first there is a wall. Glass. You can see people. They're mouthing things at you, but it all makes no sense whatever. But I can remember, within a couple of weeks I was bringing home these books in English and reading them.

What happened was I had this fantastic teacher. She was just young. Her name was Miss Hudson. What she did, she kept me after school. About an hour a day. I'll go back. I could read and write before I went to my first school in Canada, but it was in Russian. So you could say I did have reading and writing experience, and that helped. All I had to do was put the English into the Russian reading and writing. Am I making sense?

She used to stay with me for an hour a day, just teaching me English, and by the end of Grade One, I skipped to Grade Three where the rest of the children my age were. They moved me up, basing it on my math and reading skills.

There was no time when I said to myself, hey, I can speak English. But by the end of Grade One I was totally fluent in English. Totally. Exactly like any other Canadian pupil. I don't think that is too unusual. That's the best age for kids to learn a language. You learn in the class and out on the playground and everywhere.

It got to the point where my brother and I would come home and we'd use slangy Canadian expressions. My father, who had been an engineer in Russia, his English was good, but it was very, very formal, he used to get the biggest kick just listening to us talking slang English, just like everyone else, rather than what was learned in school. He just loved all our new little slang expressions.

DON'T GET THE TEACHER MAD

It was tough on us little kids. They said we had to go to school. We wanted to go to school, but when they told us we had to go to Mulvey School and we went there the first day, there was my little brother and me and they didn't seem to want to do anything with us.

I was nine and Ludwig was seven, and they put us in the same class, with all the kids who could speak English. I didn't speak any English at all and Ludwig, he was too little to speak it, either.

The principal took us to this class, and everybody was staring at me, kind of looking at me as if something about me was different. I had a white dress on with little rosettes running up the front, and I think they were laughing at my dress. It was clean. My mother had made it. My little brother wore pants and a little jacket which was of velour, dark purple, with a little flare collar, and he looked nice. I remember we both looked nice.

The teacher was an old lady. You know, a prune-face. She should have been married. Nobody would ever marry somebody like her. I think she hated teaching, and her pupils, she hated them more.

I had never been in a school. In Poland they didn't have schools for us because when I was six, when kids go to the Gymnasium to learn, I had to go and work in the potato field and help my father with the cows. The Germans made this happen. Not my mother and father. Then there was two years in the camp because we had to go to Germany, our family. The way it was, I think, because we were German. The German minority in Poland.

I didn't know what to do, and this teacher put us in the back of the room, and she didn't come down and see us. She didn't give us a pencil or paper or any books. We just had to sit there. Everybody was learning things, I think. We just sat there and the other children were looking at us and snickering. You know, tee hee. Tee hee. I hated that. I know what they meant. They were saying, "Oh, these are just these dumb DP kids and they can't speak English and look at that funny dress with the red things on it, that stupid girl."

Ludwig, poor little boy, he had a bad cold and he was snuffling and he didn't have a hankie. I remember that day so well. It is in my memory. The teacher came down and said something to him and shook him, and he started to cry.

Then a girl called over. She said, "Teacher says he has to stop snuffling." She said it in Polish, so I knew what she meant, and that was when the teacher knew that girl could speak Polish. Her name was Myrna, which is a Polish name. She told this Myrna to take us out in the hall and tell us how we were to behave. I was crying by this time, and I was nine. Ludwig was only seven. It was so bad.

Then a bell rang and we went outside, and this Myrna took us over by the goal posts. She asked about us, and I told her how we had just come to Winnipeg. She was only six years old, because that was the class they put us in, all little kids, but she was smart. She told me a lot of things and not to get that old teacher mad, and I felt better when the bell rang and we went to the classroom again.

This was a long time ago and I know now that a lot of kids had the same trouble as we did. I guess a lot had a lot more. But we had to understand, then and there, that we were going to be on our own, to learn on our own.

DAD'S HARSH WORDS GOT RESULTS!

The government put us up in an old house on Corydon Avenue. The company had a big bus, and every morning at seven we'd all be at the place, and the bus would take us to the fields and we'd work all day. I was only nine, so me and my little brothers, we carried the beets and piled them. All day. For three months, I think. My mother and father and Lena, they worked the hardest. It was hard work and there was a lot of other DPs like us working. Some lived in shacks on farms, but we were in Winnipeg where it was better.

Then at the end of October the beets are in the bins and the company says okay, that's enough. Don't come back.

My dad got a job in a wood yard hauling coal sacks and wood, and the kids went to school. I didn't have any English. Not a word. I could say "Coke." I could say "please" and "thank you," and if you went into a store and pointed and smiled, you got what you wanted and the storekeeper wouldn't cheat you. A lot would, though. They didn't like us in that part of Winnipeg.

A lady from the immigration took us to Gladstone School for our first day. She must have told the principal none of these kids spoke English because he put us all in one class with the little kids, like my brothers. Lena was twelve, I think, or thirteen. She was big and almost a woman and she didn't fit into the desk. The teacher, she just put us in four seats at the back of the room and didn't talk to us, and all the kids stared. I was wearing a blouse and a long skirt and I had pigtails on both sides of my face, and they laughed at me, poked at me at recess until Lena came. She fixed them.

Boy, that was some school. They had a fire escape, a steel tube down the side of the outside, and all we did for two days, we slid down that. Up and down. Up again and down again. The teacher didn't say anything. Oh well, maybe she didn't know anything.

We told my father what we were learning at school, sliding down the fire escape, and he went to the principal, covered with soot and coal dust, and he gave him hell. I wish I had been there. My father spoke some English because of being in the camp.

I guess that old principal, he told the teacher, and the next day the teacher gave us kids a bunch of comic books to look at. When we told my father that's what we were doing, he said, "Looking at dumb comic books is not learning English the right way." He went to the principal again. Boy, I guess he was mad that time. The same day a woman came and she took us away in her car to another school, on Maryland, where they taught DP kids, and after that it was easy. There was a good teacher, and it didn't take long, because we were in the class with other Polish kids, Ukrainians, some Estonians, and then we'd be kicking a soccer ball around with the English kids too, and it didn't take long. Oh, maybe two months and we were going real good.

They didn't like me kicking a soccer ball with the boys. I was a tomboy. They said I should be playing hopscotch with the girls. Okay, I did that, but I still wanted to be with the boys.

That year, after Christmas, we had only been in that school about two months and we could speak English pretty good and arithmetic doesn't need English, so we went back to Gladstone, because we were so good, and then that turned out to be a good school. We were smart, so Lena went from Grade One to Grade Three to Grade Five, like that, and I went from Grade One to Grade Three where the kids my age were. It was a good time after we got out of Poland.

SHE'D GIVE ME TWENTY WORDS A DAY

I'd been in Canada for a year. My uncle had brought me over to Toronto by paying my fare and letting me stay with him and my aunt.

I found later they had some sort of an assistance program, so they paid the airplane fare, but that was just for people from Norway and Holland and Germany, like people with fair hair and fair skins and who looked like Canadians. Italian girls looked different. In the district where I was born we all were skinny and had black hair. You wouldn't find a Sophia Loren in our town, hah!

My uncle got me a job in a restaurant. I washed dishes. I'd go at seven in the morning and work until nine and then from noon until two, and then from five to seven washing dishes, and then I'd wash and scrub all the floors and the washrooms. And I got thirty-two cents an hour, so you could see I was working for thirty-two cents an hour for nine hours a day, and that wasn't much money because I had to pay my uncle for the plane ticket. I got my meals and supper at the restaurant over there on Queen Street. That was the good thing.

A waitress in the restaurant, her name was Sylvia Bradshaw, somehow she spoke Italian. Yes, I think she was Italian and had married a white man. Yeah, that would be it. She said, "You will never get out of those soap suds if you don't learn English," and every day she'd come to work at noon, she'd give me a list: one word in English, like "dress," and opposite the word in Italian. She'd give me twenty words a day, and this went on for months, and she was also telling me how to connect up the words, like, "I've got a new dress." That's the way I learned most of my English and when I could get a better job in a factory that made shoes, slippers, sandals, that's when I went to night school for immigrant people. I learned English pretty good there, and it helped me get a job as a waitress for twenty-four dollars a week. That was good.

I MARCHED THOSE GUYS OFF TO SCHOOL

I got an apartment in an old house on Gerrard Street, and my wife and child arrived a month later, and we were all set, ready to go.

I had no trouble getting a job. Toronto was booming. Lots of construction downtown, and I started out as what you would call a welder, and in a week I was foreman of a crew on beam work. I forget the pay, but we did nicely.

But enough of me. The language thing. The job was crawling with Greeks and Italians and guys from all over Europe. But mostly Greeks and Italians, and not one of them knowing more then ten words of English. They were carpenters and masons and welders, skilled men, but the unions were signing them on as apprentices. Kickbacks to the union bosses from the companies. Nothing could be proved, but these fellows were being exploited. By both sides, I should say. It wasn't a pretty situation from my end of it, being a trade unionist all my life, but I just kept my mouth shut. They were good workers, but they didn't know what was going on.

To this day I have no idea what these fellows expected of Canada, although probably a lot of them are running small businesses somewhere around here, but one night I got half a dozen of the brightest after work and I told them, in sign language, gestures, the whole business, that the next night they were coming to our flat for dinner. They got the idea. A couple just knew the slightest amount of English to get the idea of a free meal and so, being the kind of fellows they were, they brought their best clothes and changed into them after the job.

I took them over to our place and the wife had made a big pot, this round, like a washtub. Spaghetti. And she threw in about two pounds of meat sauce and garlic and dill and celery and everything she thought was Italian and Greek in the way of veggies and boiled it up, and we let them go at it. You never saw any six guys finish off eighteen pounds of grub like they did. Table manners, they had them, but even so, they could stow away more food than a regiment of fusiliers.

Then it was about 6:30, and I told them, making gestures, pointing to the bathroom, to wash up, and then I marched them over to the school by Dundas like they were a bunch of conscripts. They didn't know what in bloody murder was going on. I was taking them to the language school. Toronto had several of them, set up by the federal and provincial governments, I believe. I took them to the superinten- dent I'd talked to on the phone and I said, "Here they are. Teach them English, because if they keep on the way they are, they'll never learn."

What I meant was this. These guys were finding out that they could survive quite well not knowing English. There were so many of them, and at night they'd hang around their cafés and clubs and just talk to one another. Soon they'd forget everybody around them spoke English at work and in the stores, and all they'd have would be pig- latin English.

I'm telling you this, and without a word of a lie, these same fellows were coming up to me on the job within two months and they were talking to me in English. Oh, not good, of course, but again, not bad. They were learning the basics, fast. I don't know what method they taught them, but they sure deserve some credit.

In six months they had all stuck with it, and I could see I had picked the right men. I could tell by the way they worked and acted, and they were the ones who had the respect of the other immigrants.

Another thing I liked was this. These fellows, they got their pals to go too, and soon the whole lot of them were talking bits of English, and when I'd hear them gabbing away to themselves at lunch, I'd yell at them to speak English. I'd keep pounding away at them. "You want to be a dumb Italiano all your life, a stupid Greek, a fathead?" They were a good crew, and Canadians on the job would say to me, "What in hell do you bother with the bunch of dagoes for?" I'd say, "In four years they are going to get their citizenship papers and they'll be Canadians and then they can run for Parliament. With the numbers of them in this city, do you want an MP who can't speak English?"

There was great discrimination between the Canadian workers and the immigrants on that job in those days. They treated them like so much dirt.

I got my rewards. We'd be invited to their weddings and christenings and just the parties they held, like on an Italian feast day or Greek Independence Day. The Italians threw the best parties. They made their own wine, and it was good stuff, and they imported grapes from Lake Champlain for it. The Greeks once nearly tore off my head. I was at this party with my wife and they handed me a big glass of pure white wine and said I had to drink it all off. Down the hatch. It went down and three seconds later I thought I was exploding. We had fun.

One day an Italian fellow, Joe, big guy with a big godfather moustache, kind of a Mafia type even then, he came up and showed me a picture of a tiny baby and he said, "This is Enrico." I didn't get it for a second. It was his first child, and he had named it after me. My name is Eric, so Enrico. That was certainly a very nice compliment.

DON'T SPEAK GERMAN IN THIS HOUSE

When I got to Kitimat they put me to work on the smelter site. I did menial jobs, and then after a few days I found a partner to work with, and he was German, and I made a pact with him. He spoke English good and I said, "Don't you speak to me in German unless it is absolutely necessary, to explain something important to me. We will only talk in English," and that was funny, because I didn't know any English.

That's the way we worked. That worked out pretty good. I started to learn English.

Another thing I said was, no comics. Every guy read comics. I said no. Only newspapers. Periodicals. If it was tough, someone would help me.

It was hard, you know. But if you are intelligent and want to work hard, you can do it. And, being in camp, what do you do? I didn't want to sit around and twiddle my thumbs. So I studied. I would talk to guys who were Canadian and couldn't talk German. I sometimes worked fourteen or sixteen hours a day, and I always tried to work with guys who spoke English, so you could learn that way. So even when I was working I was learning, and they'd help me. They wanted to help somebody become Canadian. Even when there was free time and you went fishing, you talked English and it worked.

I would say, in a little more than four months I had a working knowledge of English. It could be done.

Then I had enough to bring my wife and little daughter over, and I bought the tickets in Canada, and the real estate company helped me because I was going to buy a house from them in Kitimat. They sent the tickets to her, and it was a cinch, and it cost only thirty-five dollars more. The best way. In September of 1954 they started seriously building houses in Kitimat for workers, and that's when I decided to buy, and when I knew the house would be finished, that's how I timed it so my family would arrive.

It was quite an experience to watch how they built houses there. With the speed at which they went. Not like at home, where everything is done one at a time. There it was whole rows at a time.

Then on February third of 1955, my wife and daughter left, and they arrived on February twentieth. I went to Prince Rupert by boat, and then I brought them up to Kitimat, and we had a home in Canada then.

It was lucky we lived in an area where there were lots of kids for my daughter to play with, and she was just two months short of four years old. So my wife and I made a pact. We would not speak German in front of the child. That was funny, because my wife didn't speak English, and so the three of us were speaking English all the time, but I was the only one who could speak it. It was hard, and it would have been so easy to say, "Oh, let's speak German. This is ridiculous what we're doing." But we were certain it would work. We made it work. It was very hard when I look back on it.

But our little girl, she was speaking English after four weeks. I know it is hard to believe, but children have this ability to speak, to learn another language very quickly.

We felt that it was so important to learn the language quickly, and we found that even if there were some mistakes, some misspellings, some mispronunciations, nobody minded. Not at all. They praised you for trying. They liked you more for it. They treated you better, and we were glad we did it that way.

Of course, my wife didn't learn English so well and not so fast as our little girl, but she caught on quickly too, and that was good. It was all for the best.

TEN CENTS IN THE POT

We'd be with these friends and drinking wine and talking. Everybody happy that the worst of the times were over, and these, you know, we called them English nights. Nobody could speak anything but English, and if they did they had to put a ten-cent piece in the pot, which was a lot of money then. This way, you learned English fast. Friends we'd met at the collegiate, a game of kaiser, a card game, and Maria's good food and wine, and then that is when I think it started to become what we had dreamed it would be like.

SOME KIND OF FRENCH

Oh, such a bother it was, me getting married to Ernest, in Zutphen, and then they said I couldn't go to Canada. Ernie went back with his army in October of the year the war was over and, when they finally got everything fixed for me, it was February. I was mad, but my father, he kept saying, "It will be all right, it will be all right. The Canadian government has just made a little mistake."

Then I sailed on this boat with my baby, and that was the reason, we found out. The little fellow had been born too early, and not in nine months and one day. Oh, so stupid.

Ernie's aunt was at the Montreal station to meet me, and she said Ernie was working in the bush. She rode to Toronto with me on the train and then she put me on a train for this place called Hearst and, you can believe me or not, this place Hearst was way up north. We had tags, and people would come along the train aisle and stop and read my tag and look at me and then they would walk on. They were the rudest people I thought I had ever seen. Oh, some talked, said hello, how do you like Canada? Where are you going? Have you got a husband for that child? Still they were rude. We were like in a circus.

When the train stopped my husband was waiting and that was good, but he didn't look like the man I'd married. His clean uniform, the sergeant in the army. He looked like a wild man. He was a lumber-

jack, that's what he was. He was so gruff, and I didn't like him. He
didn't even seem to be glad to see me. He had a car there, and then I
thought, this is a very cold place. My nose was tingling. Little Jan was
crying, and my new husband, he drove us to a little house. An awful
place. He took our bags, and then he opened the door and pushed us
in. "Look around," he said, "and I'll be back." He said he had to take
the car back to the man he'd borrowed it from.

The place was awful. Just three rooms. All wood, you know. You'd
call it a dump now. It was a dump then. Hardly any furniture. One
tiny bedroom. No room for Jan. I was tired and the house was cold
and I couldn't find any food and you couldn't see out the windows.
They were so frosty.

Ernie came back a long time later and he smelled of whiskey and I
said, "Where is the food?" He brought things in, so we could eat that
night. I told him I would go shopping next morning, and he gave me
ten dollars.

It wasn't a very good night for both of us. I want you to believe
that.

Next morning Ernie got up at six in the morning. Just imagine. Six.
He said he'd make his own breakfast. He was driving a truck carrying
logs from the bush to a mill, and he worked by the trip. That means
the more trips he made, the more money he'd make. He had to work
hard, loading logs, driving.

I went shopping that afternoon and took little Jan with me. Well,
I'll tell you something. You just listen to this. When Ernie got home
long after it got dark, I was crying. I told him I was crying for hours. I
said nobody would talk to me. "They don't speak English in this awful
place out here in the woods. They speak something else. I don't know
what it is, but it is some kind of French."

He said, "That's okay, you speak French very well. Talk to them." I
said, "You don't understand, you dumb Canadian. The French we
speak in Holland and France, this is not the French they speak here. It
is all a mess. Nobody could make sense of what they are saying. It is
French, but it is not French."

Ernie said, "Speak English to them then," and I said, "You dumb
Canadian, these French people here won't speak English to me.
They've got signs in their store in English and the cans and sacks are
in English, but they won't speak it. What kind of a country have you
got here, anyway? Like Belgium? Where everybody is crazy like that."

He said, "Never mind, did you buy some good food?" And I said,

"Yes, they would certainly take your good Canadian money fast enough." Oh, sure, and probably cheated me too. Grrrrr! Grrrrr to them! I said I hated them and this dumb little Canadian town. I've never told anyone this before, but I wanted to leave right then. Back home in Holland people were mean to each other, but not like this.

Oh, we had a good meal. I cooked steaks and onions and fried potatoes. Things we just didn't have in Holland, but Ernie told me how. He had a bottle of rye and we had a few drinks, and the house was warm, and he said everything would be better. He'd see to that. Talk to people.

But they didn't get better. I was still "the Dutch Woman." I could hear them talking about me. I told Ernie and he got mad about that. He said Toronto or Hamilton would be better for me and the baby, and that was when we decided to leave Hearst and its mean people. We went to Hamilton in May, and Ernie got on with Stelco, and everything was good after that. A house, a baby sister for Jan, a 1936 Plymouth to go to the beach, and everything was fine. No more Hearst. No more bush. You could say our marriage would not have lasted very long there, and there I'd be, with no one to know and so far from my home.

NO LANGUAGE PROBLEM IN KITCHENER

These German immigrant wives and daughters would come to Kitchener. I don't think more than a few spoke any English, but there they were, trotting downtown to find jobs, and they'd walk into almost any store and get a job. Not a word of English.

You know why? Kitchener and all around it used to be German and, remember, it was called Berlin until the First World War, and then they changed it to Kitchener after the British general.

These canny storekeepers knew there were still a lot of the customers who wanted to speak German when they were shopping, just like the old days, and there was this woman in the store now who could speak German just like it should be spoken, and so a lot of the immigrants got jobs right off in the stores.

Go into one of them on a Saturday and there they were, rattling off the German and having a high old time of it.

MY MOTHER, HER CHURCH, HER PAPER

The ones from Italy, the kind you might call the old people, they made their biggest mistake when they came to Canada. They didn't have the right mental attitude. No, it was not what is called culture shock. I've heard that one before. It was just a belief that they could get by in Italian and they didn't need to understand English.

My mother. She wasn't like a lot of these immigrants I have seen, like those from Latvia or East Germany or Hungary who came here for a kind of refuge but felt, always, that one day they would go back to their homeland and take over again. Christ, no! That didn't happen with our people. Or the Greeks. Or the West Germans. The Yugoslavs, all five varieties of them. No, when they came to this country they knew they were going to stay.

Kids, me, my brother, my sisters, we learned our English more in the streets than in the school. We'd come home with new English words every day and we'd say, "Mama, you gotta learn English. Nobody out there speaks Italiano. Nobody. You gotta learn or you'll not be able to do anything." Ah no, not her, and when I think about it, looking back, she was only about forty. She wasn't old. She was young in a way. Maybe thirty or forty more years to live. You see? It was crazy. Nutso!

The kids in our family were between, oh, five and eleven, and we had a ball. Toronto was so different from Bari. There we were poor and we knew it. I wonder if that city has ever come along with the rest of Italy? I don't know. I've been back three times and I never bothered to go down there and see.

But in Toronto, that was a new city. This was in '50 when we came over. Everything was happening. There were lots of Italians, lots of Greeks, lots of every kind of nationality. We were all in the school and we may have been poor, but we didn't know it. Lots to eat, lots of new things to do, lots of new kids, and you could jump on a streetcar and go anywhere and you could have a ball.

But no, there would be my mother, dressed in black because she had two brothers killed in North Africa in the war there. Sitting in the little living room of the apartment we had, and we're saying, "Mama, you got to go out and see things," and she's saying no, no, she's okay the way she is. Waiting for the Italian paper to come and it is all about new things happening to us in Toronto and she's not interested enough to go out and see.

Television, and she can't even enjoy that because that is in English. Just pictures for her. That was nutso too. I know lots of people who came from Italy about that time. Whole boatloads of these guys from Italy, and they'd pick up English from the television. But my mother, no, just her and her newspaper once in a while, and it wasn't about things she wanted to know about. It was about Italians in Toronto and what they were doing and everything that was good and wonderful about Canada. It was out there on the street and in the stores. All she had was the newspapers and, ah, yes, the church. She must have gone to mass more than anybody in Toronto. Every day. One block away, one block back, and that's all she ever saw. A kind of prison.

My dad was making good money in construction, and I had a *Star* paper route and so did my younger brother. My sister worked in a grocery store. We had lots of money. Saving it too. We brought five of our relatives over from Bari, good guys, and two of them lived with us and they paid board and room and so we had lots of money. More than any time in my dad's life.

We loved Toronto, and Canada was the most wonderful country in the world to us, and it still is. But my mother? Sitting there, praying, going to church, cooking, washing, cleaning and saying she couldn't learn English because it was too hard and she didn't want to.

There were times I just said to hell with her. Italy as far as I was concerned, that part, Bari, was a garbage dump. It was a place you just wanted to forget about, the goddamned slums everywhere. And there's my mother sitting, sitting there in her black clothes and thinking it was the most wonderful place in the world. You ever hear anybody write a song about Bari? No, never. A dog's breakfast of a place.

So my mother lived and died in Toronto in '62, and she spent twelve years in Canada and never once knew this wonderful, just plain wonderful country, and I felt very sorry about that. I really did.

TOO MANY, TOO CLOSE TOGETHER

I was only three years old when Mom and Dad came out from Italy, and they came to Vancouver because there was an uncle there, but most of the people from Calabria went to Toronto.

Now I look at Toronto and I think, too many Italians too close together. In other words, they didn't spread out into the city. A few would start a little neighbourhood, a few houses, a couple of stores, a café, and others would come and say, ah, this is where they live, and soon you've got these little communities south of Bloor, all Italian, and Greek too, if you want to go farther.

I can go into the corner store for cigarettes around here and the son speaks English because he's like me, but the old man can barely get by. The mother, she's sitting in the back of the store and she doesn't know a word of English, and they've been here thirty-five years. Thirty-five years!

I'm not knocking my own people, because there were factors you won't find today. First, the father and mother were uneducated, maybe Grade Four in Italy. They thought, oh, sure, we've got to have protection, so we'll be with our own people, and maybe there are a few people from the same village already in Toronto. Okay, that's fine, but they're afraid too, you know. Everybody thinks the Italian male is a construction worker, a labourer, and so that's where they go to work. You'd see whole gangs of men on a construction job and they would all be Italians.

Look around here. They've got their church, St. Francis of Assisi, and there are others, and their community, and behind those stores and houses there's bocci. The movie shows, all Italian films, and all the food, and their own newspapers, and that's fine, and they've got CHIN, that was the brain wave of Johnny Lombardi, a smart cookie. There are Italian TV programs. And all these nationalities have the same things, but I know the Italians have the most. Ah, there's nothing wrong with that, I suppose, nothing wrong with having a couple of MPs and a few guys in the Ontario Legislature, but I think they go too far. That's my opinion.

Another thing. Can you guess just how many Italian clubs and organizations there are in Toronto? Let me guess for you. I'd say fifty, if there is one.

Shit, man, I'm not saying it is wrong and I'm not saying it is right. I'll just put it this way. What in hell are all of them afraid of? Why come from three thousand miles away and try and build up something you really didn't have back in those poverty-stricken villages in Sicily and south of Rome? Down there in The Boot? I'd like to know.

Could you see Canadians going to Rome or Naples or Florence, and if there are ten thousand of them, all of them sticking together like shit to a blanket? No, they'd spread out and get moving, get alive, start jumping and saying, hey, this is so much better than home and

I'm going to take so much more advantage of it than the next guy because I can do so much better.

Anyway, these are good people here. They're fine people. Not many kids who grew up around here got into trouble, and these people pay their taxes, drink their wine, laugh at their weddings and go to the Gardens and the Ex just like everybody in this town does, but you know what I think? In twenty years, when this second generation starts to die off, you'll see this area around College turn into something else. It won't be called Little Italy because it's not that now, but it has a Little Italy state of mind, a mentality, and I don't think that is all for the best. Oh, sure, it is good for Toronto. Ethnic flavour and tourists come to the restaurants, but I don't think it is too good for the people.

Too many of the people here still think Italy and work in Toronto, and you see, it hasn't hurt them. Not financially. There are a lot of people who are well off, very comfortable. But I would just have liked to see it done a better way.

CONFUSION AT THE CLINIC

I remember I was in this medical clinic, oh, about 1958 or so because it was the year I left Regina, and this man and wife came in, and he was pretty badly crippled up, very stiff, walked very slow and hunched over, and I was reading a magazine but I was watching.

The woman spoke just a little English, but the man didn't know a word, and the nurse was trying to tell the woman that he was to take a little bottle and go into the washroom and piss into it.

I thought the woman understood at least a bit of it, but they were obviously Russian or Ukrainian or from Poland, and finally she went to where her husband was sitting, all hunched over, and she said in Polish, "I can't understand what this crazy woman is saying."

The nurse had been talking about the urine and holding out the bottle and pointing down at herself, and that wasn't enough, so I got up and I took the bottle from her. Then I walked over to the old man and I said he had to piss in this.

Ah, ah! Sure!

He hobbled off to the washroom and I talked to the woman, and they'd just come over to live with their son about a month before.

How the old man ever got into the country I don't know. He looked like he was dying.

I said to her that she must have figured out what the nurse wanted, and she said yes, oh yes, she did, but she was too embarrassed to tell her husband to piss into a bottle.

CANADIANS DIDN'T UNDERSTAND ENGLISH

I was born in the East End of London and I was twenty and I could talk to anybody at home, but when I got here I found that although I could read a menu, I had to point out the items to the waitress. She couldn't understand me.

It was then I realized I was really in Canada and that I had acquired an English accent.

I'd say, I remember, I wanted breaded veal cutlets and pie and tea and the girl looked at me and said, "What was that again?" So I'd repeat it, and she'd say, "Sorry, but I didn't catch that."

An Englishman from the West Country could understand my accent. To some Canadians it was a foreign accent, like as if I was an Australian.

I thought at times, oh, they're pulling my leg. They're having me on. This little waitress is having a little Canadian joke on me, but it happened too often. They actually didn't understand half of what I was saying. It wouldn't be embarrassing for her, but it sure was for me. There I was, pointing at the menu, this and this and this, thank you.

It was a real shocker those first few times, as if I was in a foreign country, and here I was thinking Canada, being part of the British Empire and all that, that I would be received as a wonderful person. One of the privileged few, you know. And here I was walking around downtown Toronto and hungry and saying to myself, Lord God, do I dare go into this restaurant? It happened, honest!

THIS WONDERFUL ACCENT OF MINE!

On June twenty-seventh, 1949, the day the girl I loved turned down my proposal of marriage, and it was then I vowed I would leave Ireland and emigrate to Canada. I had always had my mind's eye cast on this country, a beautiful place I had known when I trained with the Royal Air Force in Alberta, and I vowed I would come back one day and make my home here.

Now I'll tell you something else. I had talked to my fiancée often about Canada and I'm not sure to this day, but there is forever the thought lingering that the reason she turned me down was because she thought she would have to leave her folks and come to Canada with me. Now if that be the case, Canada robbed me of the first girl I ever loved. I have regrets and I don't have regrets, and I'm sure you understand what I mean.

I had relatives in Saint John, which you know is in New Brunswick. Oh my God, they were a stuffy lot. Are you familiar with that part of the world? Just as well, because if I told you their name, you might recognize it. Very big in boats and warehousing and grubby little houses around the waterfront which they owned and rented to poor people at exorbitant rents. That's the kind of people they were.

For some reason I cannot fathom to this very day, I seemed to have a stigma on my forehead. Like a branded cross, you know. I felt that my relations didn't like the Irish although they were Irish, and I felt the goodly burghers of Saint John didn't like me, either. I had this terrible accent, you know. They'd ask me where I came from, and I would say I was born within sight of the mountains of Wicklow. You see, I was testing their ignorance and really they were an ignorant lot. If somebody said, "Ah, yes, Ireland," I'd correct them and say, "No, I'm from Eire." That shut them up and, I might say, served to shut me out.

Oh, I was a gay lad then. Just out of school, two years at the university, and I really couldn't do anything well or, for that matter, anything. I suppose if someone had come along and asked me to train a few horses for him I could have done a commendable job or arranged a fair in the county town, but these people, my relatives and their friends, they were entirely and totally intent on making money. Lots of it. Great sacks of it, me boy. Mountains of it, and even their women, I'm sure they were jewellers. They could look at your ring or the necklace on a friend at a party and tell you almost to the penny what it was really worth, what you had paid for it and where you could get one for a few quid more cheaply. That's the stuff that went on.

Of course, there was no work for me to do, and after three weeks in Saint John and a few rides around the countryside looking at the farms, I sat down with meself, this lad, and I said, "What in the name of the living saints are you doing here?" Now that was a good question. And I answered it immediately, like an obedient schoolboy. I said, "David, you are leaving tomorrow." And where was I going?

Perhaps I would go back to Ireland? No, that was unthinkable. Hadn't I just fled the bloody place, vexed because I was a disappointed swain? I thought, Montreal. Just up the railroad line, with a twist here and a job there. Besides, I knew it was French-speaking, and that was a language I was very good in. You pay a price for an Irish education, becoming ignorant of how the world works, but I did have fluent French to carry along with me as excess baggage. And so with fond good-bys to my relieved relatives—and back to their crude money-making they went straight away, with not another thought of me—I took the train and met a grand lot of fine people on the journey.

Yes, it was this powerful and deceitful accent of mine which won them over, as it still does, me boy, as it still does.

In Montreal I plunged off the train and into life. Oh, in those days it was a wonderful city. The English absolutely scorned the French. Not fit for blackening their boots, I'd say was the prevailing attitude and I found that off jolly right smart. I deliberately decided to stay with a French family, a professor and his wife and brood in a very large flat on Jeanne Mance Avenue, and they loved me. I'm not sure they loved me because I was Irish or because they detested the English more. We got along great. I'm quite sure I could have married their youngest daughter, but I would have had to work fast, as she was preparing herself to go into a convent. But, oh those looks she'd lavish upon me at dinner! Anyway, in she went. Didn't even have the one last fling that most Irish girls have because they know it's going to be plenty of stale bread and cold pudding once they enter. I'm not sure, but I think the old professor might have sided with me a bit, but my thoughts were not carnal. The girl was homely as a mud fence.

This is quite a jaunting cart I'm on, bouncing along so merrily and not saying a thing worthwhile. My first job was obtained in a strange way. I was walking down Peel Street one afternoon about five and there was a tavern and it had a pair of swinging doors. Bat-wing doors. Wild West style. I thought, this must be investigated. Before I knew it, I was sitting at a large table with a bunch of lads I'd never set eyes on before. One mistook me for an acquaintance and called me over, and when he found it was too late, being a nice chap and all that, he invited me to sit. I think the accent did it. This Blarney Stone of mine had got me into and out of so many strange situations. So there I was, in five minutes, being part of a jolly Friday afternoon scene of convivial young men my age. Of course, being modest, I can only say that a fair amount of attention was directed at me. A stranger, and an Irish bloke at that.

These lads were all limpy-wristy. Oh, very much so. But very charming, you understand. Oh, very much so. Now I'd seen a considerable amount of this gay cricket business in the university, and here it was. I thought I should declare myself. I just told them in as jocular a manner as I thought was necessary that I liked, I loved, I adored big, strong and healthy, blonde-haired and busty young ladies of about twenty who dearly loved to fuck. I just put it that way.

They just roared. I thought I was in a madhouse. And I'll tell you what it was. This was a game these lads played. They were as robust and horny as myself. Every one of them. But on Friday afternoons when they gathered, they would put on this act. A stranger would come in and one would profess to have known him, and he would be soon sitting with them, and then they would all go into their acey-deucy and "I-love-you" act, eyes, hands and foot upon yours under the table and all. Well, I ended that and became one of them immediately. Good lads, every one of them.

And that is the way I got my first job. In advertising and public relations. Perhaps four of them were in the foul, dank and dreadful game, and I was offered a job the very next week, and I loved it. A con job, more or less. Mostly more. But a chance to stretch my brain and my wits and my legs at Sunday morning rugby on Fletcher's Field, and the money wasn't too bad, either. In fact, I had a wonderful time. For several years. Five long years until I got an offer far, far, far too good to turn down. I just couldn't refuse it. I was quite a highflier in public relations by then, and this job was in Toronto, so I went. The money, you know. There I had my wings clipped and my nose bloodied, but I eventually succeeded, mainly because I absolutely refused, absolutely, to give up this wonderful accent of mine.

Just a little chapter of my life, me boy, to brighten up your book.

HOW TO FOOL A TRAFFIC COP

I've not lost my Cockney accent, and my husband hasn't, either. I'd go into a store and ask for some toothpaste or some other fool thing and the clerk would smile. They'd laugh. I know they weren't laughing at me for buying toothpaste or a pound of tea, but the way I asked for it.

It got so I didn't want to open my peeper, but you had to talk, and I was born with the English language and for a few years I thought, I'll forgive you because you're just a bunch of ignorant Canadian shopkeepers with no proper upbringing.

Oh yes, I got over that, and one time just a few years ago, a policeman stopped me for making a wrong turn, and I thought, well, why not? I gave him the worst Cockney talk you've ever heard, and he asked how long I'd been in Canada. I said three weeks, and he said I couldn't be expected to know all the traffic laws in Ontario, and he let me go.

Oh, I had a big ha-ha over that one. A nice lad, but I fooled him.

He thought he was being nice to a tourist. Mr. Armstrong and me came over in 1946, so I dare say I've been in Canada quite a bit longer than he'd been living.

THE WATKINS MAN HAD IT ALL WRONG

This was south of Battleford where we had our first farm, half a section which we moved into as tenants, one-third to the owner, two-thirds to us, and it was pretty lonely.

They had a man then who was called the Watkins Man, and he'd go around to all the farms in his little car and he'd sell things: linaments for the cattle and horses, and cloth and needles, beads, cough medicine. He had a hundred things and he was quite welcome.

The first time he came into the yard my husband was in the field, and I didn't know who he was, but he came over to the garden and told me and we went to the kitchen.

The minute he came in the door he started talking Dutch to me and he said, "So good to talk Dutch with a lady," and I thought, oh, this is funny. Why would he say that?

I was young then, and this was my first house, and I was a little scared, and with two little kids there, but I stood up to him and I said, "We speak English in this house."

You know, that man got mad. He said he spoke six languages and when he visited farms, he always talked to the lady in her language, and I said, "That's fine for some, but not for me. We are learning to be good Canadians and I don't think it is the right thing to do, to talk in a foreign language."

I am not saying it the way he did—that was twenty years ago. But he said I was denying my children their heritage. That's what I meant. I said, "No, Holland is over with, done with. I am in Canada now and so my husband and me, what we speak is English, and when the children go to school, then they will speak English too and not be laughed at."

A lot of people thought I was wrong about this, but I was right.

If you're going to be a good Canadian, you speak what Canada speaks.

5   GOT TO GET
   A JOB

5 GOT TO GET A JOB

"You got job?" Often these were the first three words an immigrant learned. A job meant money with which to live, and money was also the measure that European immigrants used to gauge their success against that of other immigrants. With a job, you were doing fine. Without one, you were a nobody.

People from Europe had all lived through their own depressions during the Thirties, and they knew the horrors of war and the hopelessness of its aftermath. They came to Canada prepared to work—hard.

They worked in the bush for long hours, encountering their first black flies and mosquitoes. Whole families weeded rows of sugar beets under the relentless July sun on the prairies. They might never have seen miners' tools before, but they were using them just ten days off the boat. They washed dishes in the back of cafés, the classical musician, the engineer, the accountant, standing at the tubs beside Canadian high school dropouts. They cleaned opulent Bay Street offices at night, slept, then reported for a labourer's job on the Toronto subway. They slaved in Montreal sweatshops at low wages, unaware there were labour laws to protect them. They picked fruit in the Okanagan and gutted fish in canneries near Vancouver. They were maids for wealthy families.

*While the labourers laboured, the professionals among them—barred
from working in hospitals, legal firms and dentistry—dreamed of the day
when the doors would be opened to them. They were embittered, but at least
they did have jobs.*

*A job was hope. A job was confidence. A job was the first thing a new-
comer needed, and it was the first mark of success in their new lives. Everything else followed. Nothing mattered more. First, get a job.*

THIS IS HONEST MONEY

The Englishmen came to this country after the war and they
had good clothes and money and they thought the refugees aren't
going to do at all well in this country, because they don't speak the
language.

I'll tell you this, because at one time I had more than one hundred
men working for me, and this was in 1948 when things weren't all that
great. It was the Displaced Persons who spoke little or no English and
had no good clothes who did well, and it was the Englishmen who
were always whining and not having the stamina and guts to stay on
the job.

Logging wasn't the best place in the world for a person to work. It
was dangerous and you had to learn the job fast, and they'd send them
over to Nanaimo from Vancouver, and they'd be shipped up to the
canal. We'd get four or five, six, maybe, a day, because maybe six had
gone out two days before, on the weekend. It wasn't the Poles and the
Czechs and the Swedes and the others who were going out. It was the
English. They could not hack it. I don't know. Maybe they thought
the work wasn't good enough for them. The refugees and the Swedes
and the Norwegians didn't think so. They just loved that kind of
heavy-duty going in the woods.

I'm not saying this about all Englishmen. No, there were some good
ones but a lot, you see, thought logging was somehow beneath them.
The foreigners, they liked the woods. They liked being in a camp with
men, nowhere to go but The Port to spend a few dollars. Sometimes
they just said after the first time out, hell, there is nothing there. So
they'd stay in camp, study English, work as many hours as we wanted
to give them, and I think they were making $1.07 an hour to start,
going up quickly if they were good. They were like the old-timers.
They'd save up for three months or so and then they'd hit for town.

But I don't think most of them got past Nanaimo. Hell, some, I'd say, only went to The Port, which was down the canal. They'd have a few beers and a big steak dinner at the hotel. Maybe a girl if they felt like it. There were a couple of cathouses there. Put their money in the bank and catch the crummy back on Monday morning, ready to go to work. That was what these foreign guys were like.

Englishmen would go to Vancouver and a few days later you'd get a letter telling the bookkeeper to send their cheque to them and, please, would they ask Edward or James or John, one of their buddies, to pack up their duds and send them. We wouldn't. I mean the company wouldn't. If they wanted to goof off that way, let 'em suffer what came next.

I liked them foreigners. They were called DPs. They'd work a year on some Saskatchewan farm and pick up some English and some muscles, and then they'd come out to the coast, or into some mine. A lot weren't very smart. I don't mean stupid. I mean not very smart. They just couldn't get the hang of the Canadian way of life. You can't blame them. Being in some army or some refugee camp, getting shot at. They were still a pretty scared bunch, most of them. But they got the hang of it later. We respected them and taught them the jobs because the boss said these guys would be round for a long time. With us, he meant. In the woods. Hell, some of them stayed their lifetimes in logging and lumbering. They're around Nanaimo, Alberni, Courtenay right now, little homes, wife, kids gone through university, and they got a camper in the lane, and they're just your ordinary West Coast retired guy.

Sure, they had a tough time of it. We were tough on them. We had to be, so they could stick with the job. They did. They were good men and good workers and, hell, many of them today are my good friends. You couldn't want to find better people. A guy's got an *ich* or *chuck* or *ski* on the tail end of his name, that doesn't cut no ice with anybody around here. It might in Ontario or Victoria, but not here.

You know what it was all about, don't you? It was like they were going to school and we were the teachers. It just took about a year for us to knock off all the stuff and thoughts that they had cluttered around their heads, about a thousand years of being a peasant and working for some king or lord or master and not having a thought of their own or a pot to piss in and a window to throw it out of.

I used to get a kick out of them. We paid every two weeks on the last whistle on Friday. They'd line up with everybody, and I'd be there handing out the cheques. They didn't know too much of this much taken off for medical, this for income tax, this for union, that for commissary, a bit for workmen's compensation, which sounds like a lot of deductions. They'd just look at the bottom line, what they actually had in their pocket. It might be something like, oh, maybe $167.40. Dollars. Canadian money. You could see wheels turning in their heads. Then you'd see them smile. You know what? Well, I'll tell you. In the country where they came from, that much money for two weeks was a fortune. A goddamned fortune, and I'm not kidding you.

I remember one guy we called Jake. A great big man from Poland, and he was about forty, so I guess he'd seen one hell of a lot in the war. He was a peasant, a serf, sure. Once he and I were riding the crummy to The Port and he said—and he was picking up English fast, which was unusual. Most of them were slow at it—he said, "Mr. Baker," and he took out five or six cheques he'd been keeping. He said, "Mr. Baker, this is honest money." You know, I never forgot it. I always thought that is the way they think about Canada, and I felt good about that.

SVARICH, A VERY SMART CONTRACTOR

My name was Jars Barasab, but when I had come to Canada and been here for maybe three years I changed it to John Barber. The letters started the same. I got the name out of the phone book. This was in 1952, I remember. I came to Canada in 1949.

I signed the papers saying I would work for a farmer. They put us on a ship and we got to Montreal and then they put about a dozen of us on a train to Edmonton, the CNR, and gave us tickets for meals, and we slept in the coaches. Three nights and two days, and the third day the train got into Edmonton. I thought, here is my new home.

I spoke some English because I had worked with the American army for a bit after we got out, and the guys said, "Okay, Jars, you be the boss." Okay with me. I kept the tickets and counted them every night, and if something wasn't right, I'd ask and fix it.

In Edmonton and the station there and the first words in my own language, a man was saying to us, "Welcome, friends." I talked to him and he said, did these guys want jobs? I said we wanted jobs and we work hard. I thought he was the guy who had signed for us, the kind of director of our contract. So he had this big truck outside and we all followed him, and when we get out of Edmonton he stopped the truck, and we walked into a field, and he told us he could put us in farm work. He said anybody who didn't want to work, then they could walk back. I think it maybe was fifteen miles, and the guys had suitcases, but nobody had no money.

This guy, Mr. Svarich, he said to me, "Explain to these guys I am a farm contractor and I will put them on farms and I will take twenty per cent of their pay." This is what he would do. I said, "What does that mean?" He said he would drive us to the farms and get us going and see that we were looked after, and the farmer would pay him the money and he would take his share and give us the rest. He said if we needed clothes he would go into Edmonton and buy things, and they would be against our account. You understand? I said, would he protect us from the police? This Svarich, he said that was why he was there. But he said there would be no business with the police because he knew them. He said one thing—the guys were not to leave the farms until he said it was okay. "Okay," I said, "I know what you are. You are a labour contractor, so how much do we make and how much do you make?"

He said I was a smart guy, and he said because it was into August the stooking would be starting, and they'd get six dollars a day, and when they started to thresh, the pay would be seven dollars a day. And I said, "That's pretty good, but you are making a lot of money out of us. There are fourteen guys on that truck." He said, "You are the luckiest DPs in Alberta. If you go to these Ukrainian and Polish farmers by yourselves, they will eat you like fat, juicy grapes. I am protecting you," he said, "and I am honest."

We walked back to where the guys were, and I told them. I said, "Look, this Mr. Svarich is not the guy you are supposed to go to. Not the people on the contracts, and they weren't there at the station in Edmonton. Mr. Svarich doesn't know who they are or why they weren't there with their trucks, but here he is and I'm going with him. I told them, "It is six dollars at first and then seven dollars, and you can't leave the farms, and Mr. Svarich will come and pick us up every Sunday morning and we will go swimming and have a place to wash our clothes."

I didn't tell them that Svarich had said to me, "You keep these guys on my side and I will make you my partner." He said I seemed like a smart guy. "Okay," he said, "is it a deal? You keep them on my side and tell me any trouble that happens with them and the farmers, and I pay you ten per cent of what I get."

You can figure that out. I was getting two per cent of his commission.

The guys, I think they were thinking, hey, I'll be getting seven dollars a day just for working, and that was so much money to them. These weren't educated guys, you know. The government, the Canadian one, I mean, they were just letting us into Canada because we had strong backs, weak minds, as if we had no brains. Not so, you know. Some of those guys are pretty big guys and well off now and have kids, teachers, managers, lawyers, all smarter than their old man.

We all worked hard that summer, but Svarich knew where to put his guys. He had about forty, all on farms around that part of the country. I figure he must have made about $1,500 a month on them, us, but it was worth it, and I'm not saying that because I worked for him. It was good for the guys. They didn't know anything about Canada and they had to be looked after. A guy gets an awful toothache, Svarich takes him to town to get it fixed. A guy needs new boots, he gets them and he doesn't waste a day's pay. Svarich had a big bunch of books that teach a guy how to learn English. He gives them out. Every Sunday he drives one truck and I drive another, and we go around picking up these guys and take them for a swim to a big pit they dug to hold water for the cattle. It isn't a lake, but it is water and clean except for frogs and little snakes, and they wash their clothes and run around naked and eat the lunches the farm lady sends with them.

Then there is this day, and we go and pick up all the guys in the two trucks and we take them to this big dugout and they get washed and cleaned up. Everyone is shiny, he's so clean. We go back to Svarich's farm, and the guys, all these fellows from the Old Country, are so goddamned happy because this is payday, and they are going to get all their money.

There are about thirty-five of them, I guess, all the guys Svarich looks after that summer, and he has a table outside his house, and his books are there, and each guy comes up and Svarich says, "Jars, is this a good guy?" I say that he worked hard. Then the man gets a sheet of paper, the days he's worked and how much comes off for toothpaste and razor blades and socks and boots and a shirt and that stuff, and then he gets his money. I checked it all, because I'd done that for a couple of days before, and each guy has a lot of money. After the twenty per cent comes off, each guy has maybe, oh, I'd say about three hundred dollars. That is one great deal of money. That is more than these guys ever knew before. Everybody is happy.

Then we go in the house and there is a feast. All the things his wife and grandmother and his daughters had worked on, big bowls of soup and food and the sweet things from the Old Country, and everybody eats a million of these things, and then they start drinking to get drunk. There is an awful lot of home-brew and beer, and we all get drunk and have a good time. No fights like that, but the guys, why they're just letting off steam and having a good time and singing away like crazy, all the good songs we knew, and it is one hell of a party and everybody is happy.

I don't know what would have happened to us if Mr. Svarich hadn't come along. We had no money when we were in the CN station, and he helped us out.

He didn't take advantage of us. He made a lot of money on us, but he was better than the government for us because he got us good work and good money, and the guy, he must have thought, somebody has to look after these little homeless children, and he did it. We can thank him for getting going okay.

I GOTTA GET THAT JOB!

You couldn't think you were a king. Or a prince. A smart guy. You just had to think, I don't care what kind of a job it is but I gotta get that job.

There was this place at Cambie and Dunsmuir where you'd go every morning about seven-thirty, and it was called a shape-up. You'd stand there with a bunch of other guys and wait for the guys to come along with their trucks, and one guy would stop and yell, "I got work for three men. We're laying pipe in Burnaby. Fifty cents an hour. Hop in." That kind of thing. Well, in those days the going rate was maybe seventy cents an hour, and nobody would move. But I did. Soon as he finished yelling I get into the truck. Nobody else. They just wouldn't work for less than they thought they were worth, and I still don't know how they figured out how much they were worth.

I'd think, eight times fifty cents is four dollars and I can buy food for three days with that, or that's my rent for my room for a week, and so away the guy would drive and I'd work all day. I'd work hard. I knew how to work. I was from the Slovene and I'd worked hard since I was eight years old.

I worked so hard that the guy would appreciate it, and I got sixty-five cents an hour from him. Any job. Laying drain pipe like I said. Tearing down a wall. Moving bricks in a wheelbarrow. Digging. Anything. I would give him an hour and a half's work for one hour and he knew it, and that's how I got started.

This was the first guy, the one I'm talking about. Drain tile. His name was Alan McKenzie, and he was a small guy in business but he was doing his best to get ahead. He was a veteran in the army. So was I, in Yugoslavia and then with Tito in the mountains. We would talk about things at lunch, and one day he said he was bidding on a big hospital job. I said good luck, and by this time I was working steady for him at seventy cents an hour and still working my guts off and I'll tell you why. I thought Mr. McKenzie was going to do pretty good in his business, although there was just him and me and his old truck, but I could see he had his eyes on something big. Not a little company, a big one.

Then about a month later he said he had got the big job and he could use me. He'd have to hire about ten guys and it would have to be done the way the government wanted it, with paperwork and hospital plan and job insurance and all that, and he needed a foreman. He offered me the job. No more little jobs, he and me, but a big one that would last maybe two months. "Okay," I said, "I'm your foreman," and we shook hands.

Now I thought, I'm the boss of these guys becase I tell them to do the work. How. When. This way, not that way. I got to teach these guys, and the bums I gotta fire, and in one case, I gotta beat up a guy because he's a damn troublemaker. But that was later. What was Mr. McKenzie going to pay me? He said, "Since Monday, Mike, you've been on the payroll at a dollar an hour." That's the kind of a guy he was. Just a real straight shooter.

So, there is a story to this story. I needed to work, to feed my belly and buy some wine on Saturday and go to dances at the Normandy Hall and meet women, and I took the job at poor pay because I would rather work than stand on that street corner and bitch my face off with those other guys.

Those other guys, Canadian guys, born in Vancouver and, because they thought laying drain tile in the rain or pushing a wheelbarrow for

fifty cents, they were above it. They had English, a high school education, and some of them had been in the war, they thought this kind of
hard work was below them. See them now. Standing on that corner,
and I guess about nine o'clock they'd say, "Oh, no good work today,"
and they'd go somewhere and have coffee and bitch about hard times
in Vancouver.

Get a job. Any kind of job. Work isn't bad. I say it is damn good. I
worked up from there, and when Mr. McKenzie wanted to sell his
company, he sold it to me. I was very happy about that too.

THREE WORDS—YOU GOT JOB?

I was a dumb kid of seventeen and I didn't know anything,
no English, sure. My uncle said I had to get work, and I didn't know
how it was done because I didn't have a job when I left Italy. I went by
ship to England and then to Montreal and that's where my uncle met
me, in Montreal, and he took me to Toronto by the train.

He said I was to go to places around, shops, little factories where
they made clothes and shoes and other things, and I was to say, "You
got job?" Those were the first three words in English I knew. He said
say it after him, and I would say it, and he said no, not like "You got
job," as though the boss had a job. I was to say it like it was me that
wanted the job. Like, "You got job?" Raise my voice at the end. To
make it a question.

This was the trick, and I guess a lot of other guys did it. It was like
you'd call it a game. You would smile at the boss and say those little
words, coming out at the end with "job" like it was a squeak. The first
day I got a job in a store unpacking fruit. I said my words, and when
the man sort of smiled, I gave him the piece of paper my uncle had
written out, and the paper told him about me. "This is Antonio
Aiello, and he comes from a hill town in Italy and he is a good boy
and a hard worker. He will work hard for you."

I worked hard that afternoon, and when I went to my uncle's fruit
stand and said I had got a job, he said good, and that he would go with
me next morning and talk to the owner, a Mr. Faber. That happened,
and they decided I was worth thirty-five cents an hour, and my uncle
would get the money from Mr. Faber and he would take half and give
the rest to me.

Sure, half. My pay came to about twenty bucks a week, and the ten he took, that went for my paying him back, my boat fare, the passage, sure. I gave him five dollars a week of my ten dollars for living with them, and I worked for him at nights at fifteen cents an hour, so I had five dollars for myself in a week, and I paid him ten for my boat fare and maybe three dollars came off it, too, for the money I earned working for him. That way I paid off my fare, which I think was about $170. Then when I paid that off, I didn't owe anything, and I could buy clothes, and I was learning English at night school when winter came, and that's how we did it. It was a good way.

Sure, I think it was a good way. I was working and paying off my uncle and learning English so I could get a good job. The job I had with Mr. Faber wasn't a good one. His son was in charge of the warehouse and he was a smart bastard, and he made it hard on me and the two other guys from Italy working there. He was a fat slob. Nothing good about him.

In two years I got a good job in Simpson's warehouse, and then I was driving a truck for them and making good money, and that's when I decided to bring my little brother out from Italy, so it started over again. He paid me back, and then my father died in Italy and we paid for the funeral, and next year we brought our mother out and a sister, and soon we had our own house. You see, we all worked together and we became Canadians.

More and more Italians came to Toronto and now there are a million.

PAY THE UNION BOSS, YOU GOT A JOB

This is what we found in Canada. You couldn't get a job unless you were in the union and you couldn't get in the union unless you had a job.

My husband was an expert shipwright in Folkstone, and the immigration people said he would have no trouble getting a job anywhere.

Those immigration people hadn't done their homework, and that was the long and the short and the tall of it.

There were shipyards all over Vancouver and they were all union, and this was in 1956, and here we were, living in a shack on a farm in Richmond because we couldn't afford even a half-decent place in Vancouver, and there was a Japanese place where he could have worked which wasn't unionized. But when the Japanese workers found out he was being hired, they wouldn't work with him. They weren't unionized, but they were the same.

Finally my husband went to the unemployment office downtown for the twentieth time and the man there said, "Well, you know what to do about it." He winked at my husband and rubbed his thumb and finger together and my husband, he was no fool, and he said okay.

He phoned up a man in the shipwrights' union and asked if Bert could come and see him, and the fellow said yes. My husband went over and gave him two one-hundred-dollar bills in an envelope, and that was money we had to borrow from a friend from England who had come out earlier, and that was the way he got work.

It was as simple as that. Bert got a job and joined the union the same day.

HE GOT CALLED AND I WAS HIRED

One day not long after we got to Toronto my husband had an appointment with a private job agency. This was in 1955, just before Christmas.

I went with him because I hadn't seen downtown Toronto yet, and we were sitting in the waiting room, and the counsellor came out and called us both in. Then he gave Hans an application form and handed me one, and I was so embarrassed because my English wasn't good enough to tell him I wasn't looking for a job. It was my husband who was. I couldn't explain I had never worked in an office and I would have to take English classes before I could apply for one.

He said, "Go ahead, fill it out anyway as best you can," and we went home, and next morning he phoned and said I could go to work with the Brunswick International Limited as a messenger clerk.

My husband thought I should go and see them, and I did, telling them what I had told the counsellor, that I did not have enough English and could not possibly do a good job for them. This was Canada, an English company, not Germany, but they insisted that anyone with a good general education, that everything could be learned. So I reluctantly agreed.

It was not easy in the beginning, but the people I worked with were kind and understanding and that helped tremendously, and in three months I got my first promotion, to clerk typist, and I worked with this company for twenty-five years.

My husband got a job a few days after I did and he stayed with the same company too, never changing jobs.

I LOVED WORKING ON THE SMELTER

When I heard there were jobs in Kitimat, I found the Alcan office there on Howe Street, and you had to have an application form from them before they would even talk to you, and they wouldn't give me one.

They said I didn't speak English. I didn't, but one of the two men there, he understood a little bit of German and he somehow understood my story and he finally gave me the application. I was lucky. He sent me to a priest on Thirty-first Avenue, and he filled it out. I took it back, and two days later I went back to Alcan and they said, okay, I was accepted.

But the man said, "Now you need thirty-five dollars for the boat fare," and my heart fell. I had no money. I was living at Immigration, but the same man gave me a slip of paper and he said to take this to the federal government and they will give you the money, but you must promise to pay it back.

So that was settled, and Alcan took me, so Thursday at 4:15 in the afternoon I boarded the *Princess Norah*. It was a big boat. The food was terrific. The scenery was fantastic. We arrived on September the ninth, and I was so proud. I had got to Canada, gone across it, found a job, and now I was on the job in the most beautiful place in the world, I thought. Helping to build the Alcan aluminum smelter in Kitimat in British Columbia. I was so happy.

On the eleventh I started working. At $1.69 an hour. There was lots of work. Twelve, fourteen hours a day if you wanted. I saved every penny. I lived first in the townsite and then in the H-huts at Anderson Creek, and then on the old boat, the *Delta King*. I never spent a cent. Everything was to be saved to pay for my family to come to this wonderful land.

JUST ABOUT THREE CENTS AN HOUR

I was fifteen and I stood up on my hind legs and I told my father I was going to Canada, and he ranted and raved in true Welsh style. But my mind was made up, and in the end I went down to Cardiff to my old auntie and I asked for a hundred-pound loan, and when I told her what it was for, she gave me the money right away. This was May of 1950, and that was worth about three hundred dollars in Canadian money. She wished me good luck and gave me a food parcel and put me on the train to London. I never saw my parents again.

I could have waited for the emigrant travel assistance program, I guess, but that would have meant weeks of waiting, so I said sorry, I can't wait. Passage on the old *de Grasse* was two hundred dollars. It was a terrible ship, just ready to fall apart and sink with all of us, and we got to Quebec City and I knew what I was going to do. I was going to the Wild West and be a cowboy, and I had forty dollars in my pocket and a headful of air. Nothing would stop me, I thought, and I booked passage to Calgary, but I got talking to a man on the train and he said there was lots of work in a town called Medicine Hat. Well, that name sounded Indian and if there were Indians, there were bound to be cowboys around and cowboys meant ranches. That was for me. You see, my head was very full of hot air.

Another man I was talking to, his name was Hargraves, and he said he was a member of parliament, and it turned out he was. He had pull, naturally, all over that part of the country, and when I said I wanted to be a rancher, he told me to stay on the train. Forget Medicine Hat. Get off there, but get on another train and go to Lethbridge and walk around to the Marquis Hotel and ask somebody to point out a rancher. I was fifteen, remember, and when somebody said all the ranchers were in the beer parlour of the Marquis Hotel, okay, I just walked in. I was kicked out in one minute flat.

There was a man standing outside and I asked him. God, I was brash then. I wouldn't have dreamed of doing things like that at home, but here in Lethbridge I was talking to strangers on the street. I asked him where I could get a job on a ranch. Did I know anything about ranching? I said no. He said, "Good, then you'll be able to get a job easy." That sounded funny, but then a man came out of the beer parlour, and this man stopped him and said, "Joe, young fellow here is from Wales. Wants a job on your ranch."

This man's name was Joe Gilchrist, and he had a big ranch and he asked me what I could do, and I said, nothing. Yet. I was just fifteen. He said if I wanted to come with him and work for ten dollars a month and grub, I was welcome. He didn't ask any other questions, and I threw my suitcase into the back of his truck and we headed out. It was as easy as that. He had a ranch, and it was a long run in those days, but we made it, and he didn't say much. I can tell you now, he kept all his talking for later.

He had this spread on Deer Creek, thousands of acres of it, and it was June and not too much work going on, so he only had two cowboys working for him and another who was a chore boy. Gosh, this guy was about forty years old and had been a soldier in the war, but he was like me, he wanted to be a cowboy. His wife was the cook. When I hired on, this guy, Brad, he went riding and fixing fences with the other two, and I was the chore boy.

After a month I found that I was a long way from being a cowboy. I milked the cow and fed a couple of pigs and looked after the cook's chickens. I made hay and I tended the garden and hauled water and picked rocks because Gilchrist had a few acres of barley and oats. I washed up the dishes and I was up at four in the morning to turn on the windmill, and I cleaned out the barn, and after a month I thought, gosh, I've been a cowboy for a month now and I ain't even been on a horse.

The first month I didn't even get paid, as boots and jeans and a shirt had cost me twelve dollars, so I still owed Gilchrist some money. He was tight as the bark on a tree, but apart from that he was a kind man. He was hard, but he was a good rancher. After a month I asked him for a five-dollar raise. He said, "Okay, go and harness the team," and I said I couldn't. Nobody had showed me how. He said when I could harness it I would get another five a month. So the cook one afternoon, she and I went out and together we learned to harness the team. It took us about two hours, and those horses were good, they just stood there. When Old Man Gilchrist came home from work that night I showed him the harnessed team, just standing there by the fence. He said, "You're mistreating those horses just letting them stand there in harness," and so I started to unharness them, and it took me a long time and the cowboys and Mr. Gilchrist are just standing there, laughing.

Finally I get the job done and the harness hung up, and I take them into the barn and he says, "Did you rub them down?" I said, "No," and he said, "Who the hell ever taught you to work a team?" I said nobody, I had learned myself. That started him laughing, and finally he stopped and he said he would give me a five-dollar raise starting the beginning of the next month. That was about three weeks away.

He said, "Morgan, do you know how much you'll be making then?"

I had him real straight on that one. I had figured it out, my working hours into fifteen dollars a month, and I said, "Mr. Gilchrist, I figure I'll be making just about three cents an hour."

God, but that got him. Right in front of his cowboys I'd made him look like a miser, and he roared, yelling about all the food I ate. I told him, "Mr. Gilchrist, if I didn't eat it, the hogs would get it. That Jennie don't know how to cook for anybody. She can't figure it out," I told him.

Anyway, that was what I was working for, fifteen dollars a month. Just about three cents an hour. In winter maybe four cents an hour, because I didn't have to get up until six in the morning. Oh well, that was long ago, and Mr. Gilchrist taught me a lot, and I got to know about Canada then, even though the ranch was miles from nowhere.

I was growing like a weed and filling out, and after a year there, I was six feet and about 170 pounds and all man, or so I thought. Yeah, I was. I could do anything around, because when the other two cowboys were let go in November and went out on the grub line, I stayed, and me and Brad and Jennie had to do everything. So like I said, I learned everything about ranching, and in two years I was only seventeen, but I could pull my freight with any man. I was real proud of myself.

I HANDED OUT SIXTY-SEVEN TICKETS!

I'm saying I was a tough one. I made it a point to be tough. In Hull and later in Liverpool you had to be. I joined the constabulary in Yorkshire in 1932 as a cadet. "Here, you, here's yer uniform and yer boots and yer nightstick, and go out with Constable Watters here and he'll show you the rounds, and don't you come back here asking why yer pay is late some paydays." That sort of thing. The whole country was in the waste of a depression the likes you Canadians never could have imagined.

Everybody I talked to on the ship, the Canadians, they all said I'd have no trouble getting on a force. Canada needed policemen, they said, and I wondered what kind of country I had chosen. Maybe, I'm thinking, Australia would have been a better chance, or South Africa. Or New Zealand. They all were looking for people to come, adverts in the paper, posters at the railway stations, the registries, all wanting us to come.

I was a free man, I was strong and healthy and with a reasonable amount of money, to be sure, enough to get me by for a few months, but you think I could find a job? Not on your life. In Toronto, Winnipeg, Regina, Calgary, right across, too old, although they didn't quite say it. Too old for what? I was thirty-four and had been a policeman for eleven years, and that was tough experience, and my papers were all first-class. Oh well, they had their reasons. Maybe I just didn't scratch the surface of the interview deep enough to show them what I really had.

In Vancouver I heard the provincial police, the British Columbia equivalent of the RCMP, was hiring, and I got on. No problem. I took my letters of recommendations in, my commendations, passed their tests and worked for a moving van outfit for two months until my turn came up and I was in. Yes, I could say I was happy to be back in police work again.

The inspector calls me in and he tells me he's sending me to Kaslo. A one-man detachment, and I perked up my ears at that one. One man, I thought! He said it is really a small place but is a city, and they have had trouble keeping a man there. He said it was a logging and mining town, by way of explanation. I should have known what he meant. He said I'd have to be tough. Lay down the law right at the start. No pussy-footing around. Get in there and show them who's boss, and then he wished me luck and told me to get my reports and expense account in on time, and then shook my hand.

I left Vancouver in my police car, an old one and pretty tired, but I got to Kaslo about four o'clock the next day and drove around, and it was the prettiest little place you ever saw, sort of half ghost town and half not, and then I thought, all right, lay down the law, he said, so lay down the law I will.

I drove back and up the hill for about two miles and I parked the car, and the first car that came from the direction of Nelson I flagged down. That fellow got four tickets for mechanical violations. Well, poor lights, no lights, no licence, no this, no that. The next car, maybe, I handed out three tickets. Remember, these were all cars built before 1942, so they were getting on. This went on for two hours. Cars and trucks. Tickets galore. I was on my second book.

About this time a car comes up the hill, and a guy gets out with two others, and says he's the mayor and what the bloody hell is going on. He's starting to get phone calls. I introduce myself as the new policeman in town, and then I walk over to his car and start ticketing it too. There were enough violations in that vehicle regulations book that even if a car was perfect, I could have rechecked the book and found a couple to nail them on. The mayor said something about stopping this bloody nonsense, and got in and made a U-turn right in front of me, and he got another ticket for that. Whew!

Until it got dark, I handed out sixty-seven tickets.

I didn't make a single friend that day except maybe the waitress in the café who I tipped, maybe, and every ticket was paid when the magistrate came up from Nelson the next week.

I don't think I gave out sixty-seven tickets in the whole of the next year. Oh, sure, I'd warn them, and if they persisted, then they'd get one, but no more tickets just handing them out to make a good impression.

I made a lot of real good friends in Kaslo, and I suppose there is the odd old-timer who will remember that afternoon. If he does, the thing he'll remember most is me ticketing the mayor twice and then the third time. I can still chuckle about that.

Yes, I got my point across, and the townsfolk accepted I wouldn't put up with their nonsense. I was there as a policeman and I was there as their friend and neighbour, and it worked out that way.

I'd have stayed there forever, but the police became the RCMP and I quit, but that little town was the nicest introduction to Canada I could think of.

THE SHOPPERS AND THE CRAZY SALESMAN

Captains were a dime a dozen, and you could find half a dozen majors in every office all pulling rank on each other, and I thought, perhaps my father is right. He'd said to go to Canada or Australia—we had a choice—or to South Africa or the Rhodesias, but even then I could see the problem with the blacks. I'd seen enough of that in Indonesia. I could have gone to Burma, but after a week of seeing the plantation, who wants to sit around watching the tea grow?

Canada it was, and Toronto, and in a few weeks I was off. One hundred pounds in my pocket, a ticket on the *Queen Mary* to New York and five hundred pounds in a money belt that the Exchequer lads didn't know about. Britain was uptight those days in currency. The economy was a dash of bitters on the rocks, and I felt I was leaving a sinking ship. When we steamed down the Channel, I looked back for the last time and saw the dear old land fading from view, and I thought, there's the prow and it's going down too.

I hopped a train for Montreal and then a bus to Toronto, and beggers can't be choosers, so I put up at the YMCA. Our family had been in textiles for centuries, Indian cotton at tuppence a yard, that sort of thing, so I went to Eaton's and presented myself to the manager of the textile department. He said to go the employment office. That was a bit of a shocker. I was being treated like a boy clerk, but I did.

I think I've always had a sense of humour, and when the manager told me they had nothing, I recited dutifully my credentials, and he said that was too bad, but Englishmen could expect no more favours than an Irishman. An Irishman he was, I suppose. Chin up, that's me, and temper in check I said I'd take any job. I didn't have to, you know. There still were those five hundred pounds I could fob off anywhere, but I was mad, clear through.

He sent me to the food department, and a nice young man showed me my job. Kraft or one of those companies had developed a new cheese paste. Lovely creamy stuff, white and gooey, and I was to stand in the aisle with a little cart and a batch of wooden spatulas about the size of a teaspoon and try and get these bloody housewives to taste it. I wasn't selling it. I just had to get them to taste this goo.

Can you think of a more demeaning job for a man? Well, I couldn't, but I had the job and I'd be blazed if I was going to fall down on it. I'd see it through for one day, and every old waddling duck of a housewife that came by, I'd damned well see that she stuck out her tongue and swilled a hunk of this. Not much luck.

I said to myself, Eric, old boy, you've got to use your wit and charm, and I turned it on, wisecracking, you might say. I raised my voice. I put body language into every movement. I told jokes. I singled out fat frumps and I told them they were lovely. I can see it now. A perfect fool was I and, if the mess could have seen me, they'd be howling into their gins. I told jokes. I recited poetry. I put on a show. I did everything but striptease. I was a bit of a mimic and I gave it to them in Scots brogue, Irish bullshit, French suavity, German arrogance, and here are they, a ring of them gaping like hungry rooks in a nest.

First I had ten people, then twenty, then thirty, then fifty, and I had the aisle clogged and mucking up the life and times of that bloody store. This is Eaton's, mind you, where everything is done by the book.

Here I was, son of the landed gentry capering like a fool, and that was not done, old boy.

A man I assumed was the manager finally broke through this crowd, and it was a crowd, laughing their heads off and having a fine time. Oh, it was a mad scene. He lost his temper and he fired me on the spot. Somebody started to boo, and there was yelling and booing, and I packed it up. Just walked away through these laughing and giggling women and I'd say half the clerks in the store.

I had nothing to pick up. I'd only been working at this dismal trade for maybe forty minutes. So I just headed for the door.

On the street I was tapped on the shoulder, and there was a man who was grinning, and he said, "You're hired. Come with me."

The upshot of it was, once the grin was off his face, he told me he was the head of London Life in one of their offices and I was going to work with him. Now selling insurance was a door-to-door thing in England, a rather unseemly way to make a living, I thought, but I was still in a rather upbeat mood, and we went to his office, and the rest is history. I became a very successful insurance salesman, and no door-to-door, I must say. I was given three weeks' training to learn the tricks of the trade, and the leads I got were not to your housewife and your bricklayer. Good solid leads. Businessmen and so forth. There was a lot of money to be made in life insurance. Oh, how those big shots wanted security. It was a sucker's game, and I loved it.

From there it led to the soap and detergent industry and then into publishing in 1953, but that's another story, as they say in the bedtime books. But it always was selling. What you sold didn't matter. There always are people who want to buy, if they think they can win. They can't, but so what!

MR. ADAMS, CAN YOU PLAY BRIDGE?

On the train to Toronto I thought, I'll go right across Canada and the place that I like, then I'll go back. I had enough money. I bought a map of Canada and I looked at it, and there it was, New Westminster. I was going to Vancouver anyway, and New Westminster looked very close. I liked the name.

I stayed in Vancouver for a day, and then I took the old tram down to New Westminster, and I remember, it was the Dunsmuir Hotel. I checked in there. One dollar and fifty cents a night, and I said I'd stay a week, and the clerk said that would be six dollars. Fine with me, matey, I thought.

Now what was I to do? I had been in the Royal Engineers, so I could do anything, and I did like the look of the city the first day. It was quite charming—along the river, Columbia Street. People I met didn't look at me and think "Limey" when I talked to them. The people were sure friendly.

I bought new clothes—work pants and a couple of shirts and some boots and gloves at Army and Navy on Columbia there, you know—and when I went back to the hotel, I asked the clerk where the classy part of town was. He said try Fourth or Fifth, Sixth. Up that way. It was a nice warm day, a Monday I remember, and the first nice house, big and white, and I thought, these people take pride in their house, and I knocked on the door.

A woman came, and I explained who I was and was there anything I could do in the yard, in the house, something to fix. And I remember her saying, "Boy, am I ever glad to see you!" Like with an exclamation point. She said, "Yes, you can start on the yard." She said her husband had been a captain in the army and now was an accountant at some mill and he'd never done an honest day's hard work in his life.

I didn't tell her I knew nothing about gardens, but along the fence and around it looked kind of ratty, so I went at it, on my knees, with tools she'd given me. I hoed and spaded and cleaned up and mowed the grass, and there I was, mowing and digging for dear life. Even I could see the place was getting to look better. I think in gardening you just have to use your common sense. I was remembering what my mother used to say about gardens and plants and flowers. She'd say, "They have souls too, Gerald, and when you don't care for them, they weep."

At noon this Mrs. Macdonald brought me out a big sandwich and cookies and an apple and some coffee, and we had a chat, and she asked me how much I was charging her. I didn't know, so I said, "Would seventy-five cents an hour be too much?" Apparently I was right on, and she looked around and she said, "But I'm going to give you a dollar an hour. It is worth it to this house. You don't know what it was like during the war, and now everybody making money in the mills and going on the tugboats and fishing. They don't want to dig in the earth."

I thought, an hour to pay for my room and two hours to pay for my food and laundry and smokes, so I said I'd only charge her the seventy-five cents. That was the smartest move I ever made. It changed her over to my side completely. She said, "You will get more work if you want it. Do you?" I said I sure did.

I fixed up her eavestrough and some cracked concrete slabs on their little patio, pouring sand under them, and when the day was over, her husband came home. He saw the work and he said, "Do you know anything about auger coal-fed furnaces?" I said yes, I did, and I didn't know what he was talking about. He said to come back tomorrow, and I did, and she showed me the furnace, and I thought, well, here's where you roll up your sleeves and start thinking with your common sense. I took it apart and found the trouble. A flange bolt had twisted, putting it out of kilter. I told her I'd have to go and find some parts. She said, "Take this bicycle. The children don't use it."

I whipped off down the hill to a shop and explained that I was a furnace repairman and could I buy some bolts. Of course, the guy knew I wasn't a real repairman. When I was leaving he said, "If you can fix that machine"—and I think it was a Forgemaster—"come back and see me. I'm going crazy," he said. "I can't get anybody to do these little jobs and it's not worth my time and money to do them." I thought, okay, maybe I'll be back.

That's the way it started. I fixed their furnace, and that was easy, and I did odd jobs around, the little things people just keep putting off. A scew here, a bolt tightened there, washers for the faucets, rewinding an armature on the washing machine, all these things. When Mr. Macdonald came home that night and I handed him a list of the things I'd done, he kind of whistled and gave me twelve dollars. The first money I had really earned since I got out of the army almost a year before. I could have stayed drunk in England for two days on that.

Work it out, that was twenty-two times six is $132. Okay, it doesn't mean much now, does it? Dinner and wine and drinks for two at some very fancy restaurant, maybe, on the thirty-fifth floor of a tower with a terrific view and a string quartet. In 1946 that was a lot of money, a lot of money. In Britain, that was about sixty dollars more than a coal miner got a month in Yorkshire. See?

Then Mrs. Macdonald, she hands me a list and says, these are the names of her friends and I can charge them. Charge them, they can afford it, yes, they can. She said she'd phoned them, and they all wanted a handyman, and she told them, "You'll have to pay him eighty-five cents an hour and give him his lunch and he'll do anything for you." She said to go to see a certain lady the next day, and she told me I could have the bicycle.

I won't go on too long on this but I think everybody remembers that first job and the first Canadians you really meet, and this is just part of this one story, but I'll say this. I worked all summer, and sometimes I'd work until eight or nine at night, and I did everything. That seemed to be the summer all those fancy auger coal-feeding furnaces were breaking down, and when the summer was over, I knew everything there was to know about every make and model of them. The guy who owned that store, the first one I went to, he was also sending me out to do repairs, and I peddled like crazy around the city that year.

Looking back on it, you know, it was wonderful. The crazy Canadians, they had all these appliances and things to make life easier, and they were buying more. Everybody had money. Cashing in their war bonds, getting raises from the union, selling old cars and buying ones a few years newer. No new cars yet, and I was the expert on fixing up cars. Four years in REME, remember? I could fix anything. For cars I charged one dollar and a half an hour, the same as the mechanics.

I know what you're thinking. I thought about it a lot. Why did I not form a little company and get a letterhead and hire a few guys to help and become a millionaire in five years? You're thinking that. I can tell. Well, I didn't want to. That summer was very happy for me, and I was making good money. For another two dollars I moved into another room in the hotel with a bathroom, and I had a little hot plate in my room, eggs and toast and an apple and a cup of tea for breakfast, and my lunches free most of the time. I was making a lot of money and no income tax, no expenses. No worries. I was doing what I wanted to and I had more work than I could do. I hated to tell people I couldn't help them, so that's why I'd sometimes work until nine at night.

One night when I'm working late, about eight o'clock, this lady calls me and she says, "Mr. Adams, can you play bridge?" I'm going to tell you something. For four years in the Engineers I played bridge every night, and with experts. I said, "Yes, ma'am, I play bridge." she said, well, I was to get in there fast and wash my hands and tidy up, because they had a two-table bridge game starting. One of the partners was a doctor, and he'd just been called out. Did you ever hear anything so nutty? In England, would you see that happen? Can you believe it? You crazy Canucks.

Let me put it this way. I think that was the night I fell head over heels in love with Canada and Canadians. They call in a handyman from the garage working on a car and, biffy jiffy, I'm playing bridge.

I remember it. I played superbly. I amazed them all, and I didn't really have such good cards. I was better than I was, let me put it that way. Hot! I amazed them, and when the game was over, I was firm friends with all of them. I won't say they were the elite of New Westminster, but, well, they were right up there.

From then on that summer, there would be a little note maybe twice a week in my box asking me to come for dinner at such and such an address and play bridge. I dined out on my bridge.

Women aren't dumb at bridge. They just don't understand it. And one night a woman said I should give lessons, and I said okay, but I'd only take four. Next week I gave my first lesson. The women played and I watched, and then we'd replay each hand and I'd explain who did what wrong and so on. That was another eight dollars a night. Two bucks each. They loved it, and I made damned sure there was no hanky-panky involved, although there could have been. Very easily.

One night in October I sat down and figured how much I was making, and it was about two hundred dollars a month, about $120 a month clear, tax-free, and I thought, this is a lot more than my old dad was making, and he was a foreman in the works back home.

I could have gone on at a great rate like that all winter, but you think, well, after all, this is a very small city and there is lots more to see. That's when I decided to leave my little room in the Dunsmuir Hotel. It was so long ago. I went to Vancouver and up to Port Alberni to work in the woods for MacMillan. The pay was better, but when they took off taxes and food and board and union and medical, it didn't work out to as much.

I will tell you why I am telling you this. In the past years I have heard all too much bitching about how tough it was to be an immigrant. Oh, I'm not discounting how tough it was if you came from the Ukraine or Latvia or some place like that and you spoke no English. That would have been very tough. I saw it in the woods later. And I admire those guys now for what they did then and what they are now. Make no bloody mistake about that. They had guts. Sure, I know, they had no other choice. Sink or swim.

But all the bitching about no jobs. Sure, there were few jobs. The country had hundreds of thousands of servicemen coming back. They were entitled to the first jobs. Their old jobs back. But there were jobs. You didn't have to become a foreman in an auto works or a shipyard here just because you had been in that position in jolly old England.

All this bitching by Englishmen that I ran across. I'd give them a good piece of my mind. "Get in and dig," I'd say. "Nothing was easy for you at home," I'd say. "Stop your whining. Get out and work. Work hard!" I think I straightened a few of those Limeys out.

SLINGING HASH AND HAVING FUN!

Can you imagine me as a waitress? All fingers and thumbs and spilling things and not being able to make cash in Canadian money and all this? Well, I was, and it was in industrial café on the highway. Rather a rough place, but the chaps who came in, tough and rough workers, they treated me like a queen. They laughed at my fumbling, and sometimes I'd put on a little act about it, and they joshed me, and the owner liked this because he said it made the café a happy place. I had a sharp tongue in my head and I wouldn't let them get away with a darn thing, and I got good tips too. A nickel for a cup of coffee. That was a 50 per cent tip in those days. It was all a lolly and a lark, and I loved it, even though the café opened at six in the morning. It was on the highway just outside of London. The old highway. Oh, it was a grand time, and it was easy to forget your problems at home. The café, being an industrial one, it closed after the afternoon coffee break, so I'd be home at four o'clock and tired from my ten-hour day. What would I find? My husband, moaning away to himself about how hard done he was.

There was a job as dishwasher came up at the café, and I suggested he take it. Oh no, oh no. God, God, no! He was in the engineering trade, as he called it, although he'd never done a day's lick at it since he got out of the trade school. I said he could do some engineering on the dishes, but he said he was waiting for letters to come back from his applications. I was bringing all the money home, about four dollars a day and maybe a dollar or two in tips, so we did okay for food, and the flat we were living in, that was free because my husband was officially on relief.

Thank God he didn't start drinking. He could have, but he didn't have the money. After four months of me working my feet off and being cheery at the café and trying to be cheery at home, I had just about had it.

He beat me to it. I came home one afternoon and he was gone and there was a little note. He said he had had enough. He was going back to England. He said his father had paid his fare and he had got the ticket that morning and he was going to Toronto and fly back. Or take a ship, I forget. Anyway, he was out of my life. I was relieved. I don't think I really loved him. Just something nice to have around. I was the man in the family, I guess. He was the puppy dog.

From that point, I settled down to the business of making a good life for myself, and I have. The only writing I've ever had from him was a note attached to the divorce papers he sent me. The lad wished me well. Fine, I thought, and the same to you, and good riddance.

MY OWN HUSBAND WAS A FOOL

On that ship! Oh, we were all so tired. We were all so tired, we couldn't even be excited. Not when we saw the shores of Canada and coming up the St. Lawrence. The ship! It was run by the CPR, and we were pushed into this corner, that corner. Do this and do that. Eat this. Eat it now. If you wait five minutes, there will be no room for you. The men and boys sleep on one side. The women and girls and the smaller kiddies, they had to sleep on another.

A long trip and bad weather. You can imagine it. Looking forward to this trip to Canada. Canada. We'd talked about it so much.

Every kind of person was on the boat. The people we talked to, they were engineers. One man from Austria, he was put in charge of a lot of us, to keep us in order, you might say. He had been a professor. There were engineers and bookkeepers and a doctor or two who looked after us, helping the doctor on the ship. There were schoolteachers and professors and lawyers, and I wonder how they made out when they went to places across Canada.

My husband had been a locomotive driver in Poland before the war, and he thought, oh, I'll be a driver when I get to Canada. He couldn't even get a job on the railroad unless he worked on what they call the gang. He couldn't do that. He had his papers. That wasn't, you know, his kind of work. Luc was very bitter about that. He thought, I can just go in and do what I did before. The company, they just laughed at him. He would say to me, "What is the difference? I drove a locomotive in Poland, and for the Germans in the war because they made me." I would say, "Maybe they know that. Maybe that is the reason." Oh, it wasn't, I know.

How could he, or maybe a doctor, expect to take over a job from a Canadian?

You know that is not the way the world is.

He couldn't see that and when we were in Sudbury and he was working in the smelter, people would say he was lucky to be working for Inco. He would say, "I should be driving the trains, not working in the yard." Every day, he would say he saw locomotices he should be driving.

Luc couldn't get it out of his mind. It was a possession with him. Sorry, I mean an obsession. Excuse me.

I said, "Luc, you are a fool. If you were a driver in Poland and a Canadian or an American came over and took your job, what would you do?" This was a good argument, but the poor man couldn't see that. He was a fool. My own husband was a fool.

Nothing was right about Canada. There were other Polish people there, and they would say, "Simma"—that's me—"Simma is right. You are lucky to be alive. They'd say, "We don't know how you even got through the war without getting killed. A Jewish wife, how did you both escape?" They didn't know that he drove a locomotive for the Germans and we ate good because that was an important job, and he was in places where the English and Americans were blowing up the trains.

Nothing was right for him. He said the city was awful. It wasn't. It was a nice city, Sudbury. You could go out and be far from it in half an hour and swim if you wanted. You could fish. There was skating. Movie shows. Lots of good stores. Nothing was wrong with that city of Sudbury but in his own mind.

I could see what was happening. He was going to lose his good job at Inco. He would have to look for another job, and he was forty-six years old. What kind of a job? Going down to the work yard when it snowed and getting a job with a shovel. That would be what he could do.

Finally, one night after he had drunk a lot, he said he was going. It was November, and he said he would be back at Christmas with presents for me and he would send some money. Oh, yes, lots of money, because he would be working for the CPR as a locomotive driver. I was happy when he left and he didn't send money. He didn't come back at Christmas. I didn't care by then. That man and I went through hell during the war and after. He was nine years older than I was and I was still pretty and I had no babies and I could work. Waitress work was good for me. I would meet people and maybe a nice man. I didn't care if Luc came back.

No, he didn't. He just—poof! Gone. Somewhere into the big of Canada. Out there somewhere. I never heard from him again. Not once. Not even a telephone call when he was drunk somewhere. Too bad. He was a nice man. Oh, yes, I loved him, but later I didn't. He was gone. Maybe he went back to Poland and was shot by the Communists. He had worked for the Germans, you see. He hadn't been taken away and put to work. He said, "Yes, you want men to work for you, and I am here."

Two years later I met this man in the restaurant where I worked, and this man was a Czech, a fine man . . . Well, this is the happy part. He said, "We love each other, but we can't stay this way in Sudbury. People talk."

This man said we'd go away, and we did. We got on the train and went to Toronto and lived like man and wife. You know, common-law. I was very happy, and he said we should get married after a few years. I asked why. He said, "Because I have a sister and a brother." That's when he told me he had cancer. He said, "If we marry, then you get my money and they don't."

"Okay," I said, "We'll get married." Nobody knew I'd been married in Poland. No records. So Larry and I got married, and then, oh, about six or seven months later, he died at home.

I was very unhappy for a long time, but I worked and worked and worked, fourteen hours a day. I had two jobs: in a factory making blouses for eight hours and a restaurant for four hours more. Keeping sane and happy, I'd call it.

Now, as you can see, I am happy again. Married with a nice man, and that is me in Canada. First me with a crazy husband. Then me with a sick husband. Now me with another husband who is good to me.

THE NIGHT THE RANGERS GOT DRUNK

I had an uncle at Chilliwack, B.C., and I wrote, and he said he'd be my sponsor, and when that was arranged, I paid my way. Had to go to Hamburg to get a ship and then to Montreal, and they told me I'd easily get a job in Montreal because there are so many cars and they need car mechanics. I knew about that.

Sure, you can figure it out. There were no jobs fixing autos, but they sent me to the Laurentian Hotel, and I was a floor sweeper. You'd call it a janitor, but I was the guy in the funny brown uniform going around the lobby cleaning ashtrays and picking up newspapers off chairs. It was okay, I guess. My English wasn't too good. Pretty bad, but when you have to talk it, you learn it. You concentrate on it, you work hard, you ask questions. I should say this, the hotel was an English hotel. I don't know where the French went, but this was English. It used to get some of the hockey teams when they'd come to play, and that was good. I got to know some of the Chicago and New York players because they'd sit around and smoke and talk and look at the women in the lobby. It was okay.

Austria had hockey teams of Canadians before Hitler came in, and that was a long time ago. I was just a kid, but I'd always liked hockey. I thought it was the fastest game in the world. It still is. It even beats horseracing. A horse runs for a minute and a half as hard as he can go, and then he rests up for a week. These guys, you'd see them going as hard as they could for thirty minutes a game. That's why I admired them.

One day there was a terrible snowstorm. It started and wouldn't stop, and soon the city was stopped. So were the buses and the trains. Nothing was running. Nothing. This morning I go out on the floor at eight o'clock, and these hockey players from New York are sitting around, and I think, hey, they should have left hours ago. But here they were and, boy, I thought, the team is losing money. These guys are supposed to be in Boston soon. They'll never get to that game tomorrow.

About three o'clock they are going nuts. This snow is never going to stop. I thought, it will be like in Austria or in the Alps, it just goes for days, and I'm telling this to their coach, and he nods yes, for days.

That's when one of the players comes over and says, "Karl, a bunch of us are going out for a few ales. That place with the swinging doors, up near St. Kits," and he asks if I want to come.

Sure, sure, and at four o'clock I run up to this tavern, and soon I'm sitting with about six Rangers, and about six o'clock we're all having fun because we're drinking a lot of Molson. There is hardly anybody in the tavern and we're whooping it up, laughing, and they're telling me about girls they've been with in other cities and Montreal, and about the other teams and, wow, what a time! Beer, ale flowing, and we're eating plates of beans the owner is making for us and smoking cigars. I'm telling them about the Canadians who played in Austria about 1935, and they're saying, "Hey, did he play over there, that guy? How come?" Things like that. It was just a job then for the Canadian players. A bit of money and a room and food and lots of Austrian beer. We have a wonderful time, and soon it is eight at night, and these guys and me, we are getting pretty drunk. Pretty drunk. I'd say.

Then there is an awful yell, a scream, and this guy runs up to the table, and he's the second coach. He's screaming at them, at me, at the owner, "Get these guys out of here, get these drunks back to the hotel, get this bastard into the nearest jail," and he means me, and that there's a bus going out because the snow has stopped and they have to get to Boston, and scream! scream! scream!

These big men run for the doors and, oh, oh, oh, I go home and, when I get to the hotel next morning for work, the manager calls me in. I've never talked to him before but he's mad, except he's laughing. He says the New York coach complained about me, that I got all his players drunk, that they wouldn't come back unless I was fired, and what did I have to say? What excuse? I just told him, honest as I could. They'd invited me. They bought all the beer and beans. They told the stories. I just enjoyed myself.

So he said, "You're fired, Karl, but only from your floor job when the Rangers come to play. Just stay out of sight. Help the girls upstairs, but keep out of sight." He said, "If the team loses this game, if they get there, all the snow, they're going to be madder at you than ever." Next time they came, I just took the day off.

That's the thing I remember most about my first year in Canada. Not being an immigrant, tough times. No, getting the Rangers drunk.

JUST IMAGINE! EIGHT THOUSAND BEER BOTTLES

When I look back on it now, it was idiotic, I know. We knew nothing about homesteading and nothing about British Columbia, except it had mountains and the seashore.

When we got to Victoria, we saw that homesteading was quite out of the question. It was quite funny, really. Vancouver Island was not for people from England who knew nothing about farming. But my husband, all the time he'd been in the navy, I suppose, he had had this dream. I suppose he'd read about homesteading somewhere.

Then we saw this advertisement in the paper. This Englishman who had come over in the Thirties, he had a quarter section at Campbell River, right where Painter's Lodge is today. He wanted to go back to England for the winter and he wanted a couple to look after his farm. We wrote him, and he said we could come up. He said he lived on forty dollars a month, so that's what he paid us.

So we went up. Ignorant us. It was in the fall and there was no dried wood for winter, so our first job was to get wood in. Most of it was wet and it stayed wet. Keeping the stove going seemed to be our number one job all that winter.

We couldn't live on the forty dollars a month, but we did have free eggs and chickens and turkeys, and we'd kill chickens and turkeys to eat. That was our meat. The man had told us to sell the sheep to the butcher in Campbell River, and he gave us the livers. Said he couldn't sell them. The butcher kept the money for the sheep for the Englishman when he came back.

Then the fishing guides and the fishermen, they got to know us, and they'd drop off big chunks of salmon. Just lay it on the table outside the door and we'd find it, and that kept us going too.

Oh, there was another thing. When they built the dam above Campbell River, there was a camp beside the little railroad up to the dam, and the bull cook at the time was a friend of ours. His name was Art. He had collected empty beer bottles and he had a pile of them, and we bought them off him for a few dollars. There were seven hundred dozen. That was more than eight thousand beer bottles. The farmer had an old army surplus truck, a half-ton, and we put the beer bottles in sacks and trucked them down to Nanaimo where we could sell them. Maybe we got one hundred dollars for them. I'm not sure. But that kept us going.

Anyway, we lasted out the winter. We had eggs and turkey meat and fish and what we bought from the store, and we didn't do much.

Apart from taking the bottles down to Nanaimo to sell, I think our main job was trying to keep the stove going with the wet wood so we didn't freeze to death.

And keeping the house propped up. That was another thing. It was the prettiest little house you ever saw, but he had his own ideas of construction, and when he showed us around he said, "Now, when the southeasters blow, you go in the shed and get those poles that are there and you prop up the other side of the house so it won't blow down." Oh, it was crazy. But he was right. The poles did stop the house from falling over when it blew so hard those days.

The plumbing! Now, that was another matter. The biffy was out in the open. Right behind the stove. Just great when you had people in visiting. And the hot water. There was a big tank in the kitchen, and after an hour or two, it would give about a pail of boiling water and that was all. Not a pennyworth's more.

No electricity, of course, and, oh yes, there was the sleeping arrangement. He'd put poles across the rafters and hung ropes to them, and his bed was suspended from the ropes. About three feet off the floor, you see, and down below was a big hole in the floor and down there he had kept his dogs and cats and pigs in the winter. That was another thing that really surprised me. I was afraid of falling in, especially with an oil lamp.

Anyway, it was an experience, I must say. One fall and winter was certainly enough. It was fun if you look at it now and think that you were young and didn't know much.

Then he came back and it was time for us to go. His name was Tom Hudson. He's dead now. But he had a good life there himself and he was, I think, the happiest man I've ever known. But his life was not for us.

KEN, YOU'RE A GOOD COWBOY!

One day I decided I wasn't going to work at this kind of work any more on a British airfield, although the food was good compared to what I'd been used to, and that's when I decided to leave Germany and go somewhere else.

The planes from the airfield were going back to Britain all the time. It was the Royal Air Force. I just got on a transport plane with my suitcase as if I belonged, and it went to an air base in Sussex, and I got off, just like a passenger, and nobody said anything. It was kind of crazy. This was the Berlin airlift time.

Then I went down to Southampton and walked around the docks, and because I could speak good English and was young and small, I guess they didn't think too much about me asking where each ship was going, and I found one going to Montreal. I bought an extra suitcase and filled it with food and walked up the gangplank one night. They just maybe thought I was a new crew member, and I went to a lifeboat and got in and pulled the cover over, and I had my blankets and food, and then the ship sailed.

It was May, and I only got out three times, at about three in the morning, and I'd empty my rubber balloon of urine, the French safe, and go to the bathroom on a piece of cardboard and throw it over. It wasn't cold. The weather, oh yeah, it was good.

Nobody found me, and that's how I came to Canada. You couldn't do it now. Everybody takes airplanes.

I figured, I've got no papers and I've got to get some, but how could I, and I went to the seamen's mission and talked around until I found a Danish fellow I thought I could trust. He didn't know, but he said, "You get yourself far away from here and work for a year; don't go where there are people. Maybe a farm," he said. "Then when you have been there a year, go to the police and they'll let you stay."

I got off the train in Calgary and spent a day there just walking around, but it was no place to live. The wind blew and the streets were always full of blowing dust and sand. Nothing was green. It wasn't far enough into their spring yet. I said no, I'll come back, Calgary, when you have grown up.

On the train I met a man who said he was going to a town called Williams Lake where there was ranching, and I thought, oh ho, nobody would find me on a ranch. Out in the hills and mountains with the cattle all day. Riding a big horse and wearing a big hat and a six-gun to shoot rustlers. You can see I saw too many American western movies at the air force base.

His name was Drummond, and we talked for a long time, and he asked if I wanted a job. He was foreman of a big ranch in the Chilcotin. That is a big country, but his ranch was west of Meldrum Creek. I told him my name was Klaus Braun. From then on he called me Ken Brown. He said he couldn't be bothered with foreign names. Okay with me. Just fine.

Mr. Drummond offered me my first job in Canada and I took it. The pay was sixty dollars a month, which I thought was pretty good, seeing that he was doing me a favour, but not knowing it, by hiding me out. I worked there for a year, through one very bad winter and four blizzards. I didn't get to do much riding on big horses. I found a cowboy's life was looking after cows, making hay for the winter, rounding up, branding in spring. Very cold and hard work in winter, and just about one of the hardest jobs I ever had. I wouldn't have missed it. Not ever. It was just good fun to me. I was only twenty-two, and the only time I went to Williams Lake, just the once, was to a big party that lasted three days. That was at Christmas. The rest of the time I stayed on the ranch. No spending money, and I met wonderful people. The Chilcotin Indians—they had a life worse than the refugees in Europe. No hope then, no hope now. That's something else about Canada. They treat their native people like dirt!

After a year I took my gear to Mr. Drummond and said I was going to Vancouver, and he said, "Ken, you're a good cowboy." I was proud, and he gave me a letter of recommendation, and I went to Vancouver and then worked in the woods for two more years at good money, like $1.65 an hour to start, and saved a lot and bought a truck and that's how I got started.

The immigration business, that didn't matter. In 1957 I went to the immigration people in Vancouver and I said I had lost my papers. They said, "Okay, that's too bad. Fill in these forms." So I did. I didn't make them suspicious. Sure, by that time I was as Canadian and British Columbian as they were. I don't think they even checked on me. Just made out new papers, with "Duplicate" stamped across them, and that was all there was to it. Easy. I laugh now when I think how worried I'd get when I'd see a Mountie. Nothing to worry about. That's the way the Canadian way used to be. All good things for everyone.

6 EXPLOITATION AND DISCRIMINATION

6 EXPLOITATION AND DISCRIMINATION

Canada in the late Forties and early Fifties was not the nation that we know now. In those days there was open racial discrimination, and if you were not English or French, then you were one of the "others."

In schools, immigrant children were taunted with the words "Dirty DP," and there was also discrimination in housing. Newcomers looking for a place to live were often turned away with the words "We don't want Hunkies," a racist word that was then an accepted term for an immigrant.

Discrimination was most prevalent in the workplace, where immigrants faced a no-win situation. Canadian workers accused newcomers of taking jobs away from them, but most of the jobs that immigrants did were menial, low-paying ones that Canadians did not want. Canadians also complained that immigrant workers undercut them by accepting wages below the prevailing levels but refused to allow newcomers to join unions. Exploitation of immigrant workers was a common practice, and their lack of English and lack of familiarity with Canadian ways made them easy targets. Canadian employers who took advantage of these workers were not considered to be committing a sin; on the other hand, immigrant workers were scorned because they worked too hard.

A STRANGE CITY, AND $3.87

The only bad experience I had coming to Canada was the train. We got on at Quebec City after coming from Rotterdam, and there were many of us. This was 1953, but I must say I think the cars we were put in were early 1930 vintage. They were deplorable. I must say that.

There were four cars, and they put them at the tail end of the train. One for B.C. and the other three for the prairies. Then they would drop each one off.

They locked the door so we could not go into the other part of the train, where the Canadians were. It took us five nights and four days to come to Vancouver. It was very hot that summer. It was stifling, and all those people with little children. Oh God!

We couldn't go to the diner because they had locked us in. The train stopped only at the big stations where you could buy something, but everybody from the other part of the train was doing that, too, and we were stopped far down the platform, you see. I didn't speak the language, and it was a long run, and the first time I tried it, I was at the end of the line, you see. So in ten minutes when I still hadn't reached the food, they yelled that the train was going. So that was the first time, and I didn't dare do that again. So from Quebec City to Winnipeg, all I had to eat was one loaf of bread and some sausages I had bought in Quebec City. Then at Winnipeg, where there was a stop of an hour or more, we bought lots of food from a little store that was across from the station.

From then on it was better. Despite the heat, despite the lack of water, despite not having much food, everybody was upbeat. We knew we could hold out. A new beginning. Then the prairies were finished and we came to the mountains. As you know, Austria is mountains, and I felt much better. This is what I had dreamed of, the mountains. What I had read about, and they were wonderful.

I didn't think any more about how we had been treated. No water. Not being able to go to the dining car to get a meal, but I must be honest. I couldn't have gone there anyway. They allowed each person sixty dollars Canadian when we left Austria. I didn't have that much anyway, and when we got off at Quebec City I had eight dollars. When I got off in Vancouver I had $3.87. I remember that was what I had.

A new beginning. It was hard, but I made it.

EXPLOITATION, THE CANADIAN WAY

On the train the interpreter told us, "Just do your job, work hard and do as you are told."

That sounded familiar, like my father on our farm and then the army and the work camps in Germany I'd been in, and now I was in Canada with a bunch of other guys, and they were saying the same thing to us, but we were going to get paid for it and pay off our contract.

It was in the first part of September when we got to Winnipeg, and they put us in a building for two days and wouldn't let us go out, and then they called out names, and I was called. We got our things and got on this bus. It took us to a big farm near a little place called Letellier, and they lined us up and I thought, now we're going to be shot. Some farmers were there, and they went down the line and pointed at him, him, him, me, him, him. We were to work for these guys. And when the picking had been done we were told to go to this truck, that truck.

The farmer I got was French, but I didn't know it for a while because, honest to God, I couldn't understand what he was saying, although I speak, or I did then, I spoke some French. This was some kind of new French and I could only get a vague idea of what he was saying. Everything seemed to be slurred or, oh, I don't know what.

He showed us where we were to live. This guy spoke English, but he wouldn't to us, so his hired man talked to us in English, and that was okay. I'd been for two years where English was spoken in the camps and I knew my way around in it. The hired man, his foreman, said this shack for the five of us was where the Japanese had lived two years before and we'd have to clean it up.

It wasn't bad, but I kept thinking who were these Japanese? It wasn't until a long time later I found out they were Canadian Japanese who worked for these farmers doing their beets. Whole families of them, and if they lived in that shack we had then, I pity them. Yes.

We go to work next morning and we get breakfast, which is a bowl of cabbage soup and a bit of bread and coffee, and I think that is it, and I mean that is not enough. The foreman shows us how to pick up the beets with the hook of the knife, flip it, catch it and slash off the tops and bottom stem. You did two and then you knocked them together to take off dirt and then you threw them on the pile.

These beets were big, and by noon we were pretty well finished. It was hard work, and that night we were so tired, we hardly could go and eat, and then the foreman comes out to this little shack and he says we're not working hard enough. We've got to do more. He says the plant is yelling for beets, and I say, "We don't even know how much we are making." I think he thought I was a smart guy by then, because I was the one who said breakfast was not enough; we needed more. He said the pay was twenty-seven cents an hour like everybody else got. And because I'd been in the camps and knew some of these things, I asked about our food. He said, "Oh, well," he said, "you don't expect François to feed you too," and that's another $1.50 a day, and if we used the washing machine that was twenty-five cents, and if he drove us into town that was a dollar each, and other things. You know, I'm making up these prices. I can't remember just what they were. I did some figuring after he left, and I think we would be making about one dollar a day and living in this dump, five of us in this goddamned garage and making one fucking dollar a day. I told the guys, these fellows who had been in the camps like me and trusted Canada, I said this was no fucking good.

They thought, oh well, maybe it isn't so bad. But they hadn't an education like I had in Croatia, and they were just dumb goddamned peasant boys, and I said, "Okay, we work two more days and if we don't see things better for us, then that's the end of this horseshit." Boy, I was mad. I can still get mad when I think of that. We were working for less than ten cents an hour, and here is this Frenchman thinking he is doing us a big help. Hah!

On Saturday night I ask for my pay, and the other boys too, and I'm right. It works out to just about three dollars for those three days, and the next day is a Sunday, and I tell the guys, "Are you coming with me or not? Come, or stay in this dog pen."

They say they'll stay, and I say, "Okay, but I won't be here to protect you. You're just a bunch of dumb foreigners to these guys, so look out." After dinner I get my stuff and I sneak out and all night I cross fields and go along roads, and it is only about thirty miles into Winnipeg. A truck gives me a ride the last ten or fifteen miles, and by morning I'm in Winnipeg. I go to a hotel on Main Street, an old one, and I have a good breakfast, and then I go over to the Unemployment Insurance place which was behind the old city hall, I think, and I go in and see a guy.

He says a few things and brings out a file and says, "Hmm," and there's a job for men at McDonald Brothers out at Stevenson Airport.

That's the international one now. The pay is sixty-five cents an hour, forty hours a week. I say, "Okay, how do I get there?" He says to put on old clothes and take an Ellice bus or streetcar, I think, and report to the office there. I do what he says, and after lunch I'm working with a bunch of other guys and making sixty-five cents an hour which is, let me see, about twenty-five a week.

I've been asked when I've told this story to friends, didn't they come after you and say, "Juroslav, you're coming with us. We're sending you back to the camps. You broke your word."

Nothing like it, nothing. No letter comes to me. No cops. Nothing. I pay off the government in the next two years, $150, something like that, and nobody says nothing. I think all this business of going to work for farmers for a year or two years on a contract, and like he can have you deported if he thinks you're not smiling enough, I think that was bullshit. I never heard of anybody being sent back. They just said these things to scare us, like those four other boys back on that Frenchman's farm. They should have come with me.

LIFE IN THE SUGAR BEET FIELDS

Everybody was very hungry. When the train stopped, we would run to the nearest store and buy bread and butter and tinned stuff, anything that was food that you could eat. It was not the bread we were used to. It was this soft, mushy Canadian bread and the butter was salty. We hated that, but we got used to it. That's how we made it across. We were stupid, with no money.

But the prairies. It was endless. It never stopped. You'd look out the window at noon and there would be the endless nothing of it. At midnight, black as night, and way off you might see a little farm house light and that was all. You felt so depressed.

People were saying, this is not what we were told. This can't be Canada the way it is. They just didn't know. For two days. Endless. It never stopped. People would start to cry.

Then we got to Lethbridge. It was really awful. Everybody got off the train from our car. And we were lucky, we were so lucky. We had friends to meet us. People who had come over a year before. But it was so sad. Imagine, a young couple, maybe no children, and they don't speak a word of English, they have no money, maybe only two suitcases, just clothes, and they've got to work for somebody who has a contract that says they have to work for him. Doing anything he wants them to do.

The last hours or so, people were going into a trance. Two days of the prairies and they were getting to be terrified. This was not the Canada they had dreamed of. They thought it was a terrible place. People were crying when the train stopped. They were tired like they were dying. They were covered in coal soot from the engine. They had no money and nobody to meet them. They knew no English. They didn't want to get off the train. Some wouldn't, but they had to, you know.

We were lucky. We had our neighbours from Germany and they could talk to us and tell us about what this was like and what we had to do, and the farmer, the one who we would work for, they would interpret for us. So we got a bit of a start that way. Not like those other people.

That was in the summer, and we all worked in the sugar beets and lived in the sugar beet houses. We found out where everyone else was and on Sunday we'd go visiting, and even after a few months, we'd still cry on each other's shoulders and comfort each other. But then it got better.

MAKING SUPPER: THE CRYING TIME

Henry, my husband, would ask for money for food, and this Mennonite farmer would say, "Go to the grocery store in Chatham and get what you want and I'll pay him." We were in misery. Rice—I'd never cooked rice before—potatoes, and we'd have hamburger only for Sunday night dinner. It was rice, potatoes, turnips, all these things. They were just starch, and we had to work in the fields for months, to the end of September, and we were always weak, but we knew we had money coming.

An hour before supper I would leave the field and go to the awful shack, and I'd cry all the time I was making supper. It would be soup with rice and vegetables or potatoes. This was the only time I could cry. When I was alone. I wouldn't let them see my crying. Making supper was my time to cry.

When the beets were in, the farmer took us to Chatham and he went into the bank and came out and gave Henry three hundred dollars. He said that's what we had earned. We were not good workers.

He said, when he had the Japanese they worked, and we are not as good as them. That was three hundred dollars for more than three months' work for five of us. If you work that out, you will see what kind of a man he was.

That was the worst time. Everything was better after that.

HE COULD NOT CRY FOR HIMSELF

We came to Canada. It was to Kirkland Lake. My husband said he was a teacher. "Look at my hands," he said, "I am a teacher." They said there was not a teaching job in Ontario until you have worked for a year. Maybe two. Maybe forget it. So they sent us, and he worked in the mine. Not the warm underground but cold and hard on the surface, and he would come home to our little house and he would walk in the door and he would do this.

He would come through the door, like this, and then he would take off his coat and hat and mitts, like this, and then he'd sit at the table and he would put his head in his hands and he would sit. You see how I am sitting. Maybe ten minutes. He was so tired. So cold. The winters. So tired. I cried for him because he was a grown man and he could not cry for himself.

Then I would bring a wash basin to the table full of hot water and I would bathe his face and hands, and he would look at me and say, "Wife, you are the best woman in the world."

If it was an especially cold day, I would give him a glass with about four ounces of whiskey in it, and he would sip it and then he would start feeling cheery. Not happiness, but happier.

Every night then, at that time, I would put on some Czechoslovakian records on the gramophone we had. I would put on my Czechoslovakian dress and an apron with blue flowers on it, and we'd do a little dance to the music.

The children would be there and they'd think, this is crazy. They never said anything, but we'd been at the mine for almost a year by then, and they were so Canadian you just couldn't believe it. They spoke English so well and were doing so good in school. Just as if they had always lived in Ontario, up there in the north at the mine.

Then it was usually Friday when my husband Jan had these attacks of sadness, and that was the night I'd make svickova. That is like our national dish. You have beef and dumplings and cranberry sauce, lots of it, and before that, we'd have liver dumpling soup, which is almost like another national dish, and then little cakes and a bottle of wine. A party. Yes, a party in that little house with the cold outside but not able to get in to our party.

THAT FIRST AWFUL WINTER

My mother had a baby that first winter, and it was stillborn, luckily, because it would have died when she brought it back to the shack we had to live in that year.

It was thirty or forty below, and you know prairie winters that last so long and it is so cold and we had nothing to keep us warm, just a stove that burned coal, and everything that was wet froze solid at night, and our hair would be frozen to the blankets, and that was the way it was. Nobody had told us what it would be like in a Canadian winter with just a shack, boards and tarpaper on the outside, and the people in the farmhouse, they were all snug and cozy and with a warm fire. Our whole family, five of us, nearly dying of the cold, and no one to help us. All the other immigrants around us, they are all the same way too. It was awful.

YOU ARE GOING TO PICK ROCKS

When we came to Canada in 1947, we came as man and wife, and as everybody knows now, the Canadian government didn't want us as citizens to help build up their country. They wanted us for our strong backs and weak minds.

Work for a farmer for a year and then you could do what you wanted, and the work part was, we found out, that farmers in Alberta had had German prisoners of war working for them for about a year after the war and they wanted more labour like them. We would be that labour.

The pay would be forty-five dollars a month, and they said the farmer would give us a place to stay. Then we would see what we would do. We would learn more English. I didn't speak it then, but in the camps in Austria my husband had learned some of it and he was kind of an interpreter for the Yugoslavs. He had learned some English there. Just enough to get by.

The farm was north and east of Vulcan, and the farmer met us in Lethbridge. They lined us up by the train and called our names, and the farmer came and picked us up. I won't tell you his name. He might still be alive. He could be. He wasn't too old then, about thirty, maybe.

He drove us to his farm and all this flat land, and it was in May, and he didn't say one word to us in the truck. He didn't even answer the questions my husband asked him. He just went awful fast and made the ride a terrible one. I don't know why he did it. I think he was trying to show who was boss. I remember that.

The house we were to live in was a granary, a shed, you see. It had nothing but two cots and a pail and a little woodstove for coal and a lamp and some dishes and a fry pan. I thought, just a fry pan? Nothing to boil water in?

Next morning somebody blew on a horn, and my husband went to the house and brought back our breakfast, and I remember it. Two eggs and some white bread and a pot of coffee, and that was all, and this was six in the morning. No place to wash. There was nothing. And we'd been cold all night because we only had two blankets. That was the way it was in our first place in Canada.

This was when the farmer came over, and he told us to come with him. My husband went out and the farmer, this George, he said I was to come too. My husband said he was the one who was hired, but the farmer said, "No, I hired you both. You both work for me. That's the law." We didn't know anything, and we didn't have any old clothes for working yet, nothing, and I had city shoes and Dimitri had oxford shoes. Then we get in a wagon and go to a field, and the farmer tells my husband, "This is the field where you and your wife are going to pick rocks." There sure were a lot of rocks in that big field, and I could see you would have to pick up every one. One, you'd bend down and put it in the wagon, and then another, and they were bigger than big apples. Some were like the size of eggs, though.

"Just pile them up along that fence," the farmer, this George, he says, "and I'll blow the truck horn when it is dinnertime," and it was only about seven in the morning then. That meant we had to work for five hours before we even got a glass of water.

We tried, but the sun was hot and you had to pick up every rock and throw it into the wagon, and we had no gloves. We had nothing, and in our good clothes. I mean, we didn't have work clothes. We didn't have a watch. The sun got hotter and hotter, and I thought, I can't do this. This is crazy. This is not what they told us we would be doing. They didn't tell us Canada would be like this. What is it going to be like in the afternoon when it gets very hot? There was a little wind blowing and it blew dust at us. I guess when we thought it was time for dinner it was maybe only ten o'clock.

We filled the wagon up, and Mother of God, it was hard work and it took a long time. Then we found the horse couldn't pull the load. It was so heavy. We didn't think of that. We hadn't worked on a farm in our lives. I get excited even when I tell this. It was so crazy. We found we had to empty half the load before that horse could pull the load. Then we emptied it, and so we had to go back and fill up the rest and do it over again.

I remember I was crying, and Dimitri had stopped telling me it would get better. It was so much worse. My arms and back and my legs, they were aching, and I told Dimitri we should have stayed in the camp. We didn't have to suffer like this when we were there. I was crying all the time, and Dimitri said, "We won't stay here," and I said, "We have to. They'll send us back if we go away from here, this place." The farm.

Then the horn blew and we went into the farm about half a mile away, and the farmer said, "Where's the horse and wagon?" Dimitri said he didn't know anything about horses. He said, "We're not staying here another hour," and the farmer started yelling and screaming and his wife came out and told him to shut up. To go and get the horse and wagon.

Now what I am telling you from now on is true. What I have told you is true, but this is true too. This was the first time we had seen this lady. She told Dimitri and me to go. She said her husband was a horrible man and somebody would kill him some day. She said all these farmers were crazy, so greedy. They were crazy for money. This woman said, "Go now, get washed up and go out on that road with your suitcases and start walking to Vulcan. Hurry. Somebody will pick you up. He won't go after you." She said she'd protect us, and she did. We got ready and she gave us water to drink and then we ran to the road and started going to the town. That was it. He didn't come after us. We didn't see the police. We got a ride into Vulcan and asked the man in the drugstore for some band-aids for our sores on our hands, and he put them on for us. A kind man. He told my husband we were lucky to get away from that guy.

So we went to Calgary and we worked so hard, hard, hard, hard, but we made good money. My husband owned a machine shop until he retired, and we have a nice big house and good friends, and our two kids went to the university. She's married and he works for an oil company. We can laugh at this story now, about our first day in Alberta. I guess I have told it a hundred times. Nobody likes to believe it, but they know me, so they know it is true.

WHAT IN HELL AM I GOING TO DO?

The farmer picked me up at the train station at Chatham, and the minute I met him I knew it wasn't going to work out. He was big and he was mean and he was drunk, and there he was, and little me, and when we got to his truck he told me to get in the back. He wasn't going to have any goddamned German riding with him in the cab, and this was the guy I was supposed to work with for a year.

I had had enough of all that in Russia for six years, and he drove away and then stopped at a hotel, and he told me to stay right where I was. I knew why he was going into that hotel. For beer, because that's what it was, a beer parlour. I was scared. I was afraid for my life and I thought, what in hell am I going to do?

He was going to be bad for me this guy was, I knew. And something just came over me, and I grabbed my bag and jumped out of that truck and I walked very fast down the street, and there was something I had to do. I had to get out of there. This town wasn't big, and I walked about ten minutes out on the road, and I didn't know about hitch-hiking. All that was new to me, but trucks and cars were going by, and I turned to one and I sort of put out my hand. No, not my thumb. I just sort of waved my arm a bit, and the car stopped, and it was a guy going to St. Thomas. I didn't speak much English, but he asked me were I was going, and I pointed up the road, and he asked me what I was doing. I said I was looking for a job.

St. Thomas wasn't far and he was going fast, and that was good for me, and I told him I was a German and looking for work, and he said that was fine, lots of work. We stopped in St. Thomas and he said, "If you go in there, you'll get work."

Then he said, "Oh, I'll go in with you." And we went in and he said, "Joe, here's a guy I picked up on the highway and he's an immigrant. Know any work for him?" Just like that. The guy Joe says sure, and in one more hour I'm working on this farm and the family is named Metcalfe, and they are very good people and I work for them a long time. Three years.

CANADA WANTED LABOURERS, NOT PROFESSIONALS

I started work as an accountant for a large importing company, fruit and vegetables, and one day in September I got a phone call from a man named Calvert, who said he worked for the government and would I come and see him. I thought, oh, oh, this is bad news, but it was good news in a way. He had heard that I spoke several languages and he asked if I wanted to work in the department which looked after immigrants, refugees, Displaced Persons. The thousands who were coming over from Europe under the various assistance programs which had been set up.

The salary, of course, being government, was less than I was making, but not that much less, and I said I would. I felt it would be an opportunity to help these people, as there had been many very disquieting stories circulating about Winnipeg about them.

I spoke German, Polish, Russian Ukrainian and of course Yiddish. I had worked for the govenment in Poland before the war, before I got out of Europe and got to England and joined the Polish government in London, so I understood how government worked. All governments worked the same.

From the first, a pattern emerged. I dealt with the mature male, the European male who had been, well, you might say of the officer class if they had been in the army in Poland where I came from, or had been in the professions, and it was very disquieting to me.

These were men who had been doctors, lawyers, accountants, engineers, men of quality any country would have been happy to have. Men who had a purpose in life, a sense of achievement, a large measure of pride and would have contributed a great deal to Canada, but they were being shut out.

I found they had been told when they were in the camps overseas that they were to downgrade their education, their skills, their accomplishments, in order to fit into certain slots the Canadian government had set up. I mean labourers. That really was what it was all about.

It was very disheartening to me, very disquieting, to have to tell these men they could not work at their professions. No medical association, the great god of the professions, would allow them to practise, and they could not work as engineers or lawyers. This, in a way, they did understand, as Canada was not prewar Europe. While students were jamming the universities in Canada taking medicine and engineering and the country was crying for doctors and engineers, they could not even work, even under a temporary licence. Lawyers, of course, were a different matter altogether. That was a closed shop, completely, for years. Well, for that matter, so was medicine.

Time after time I would have to tell superbly qualified men they would have to work as labourers, unskilled tradesmen at low wages, and I could only sympathize with them, tell them I hoped that things would improve. I'd, well, try and give a bit of a boost to the morale I could see fading from their eyes as I explained the situation.

I know they didn't blame me. They knew what government regulations were, and they knew of them in the Old Country. It didn't matter if they had the skills good enough for fine Polish or German hospitals. This was Canada now, and I'd tell them, frankly, they were imported for jobs which the ordinary Canadian did not want. It is the same today with the boat people and the Filipinos, and there are many in Winnipeg today. It was the same then. They were the boat people.

They didn't consider me the bad guy. Oh no, I must emphasize that. I think they must have known the pickle they would be in even before they came to Canada. It was Mackenzie King's policy, the policy of the almighty Liberal party in Canada. Nothing else mattered.

Do you know what I would tell them? I would say to work hard at any job and save and then go back to England, as a lot had eventually wound up there, and apply from there to go to the U.S. or Australia. I told them, because I knew from friends I had who had gone there, I knew they would do much better. The climate for new people would be much fairer.

As far as I know, not one took my advice. They settled down in Winnipeg or moved to another city with what they had and tried all over again. But I do know, from what I have learned since, that most of them did well, very well, or very, very well. You understand? They had it within themselves from the beginning to get ahead, to succeed, and they did not let a thing like this blatant discrimination stop them. Yes, you could bet the farm they all did well.

THE OXEN OF THE FIELD

If I was doing it, based on my observations then and what I know happened to other people, I would have given more practical aid to those people who came over from the refugee camps.

Many were classed as political refugees and being supported in the camps by the United Nations Relief and Rehabilitation Association and later the International Relief Organization. They were a pretty forlorn lot, the ones who came over on the ship with me.

They had papers on them and they didn't understand what they meant, and they were ticketed, like children, and ordered here and there, and had no idea what each order meant, its purpose. Like beaten animals, I would say, and tragic to watch.

When they got to Halifax or Quebec City, Montreal, Toronto, there didn't seem to be much organization, and that was the government's fault. You just don't bring people over to work on the farms and in the woods and then abandon them to the mercies of their employers. I never heard of any supervision, government staff going into the fields or the woods and finding out how these people were making out and, from my knowledge, a lot of these people, a great many, were exploited terribly by you Canadians.

You were going ahead full-blast building your industry, your cities, your highways, and bringing in these poor beaten people as the bull labour. The low-pay workers. The oxen, if you will. It was outrageous, and for years I believe a lot of them continued to be exploited because there was no kind voice of government to tell them, "Look, you don't have to work for nothing for this farmer, or at twenty-two cents an hour and a twelve-hour day for this Montreal clothing manufacturer, or you don't have to risk your life in the woods and the cold and be kicked out in the spring to do ballasting and pick-and-shovel work for the railways in the summer. You don't have to do that," the government should have said.

Oh, no, but that wasn't why they were here. They were not wanted in the cities because the cities were filled up with Canadians making fairly good money at easy jobs. So it was the landed immigrant who was the ox in the field, and they knew no better because nobody was there to help them. Not with their papers they might have to fill out. Not with the need to learn English. The unions ignored them, as they were getting "fat cat" by this time organizing the big industries. The churches, well, how could they be out in the bush or on isolated farms? It was too bad.

But, as a landed immigrant myself, I suffered none of this, because my degrees from the universities and my prewar contacts with Canada spared me and my family. But at work I would hear people say, "Oh, isn't it wonderful? Aren't we a generous country? Aren't Canadians so big-hearted? Look how we opened our doors and brought in these poor peasants from Europe and let them enjoy the wonders of Canada!"

Balls! Balls, my friend. They were brought to Canada to do the work Canadians wouldn't do, just the same as the Vietnam boat people thirty years later were brought to Canada to do the work Canadians wouldn't touch. The difference is, hah, the boat people opened restaurants.

From my vantage point, Canada had very little to be proud of in the way these postwar immigrants from Europe, the Slavs mainly, were handled. I hope they have forgiven you and this country.

WE HAD OUR PRIDE . . . BUT WE HAD NOTHING

Oh, sure, you'll hear how everybody came to Canada and then they started to prosper and the money flowed like wine and everybody lived happily ever afterward. That's a fairy tale.

When we went to the Immigration in Canada House, they told my husband he'd make at least one hundred dollars a week in Canada and mind you, this was in 1948, and that would be about two and a half times what we'd have in Britain, and still the wartime shortages and all of it.

We sold everything, the furniture, the beds, the books, everything, and when we got to London, the London in Ontario, we found it was a load of malarkey. There were no jobs, not at one hundred dollars a week, and not even too many at thirty-five dollars a week, and none for accountants. No accountant in London made one hundred dollars a week, my husband can tell you that. He'd have his brief interview with an office manager, and the man would say, "We're sorry, but there are no jobs." When my husband would tell them about the $100-a-week business, they'd laugh at him. Why, these men weren't making that much, not by an eyeful.

There we were, in this little shack we'd managed to rent, and we agonized. Should we go back? Should we go back? We had our pride, but another thing was, we had nothing. We had no home. We'd sold the lease, all my lovely things, and I just can't describe the anguish we went through.

People say, oh, immigrants came over here with nothing, but they worked hard and made good. That's true for some, but with us and a lot of others, we came over here and we went downhill, compared with what we had in Britain. When you're an Italian from a poor village and you scrape and scratch the ground for a bare living, coming to Canada was something, because you had nothing. When you had a fine home and good friends and good money and you come to Canada and you come up against what we did, then the shoe is on the other foot, wouldn't you say?

Within two weeks we knew that coming here was the worst mistake we'd ever made. But we had to live with it. We couldn't go back home, because we couldn't afford to. We were stuck, and we were barely getting by on Bob's wage, and that wasn't much. About thirty-five dollars a week.

Oh, we agonized, and we suffered and strained, and we got by. And finally we began to see some hope of leading the life we had hoped to find, but I'd be washing the dishes and I'd think, oh, how the Canadian immigration people, how they deceived us. They must have known. Not must have, they did know. I'm convinced of that.

WE CRIED OURSELVES TO SLEEP

Peter was to cut wood for a company up on Lake Nipissing, and they gave us a cabin. It was made of logs. It had a bed and a stove and a table and a kerosene lamp, and there were some sardines and raisins and biscuits in the cabin, and that's how we had our first dinner in Canada. This sounds awful, doesn't it? It was worse.

Oh, I shouldn't say this. We cried ourselves to sleep that night, but next morning he went and found where he was to work, and they gave him the right clothes. Poor man, he'd never cut wood in his life. But he managed, and came home that night with a bag of food. They'd taken him to the store and told the storekeeper he could have credit. That's when we learned that people would trust you if you have a job.

The rest was not too bad, although it was still pretty awful.

That night some people came to the cabin, and they spoke German and they were nice. They showed us how to do things, like make the stove work and how to make it burn all night, and things about the lamp, making it work, and they brought us bread they'd baked and a pie, and this was good.

Not what we'd hoped. He was an accountant before the war, and wood cutting, well, he just wasn't used to it, but that job lasted another month before spring came in April and things got better.

I made the cabin nice and he got a job on a truck. There were four trucks loading wood and other things. He didn't drive—he went from truck to truck, just helping to load and unload. This was hard, but I think he got sixty cents an hour, and you can see it was money coming in.

We began to teach ourselves English from the *North Bay Nugget* newspaper and the *Saturday Evening Post*. There was a big pile of the magazines in the cabin. We had an English dictionary and Peter was learning a bit of English from the other men he worked with and, well, this was 1947, and we were away from Europe and the camps, so this was better. Awful, not like the home I had had, but so much better.

I had my baby girl in June. We now have a nice home. My husband Peter is retired now. He became an accountant with a big firm that needed European people. We have a nice car. We bought our first new car in 1952, so you can see we worked very hard.

Canada is the best country in the world. I hate it when I read the newspapers and see people are attacking it. They just don't know.

SOME EMPLOYER! SOME CANADIAN!

When we got off at Vancouver we had to go to Immigration by the CPR station. I stayed there four days, and I wanted to go to Kitimat. That was my goal. I had seen the posters and the information in Austria, where I had got my medical exam, and when we had sold the lease of my apartment in Linz to get money, then I could come to Canada. My wife and daughter stayed behind. I would bring them over later.

I had no money and I didn't speak English, and so I stayed in Immigration for four days, and I knew I had to get a job to get out of there. There were guys who came around and said they wanted workers, but I was not chosen. Then a guy came and he said he wanted a plasterer's helper. Somebody translated it for me, and I didn't know what a plasterer was, but I thought if he wanted a helper, why couldn't I help him?

I was the only one of the forty-seven guys in that room who raised his hand. I don't know what those other forty-six guys were doing. That was what concerned me about immigrants then. To me, you wanted to better yourself. A job was a job. They seemed to be happy just to sit around Immigration and play cards and be fed and not try to work.

I lasted three and a half days. This was down in New Westminster. You have to mix the plaster and there is a lot of lime in there, and I didn't have gloves, and the skin, it affected the skin badly. The guy wouldn't give me any money for what I had worked to buy gloves, so I got bad sores on my hands. Somebody else on the job saw my bloody hands and they took me to the Workmen's Compensation, and there was a doctor there and he put stuff on and bandaged me, and so I went back to Immigration.

That was my first job in Canada. I didn't get paid. And that was my first experience with a Canadian boss. Thank God, it was the worst one I ever had. The rest were better.

NOT THE LIFE I DREAMED OF

This life of mine, it has been very hard. I guess I have been just unlucky. I have worked so hard to try and be like Canadians, but there is always things that get in my way, and people say, "Mary, you should have done this." I seemed to have done other things all the time, and that is what made my life so hard.

We came over on a boat from Le Havre, where they sent our family. This was in 1947 after we had been in the refugee camp. The UNRRA people looked after us, and when my father said he wanted to take us to Canada, they sent us with a lot of other people to get the boat. I was sixteen then and my brother Nick was fourteen and another brother, Franz, he was a prisoner with the Russians, and what happened to him we never found out.

On the boat my mother fell in love with another man. We didn't know it. She kept quiet, but when our train reached the city of Montreal she was there, and half an hour later, where? People looked everything around. I mean everywhere. But she was gone and so was this other man, this Austrian engineer who had been half in charge of the forty or fifty of us. Then somebody said, "I know. She has run away with the Austrian man who looked after our papers on the boat." That must have been it. We never saw her again. My father, he was very upset, but he didn't stay and look.

The tickets said Regina. We didn't know where Regina was, but the Red Cross said, "Get on this train and don't get off until you come to Regina." That meant, all of us thought, we couldn't get off the train, and we should have to buy food in the stations. We had been in the refugee camp so long. In the war before. We thought, if someone says don't get off, don't get off.

In Regina we were taken in a truck to some place and they fed us, and by this time it was night, and the men and boys had to sleep in one room and the women and their little children and the girls like me, another place to sleep. It was warm in the place. I remember that.

My father went out next morning with other guys and they said they were going to find a job. I didn't speak English and I don't think none of the women did, but a woman from the government came in and asked in German, "Who speaks German?" I said I did and some other people did. They all wanted to know where their husbands were, and the woman said they were getting their papers checked and then they would be given jobs. My father found a job. It was winter, and he got a job on a coal truck. I remember he didn't have the clothes and the boots, but he worked, and the man gave him four dollars for the day. That was good. It was what Canadians got, he said. He bought some cookies and candy for us, and we sat in this big room that night and talked.

I told my father I had told this government lady I would go to work for a German family. Their farm was near Davidson, and the next day the farmer's wife came to Regina and got me. Their name was Nixdorf. I worked for them in the kitchen for two years, and then I came back to Regina. They were good to me, and I saved $120 in those two years. Those were my wages, all I had left, because I had to buy clothes and shoes, and when we'd drive to Davidson I'd go to the show. I went to the show every night for two years of Saturdays, and that is how I learned a lot of my English. Listening to the actors. I didn't really watch the movie and what it was doing, you know. I was with the words. The movie house is a good place to learn English. You are alone, and they are doing things on the screen, and you can figure out. There was a German-English dictionary at the farm too. Mrs.

Nixdorf gave it to me when they sold the farm and moved to British Columbia. That is why I left the farm and drove with them to Regina. I was eighteen.

My father was sent to jail for something. He wouldn't be a thief, so I guess he hit somebody and maybe hurt him or killed him. I don't know. My brother told me he had heard my father was in a prison.

I have always worked for other people. Wages are good now. Pay—like with the Nixdorf family I got fifteen dollars a month, and I worked until after dark—it got better. I love little children and I have always worked for people with little children. One man in Calgary who had two little children and his wife had died, he had this big house and a summer home at Windermere and he wanted to marry me. He may have liked me, but he didn't love me. He couldn't understand why I wouldn't marry him or go to bed with him. To sleep. I mean make love. I couldn't. I kept thinking of that mother of mine.

This way, it has been a hard life, but I think it is better now. Rich people want what they call a nanny. They have children, but they want to make more money working. They want to go to parties. You know, a trip to Europe and have a good time. If they have a good nanny, they don't worry. I'm good. I know it. I could work anywhere in Vancouver and I can get any job. All their friends say, "Oh, how did you get such a good nanny?"

Now I make seven hundred dollars a month, and I save it mostly because I have my own room and bathroom in the basement and I eat their food, and if I want to go to a show at night, they will give me one of their cars. This is the way I live. It is not the way I wanted to live, when I think back to when I was a girl. I had dreams then.

HOUSEWORK, HARSH AND HARD

My sister married a Canadian soldier after the war was over, and she'd write back telling how wonderful it was in Canada—how beautiful the country was and she now had a baby girl and her husband had started a hardware store in Vancouver and the government had given him $5,000 to buy it and it never got cold there, and I thought, why am I here in Rotterdam? Everything so hard for my father and mother and me, and I wrote my sister, and she said she'd sponsor me.

But when I went to the Immigration, they said, "You will have to work in a house for a year." I asked, "What do you mean?" They said, "You will have to work in a house for a Canadian woman, and she will pay you, and when a year is over, then you can do what you want." I said, "But I will be living with Anna." "No, you won't," they said. "They want girls in Toronto and that's where you will go." I told my parents and they said beggars can't be choosers. So I went, and this was in 1948, and I landed in Toronto with a lot of other Dutch girls, and they called out our names, and when they called me, I put up my hand and I found out then who I was to work with.

I won't mention the name, but her husband was a manager of a big bank. A director, we'd call him. They had a big house, and I had to do all the cleaning and the scrubbing and the washing, and the woman would say, "We're having six people for dinner on Saturday and this is what I want you to cook." I hadn't done any cooking at home, not for eight people, but I'd manage, and then I'd be in the kitchen until eleven at night, washing dishes.

You didn't eat with the family. If you thought that, you were crazy. I would eat what was left after they had eaten. I mean the scraps. A bit of meat off one plate, potatoes that hadn't been taken out of the pot. Maybe a piece of pie and lots and lots of that awful Canadian bread. Weston's bread. Fluffy stuff. I hated that house.

I was just a young girl of nineteen, and I guess you could say now I had no backbone, and so I got pushed around, and I was supposed to get Thursday afternoon off to go shopping and maybe a show downtown, but I never did. I'd write my sister and tell her and she'd say, "You have to stick with it. If you run away, you can't come here. You'll have a mark against you, and I don't want the police coming around, because of the neighbours." I think she was afraid of the police, and I was because of the German soldiers and the Gestapo all those terrible years in the war.

I'd cry at night. I was in a little room in the basement, and the woman's husband would come down to fix the furnace for the night in winter, and he'd hear me crying. I'd hear him stop outside my room and I wished he'd just knock one night and ask what was the matter. Then I could have told him how awful his wife was. What a brute that woman was to me! But then I'd hear his feet going up the stairs.

I got thirty dollars a month, and remember, that was only a dollar a day. I paid ten dollars of that to the Canadian government to my fare, and so I couldn't save much, but when I had $125 I thought, I can't stand this any more. I'll be dead of hard work and not enough food before I can get out. So I ran away. One afternoon I waited until she had gone out in her car, and I took my bag and I called a taxi and I bought food, chocolate bars at the train station, and then I went and asked how much it cost to go to Vancouver. I thought it would be a terribly large amount, oh, five hundred dollars, and the man said it was sixty-five dollars by coach, and I didn't know what "coach" meant, but I got a ticket and kind of hid until the train left that night, but I was on it.

You had to sleep sitting up, but I didn't care, and next morning when everybody was going to eat, a lady I had been talking to, she said to come with her, and that's when I had my first Canadian meal. In all those eight months I had not had a Canadian meal. Just the scraps and what I would get from the refrigerator. I couldn't believe it. I didn't believe there were places like this. A Canadian dining car. The silver. The linen. The nice, coloured waiter. The food. You had to be there to see my shining face and the big smile.

Then the lady asked about me and I told her. I had to tell somebody. I said I was afraid they would send me back, and she laughed. She said, "Child, if they come along, and they won't, I'll use my six guns on them." I laughed at that. Mrs. Camden. What a wonderful woman! I rode with her until Winnipeg, and she told me all about Canada and gave me her address and told me if I was ever in trouble, I was to phone her.

After that I just looked out the window and ate the meals in the diner and thought, my goodness, what a wonderful big country this is, and I thought, I'm not a weakling for leaving the way I did. I'd say, I am strong, I am strong, I am strong. You know the way a wheels go over the ties on the track. They'd make this click, click, click, and I'd be saying, I am strong, I am strong.

The Rockies, oh, that sight! Then the train got into Vancouver, and I went to my sister's house and everything was fine. She wasn't mad at me at all. She loved me and I loved her.

TORONTO IGNORED ITS ETHNICS

You could pick up the Toronto *Star* or the *Telegram* in those days and there were hundreds of jobs. Not good paying ones, by any means, but there were good ones too.

I had been a fitter in Britain, and a good one. I picked a General

Motors ad because I was familiar with the name, and I hopped out
there on the streetcar the next day. I remember it was about 7:20 A.M.
and it was a workingman's streetcar going out to the plants and
warehouses, and all you could smell in that streetcar was garlic, and
you could hear a dozen languages. I got a job right off. No trouble. I
thought, this is too easy, and I laugh now. The pay was easily twice
what I'd been making in Britain.

You worked a six-day week in those days, and every Sunday I'd go
on my own walking tour. All these little districts, quiet little corners
of Toronto where all the immigrants from Europe had piled in. Their
stores, their shops, the restaurants, Greek, Italian, Russian,
Armenian, I suppose, and God knows what else, but there would be,
say, Gladstone and Palmerston, streets with the names of famous
English prime ministers, and here it would be, Little Europe.

It was a revelation to me, and all these little corners of Europe were
totally ignored by everybody in Toronto. I don't know if they hoped,
perhaps if they didn't say anything, they'd go away. Or if they didn't
say anything, they would not spill into any of the old Anglo-Saxon
areas, and you must remember, Toronto was a very stuffy place in the
late Fifties. Very. Oh yes, very.

Everybody in those little neighbourhoods, they spoke Greek or
Italian or whatever, and here were dozens of these little shops in the
front of these old Victorian-type homes, with an immigrant in each
one and, well, here's an example.

You would walk into a little corner store, maybe cigarettes and pop
for sale, Canadian stuff, and the rest would be all these exotic foods
and packages and bags of this stuff, and their olive oil and the magazines from their home country. The store was fourteen feet deep. Behind it, through a curtain, you'd hear noise, voices, and men coming
and going through the curtain. If you poked your head in, you'd see
card tables, men gambling, drinking wine at tables at noon, which
was something which did not happen in stuffy old Toronto. I'd get
some pretty hard stares from some very tough-looking characters. This
was their territory. They were doing what they would have done back
home, and I don't think it was worth my life to hang around there.
No, it wasn't.

In the bright sunshine even in the morning, my God, the fantastic
street life that was going on. The vegetables and the fruit they sold
outside these grocery stores, and there seemed so many stores. The
thing is, I don't know where that produce came from. Little farms in

their back yards? I don't know. But, you know, you couldn't find that
kind of stuff in any other part of Toronto. Those people. They'd come
over here with nothing, no English, and in months, a couple of years,
they've got things going for them. Happy as hell.

Funny, you know, but that was a part of Toronto that was never
touched by the papers. They were in a circulation war, the *Star* and
the *Tely,* and you'd think there would be plenty of new customers out
there among the immigrants. But there was never any ethnic
news—the whole thing was ignored. As if they weren't there. Didn't
exist.

I'd think, here is a whole new life going on here, something so different and exciting and interesting from the Toronto I'd seen, the
Anglo-Saxon Toronto. Right under their noses, all this going on, immigrants pouring in, living in a cheap room, four of them, working
their little old guts out and putting a down payment on one of these
old houses. Then they'd fill up the rooms with their own people, all of
them jabbering away like maniacs, and when they got that half paid
off, they'd buy the one next door or across the street. Little neighbourhoods were being created, and when I'd walk around, I found it
the most exciting part of the whole city.

But no—and I'm sure I'm right in this—the only time there would
be something about a new immigrant in the paper was when one
knifed another.

I got to be kind of known to some of these people. Just by being
around. Oh, I lived nearby, so I'd be around there in the evenings as
well as Sunday, and I got to know some of them. They were quite
friendly too, once they got to know you. I remember once I was invited to an Italian wedding. A Greek wedding once. Armenians, I've
had lunch with one of their big families. It was all very fascinating,
and yet, here all of this new upheaval of new people and new ways was
going on in Toronto, south of Bloor Street, and nobody appeared to
know what was going on, and, you know, those very people did an
awful lot to shape the cultural environment which Toronto was eventually to move into. It was exciting for them, but not for your average
Torontonian who, quite frankly, I found to be a very, very dull clot.

DIRTY, DUMB FOREIGNER

I had been a corporal with the Polish Second Corps, and so we could go anywhere we wanted when the war was over, and only a crazy man would want to go back home, because the Russians were there. We knew all about the Russians.

I said I wanted to go to America, which was the U.S. in our minds, but the officer said that Canada was making a special section for Polish veterans who had fought for the English. I came here to Winnipeg in 1948, and they gave us places to stay until we got jobs. We weren't like a lot of them who were shipped off to the mines and lumber camps, just told, "You go there and find out what it is like to be a Canadian. You'll learn there." We had a special status, you might call it.

There was a little restaurant on Selkirk Avenue run by a Polish woman and her daughter, and I used to eat breakfast there before I would go out looking for work. I had been going there for maybe five, six days. They were friendly and would ask me a lot of questions.

One morning the mother and I were gabbing away in Polish and a man in a booth called over and asked what I was saying. This guy seemed to think it was his business. The lady said, "Oh, we're just talking about the Old Country. This man is just new in town. He is a Polish war veteran and was in Italy, and he's looking for a job."

The man got up and said, "We don't want any goddamned Bohunks here. Enough of them here already. My father came here from the Ukraine in 1913 and he's made a good life for himself, and we don't want any Bohunks spoiling it for everybody." That's just about what he said. Of course I remember it. He didn't know I spoke English very well. We had a lot to do with the English in the war.

I didn't know what the word "Bohunk" meant, but the way he used it, well, I knew it was a bad word. I asked her what Bohunk was, and she said, oh, she tried to find a Polish word for it, but finally said it meant a dirty, dumb foreigner.

I said his father would have been a Bohunk then, wouldn't he?

This woman, the café woman, she laughed and said yes, his father was a Bohunk, and she thought it came from the word "Hunkie," but she didn't know just where that word came from. It didn't matter whether you worked on a pig farm or were a professor in the Warsaw university, you were a Bohunk.

She said she was a Bohunk too, for what it meant, and she didn't let it bother her, but she said I'd hear it a lot when I got working.

She was right. I did. Even I used it, maybe when some other immigrant who worked with me at Canada Packers, this guy would do something dumb, and I would call him a dumb Bohunk.

I've got to admit there were times when I wish I had a word like that to shout at some of the English, the Canadians I worked with in the first few years. I always thought just the sound of the word Bohunk made a person worse off.

People still use it, you know.

WE WERE THE SQUAREHEADS

Oh, it was a big joke. Some of the guys were really upset about it when they heard, but when they knew what it meant, they just laughed.

When we got to the immigration shed in Montreal, there were about three hundred of us, and the officer in charge, he said, "Single men over here and married men, women and children, over there," and so we were split up. That was okay. None of us knew each other. We came from all different countries and the orders on the ship's loudspeaker were in English, Polish, German, Ukrainian, Russian, and so everybody did okay for meals and inspections and lifeboat and that kind of thing. Besides, a lot of us knew some English anyway.

Then a man who didn't wear a uniform, he asked the single men who wanted to work in the bush that winter. This was October 1950. He said it was a big company with good bunkhouses and good food and the wage was $1.50 an hour. That would be about fourteen bucks a day and they took four bucks off for transportation, insurance, hospital, food and your bunkhouse. That left ten, and that was good, and I thought, winter is coming, no job, no nothing, and why not? Sounded good. I'd have a lot of money in the spring. I knew what ten dollars was.

We hadn't been prepared for this, jobs right away, but a lot of us put up our hands when he had rattled through it in English, German and Ukrainian.

Then he said—and I'll always remember this—"Squareheads, over here. The rest, over there."

I didn't move, and I don't think anyone did. And then he said, "Okay, sorry, Ukrainians, Russians, Poles, over here, and the rest of you over there." We were the squareheads.

Ho, ho, and that's the first bit of slang I learned in Canada.

PUNCH-UP IN THE SCHOOLYARD

The boys would pull my pigtails. I was the only foreign DP girl in the class and they'd pick on me. I knew they were calling me names because they had mean faces when they did it, but I didn't know what they were saying.

I was born in Holland in a village in 1941, and we came to Canada to Owen Sound in 1949, so I was eight.

You get so you can't stand it. One day there was this big girl, and she ran the kids and she wouldn't let me play with them, and this time she shoved me and, boy, did I ever go at her. Punch, punch, punch, and I was screaming, and I was screaming, "You bitch!" because that's what the girls would yell at me, and I pushed this big girl down, and the other kids stood around and yelled and cheered. I was punching this big girl, and the other girls, all these ones who had yelled at me all the time, how they were cheering! Why? Because they could see I was beating up the bully, the girl.

There was a lot of trouble. This girl's father came to the school and my father had to come, but everybody found out what a bully this girl had been. I got into trouble, but what it was, I forget. This was about 1950, I guess, but I still went to the school, and now everybody was nice to me. They'd help me and give me part of their lunches, because my father and mother were very poor.

But it was nice for me. The teacher still didn't like me and wouldn't help me at all, not even giving me books to look at, but the other boys and girls, just so nice. They say you can't get an education that way, with a person not knowing the language, but writing and arithmetic was the same, and I had two years of school in Holland and, oh, I don't know how it happened, but I just picked up my English from playing with the kids, talking to them.

Next year that teacher left and one named Miss Marks came, and she helped me so much, so at the end of that year I won the prize for composition in the school and went up to Grade Four with the other kids. I mean, I'd been in Grade One the first year, and then whoosh, I'd caught up.

AN EVENT AT THE LOCAL STORE

We didn't have much money, just enough to pay the rent and the heat. There was no money for anything nice, just for food, and we still had all the clothes and things we'd brought from London in storage.

Then one day a letter came for my father. This was about four months after we got to Hamilton, and it said there was a job for him as a sheet-metal worker at this factory that made car parts. That was in July of 1947, and my dad went out and bought some nice food and a small bottle of whiskey and some Coke for my brothers and me. We had a party.

After his first pay cheque my mother went to the local store and she bought a lot of things, and I was there and she was different. She was happy. Laughing, and like in London she started chatting with the storekeeper, and he said how happy he was that my father had got a good job. She was laughing and talking to him, and this woman was standing there, and she heard my mother's heavy Cockney voice and she just let fly at her. I don't know who was most surprised, my mother or me or the storekeeper, but this woman started to scream that my mother—she called her you goddamned English—that we were taking all the good jobs away from Canadian boys, and it was the Canadians who had gone to England and saved England from the Germans. They'd died at Dieppe and at other places. And honestly, I thought that woman was going to hit my mother. She was screaming. Yelling. Cursing. Finally the storekeeper came around the counter and pushed her out the door and said, "Sorry, her husband has been out of work for months. I guess she's upset."

Oh, you know, it was just such a shock. We didn't know Canadians felt like that about us. I never ran into it again, although my father said he did, later. We didn't know there was a recession in Canada and we thought, we are the only unlucky ones.

It was funny. The first Canadian woman who would talk to my mother was one who gave her holy and complete hell because my father was lucky enough to get a job.

CLOTHES, BUT NO HOSPITALITY

The first few months, my husband could only get jobs around Delhi, working for other people. We'd got there too late for the tobacco and there was no other farm work, and the farmer told us if we promised to stay until October the first of next year, then we could live in the migrant shack, and we said we would.

My husband said, "Well, we've got to live," and he'd go around to the farmers and they'd give him work, not much, but if he worked three days a week he'd get maybe fifteen dollars.

I had five mouths to feed and I thought, this shouldn't be a problem. And on the weekends we got this farmer's wheelbarrow and a bunch of sacks and we went around to people who had big gardens. We'd ask if we could go over their gardens again. They'd always say yes. We'd find potatoes they hadn't dug, and all sorts of vegetables, and there were lots of apples on the ground that were okay. We'd get a lot. When my husband was working, I'd do it with my little girl. The two other kids, we put them in the school.

Women, the ones I'd ask if I could go over their gardens, they'd say, "Oh my, you speak English, so why are you begging?" I'd say, "We are from Hungary," and I could have said, "You know, Hungarians are a very civilized people, and what we had there would make you look like people who go out in the forest and get dead branches to sell for kindling." But I didn't, and these women would say, "My, I just can't get over how you speak such good English." I could have said I had been to two universities and I was a biologist and my husband was a music teacher, but we had been in the war for six years. I didn't say that to these women. They were being nice, the way they thought they should be.

"Have you got clothes?" this woman would ask, and I would say, "Yes, some very good ones, but they are in Budapest and I won't be getting them for a long time, because I think the Russians are in my house." Oh, something like that. It didn't matter what I said. These women didn't listen anyway.

They'd say, "What do you need? Where do you live? My husband will drop off some warm clothes for you," and maybe she'd give me some food. Fruit she'd canned or bottled, peas, beans, all these things that Canadian women on the farm seem to do.

Then it did happen, and I was very surprised. Her husband would drive to the farm with clothing and things, and sometimes another car would come, because these women would phone their neighbour and say, "Oh, Myrtle, there is a poor Hungarian family at the McCormick farm and they need help. Anything you can send?"

It was funny. We could have got along easily with nothing from them. I could feed the family very well on the fifteen dollars my husband made. It was hard on his fingers because of the violin he played, but it had been so long I guess it didn't matter. We didn't need their clothes and bedding and blankets, although it was kind, but it would have been kinder if they could have invited us into their homes.

It was too bad, but nobody did. We were just immigrants. DPs. A DP is a Displaced Person, which is all that it means, but I used to say it means Dumb Dog. That's the way we felt, the first two years.

WE WERE FOREIGNERS

I remember a lot more discrimination in Ontario than when we moved to Swift Current. DP Kid, and all that. Displaced Person Kid. I guess it was because there were more of us there.

We got a lot of that thrown at us. Oh, definitely. In this nice little quiet town in darkest Ontario.

And yet I remember the street we lived on. It was a block long, and I don't think there were two nationalities the same. Italian, Greek, a French-Canadian, Hungarian, you know. Everybody was different.

But the funny thing was, all of us kids, and none of us could speak English, and not one of us could speak each other's language, but we managed to communicate. Everybody was different, but we played together all day long. Everybody was different, but we were all the same.

But when we moved to Swift Current, there was no discrimination. Maybe because there were no other recent immigrants, and again, a lot of the Russians and Ukrainians and Polish who had come a long time ago, a lot of them couldn't speak English even then. So I guess the people of the town were used to that sort of stuff. Been there for fifty, sixty years, and they didn't even speak English.

My father spoke good English but my mother, until she went to work in about 1952, she didn't speak English. She learned, but she never spoke good English. She'd waited too long, I guess. She could make herself understood all right, but it seemed she was thinking in one language and talking in another.

But for me, as a kid, I had no trouble. It came to me easily. At age six, when I went to school, I didn't know a single word, I think. But kids are good that way. If you start them early and with kids all around them, they know they have to get going and learn, and they do. The nice thing about it all, I think that I was learning English and yet I didn't realize I was learning English. There I was, just kind of moving into it, and all of a sudden I was talking English, and other kids were talking to me in English and, "Hey," I guess I said, "look, Ma, I'm talking English!"

Kids had an easy time of it. It was the parents who had the tough time.

I think it was not good that they all clustered together. If there was a Hungarian family in town, then they'd go over and visit, and they would meet another family through them and they'd say, "Oh, well, we've got all these friends from the Old Country and we don't have to learn too much English. Or not right away." That's the mistake they made. They should not have gone so much to these friends and they should have tried to get going in English with their neighbours and that.

Kids, they meet in the schoolyard, on the street, and they pick it all up that way and it is easy for them.

That's when the discrimination, it goes away then. You don't hear people saying, "DP Kid!" That hurt, because I knew it meant we were poor. We were foreigners from another country and being in deep and darkest Orange Ontario first, we sure felt a lot of that.

Out on the prairies, people, they are more free out there. They are more willing to accept people. You know, people have to help each other in the West. In southern Ontario everyone has been there a long time. They are suspicious, unfriendly. They thought, maybe, because we were from Estonia that we were Russians and peasants and serfs and all that. They were wrong. The people who came out from the Baltic countries, they weren't like that. They were the educated class and they had the money to pay their way. They were a high class of people. But still they showed a lot of discrimination against us.

LOOK AT YOUR OWN GRANDFATHERS

The first few years I got sick and tired of Canadians reminding me, us, what a huge favour Canada had done by letting us come into their country.

Hamilton in those days did have a racial mix, but it was mainly English and Scots with a few shanty Irish thrown in for good measure. I would think, why these silly questions about where were you born? What did your father do? What kind of school did you go to?

I'd tell these oh, so very nice ladies that I was born in a large house in Gloucester and my father was a solicitor and had been a wing commander in the Royal Air Force and my parents had sent me to a very posh school. I should have said, "My ancestors are superior to yours because yours came over to Canada to escape poverty and the mill towns. My husband and I came of our own free will, and we had money and we brought our furniture and our fine things with us."

Oh, I know it is silly to say those kind of things now, after nearly forty years, but this prying, this wondering, this suggestion that we had come to Canada to escape a poor social situation, that can be very grinding, you know.

Even today, just because I still have my English accent, these silly questions come at you, like, when did I come over from the Old Country? What they are saying, in effect, is, "You're an immigrant, so don't try and play the fine lady with me."

It would interest me very much to know the backgrounds of the grandfathers or great-grandfathers of these people. Probably farm labourers on some estate at two shillings a day and a cottage for the wife and brats.

Canadians like these people show very little breeding, in some ways, but some do think they are superior. Don't laugh.

HOW TO MAKE HOT WATER

There were twenty-two of us and most of us spoke English. We could read and write in English, and some of us had been at the university, and when we landed in Halifax, we were in a big shed. The official in charge, he said we would have to wait for another ship that had other Czechs on it and we would all go on to Ontario together. He said it would be two days and we would stay at what you would call a hostel now.

They had a bus for us and they took us to this hostel, and the lady in charge, she took the women to one side and told us we shouldn't walk on the streets alone. We must go together. Then she took us around and into the washroom, and she would say, "Now, I want any of you who speak English to tell your friends," and then she turned on a tap and said, "This is a tap and when you turn it this way, cold water comes out, and when you turn it this way, hot water comes out." She went on and on, showing us how a toilet flushed and how a bathtub worked, and on and on.

Someone else was telling these things to the men, and some of the men were university professors.

I felt like telling her that when I lived with my parents in Prague, we had a seven-room apartment and three bathrooms, and that Canadians didn't invent hot and cold running water and the bathtub.

I don't know who she had been dealing with before, and this was in 1947, but we weren't exactly Russian peasants. It would have been mean to tell her Czechoslovakia had been a civilized country when Canada had been owned by the Indians.

MRS. THOMPSON AND HER APPLIANCES

You Canadians! I could spend hours talking about you. You weren't ignorant and you weren't dumb and you weren't stupid but, okay, you just didn't know anything.

I am Ukrainian, and my father's home was in Cortkov, and if you don't know, it is a small city in the Western Ukraine about one hundred miles west of Kiev.

I got to Canada because I said I would work for a year for a lady. I didn't know which one, but they said you work for a year and she will pay you forty dollars a month and feed you. Then it is up to you. When I got to Toronto after a long journey, I was told by the government people that the lady was named Mrs. Thompson, and here she is, and she's standing there with some other people, and they introduce me to her. That's nice, I thought.

Oh, don't get me wrong. I am not being sarcastic. She was a wonderful lady, and her name was Katherine Thompson, and she's dead now. She died a long time ago. She had two daughters much younger than me, seventeen and fifteen, and a nice house off Avenue Road and that was a nice place to live then. This was in 1949, and by this time I had quite a bit of English, because we had been in three camps.

So this morning, Mrs. Thompson drove me home and gave me a little uniform to wear, and with nips and tucks we made it fit, and she said, "Oh, you do sewing," and brought out her Singer to show me. "You push this, you move that, do you understand?" and I could have said, my mother in Cortkov had a better one than that. My father was a middle-class merchant.

We went through the house. The toilet. "See," she'd say, "you press this and it flushes and all the bad stuff, ugh, it goes away." We had always had plumbing and showers and bidets and everything in my home in the Ukraine. See what I'm talking about.

It was the same with all the appliances. This is how the stove works. When this element gets hot, you're ready to boil water for our eggs in the morning. And this is a washing machine. It was one of those old copper things in the basement. I could have told her that my mother had a better one before the war. They were one of the things my father sold to the wealthy merchants like himself. I'm making fun of poor Mrs. Thompson, I guess. I could have told her that the middle-class people in all the cities of the Ukraine had a standard of living as high as the Czechs or the Germans.

She had read too many books, I guess. About the poor Ukrainian peasants and how they came to Canada about 1910 with nothing and no education. There were those people there, many millions, but the Ukraine is a huge and rich area.

She'd just tell her friends—and I'd hear her—what a genius I was! How I could pick up the use of all these new Canadian kitchen gadgets, these things, and how smart I was! I laugh at it now.

WE DIDN'T LOSE OUR DUTCHNESS

I still find it prevalent among Canadians, the misconception that if you were an immigrant you not only came over on a jammed boat with a lot of poor and beaten-down people from war-torn Europe, but you paddled by hand all the way. That sort of thinking.

They assumed that all immigrants came from an impoverished background. Otherwise, why would they have come to Canada?

We were quite well-to-do. We flew over, and we paid our own way, and we travelled by train across Canada, sleeping in compartments, and we ate well in the diner, and in that sense we were no different than other Canadians who travelled well.

I remember my grandmother who came with us, why, she just revelled in that train trip, and while the meals in the diner weren't all that good, she admitted, my, my, these Canadians sure could make coffee! They weren't bad at polishing shoes, either. That was when you put your shoes out in the corridor, and the porter polished them while you slept. And there were other things she liked.

We travelled in style, and when we reached Vancouver Island, we bought a big farm, and when you went through our gates you knew you were on Dutch territory. My grandmother had brought over antiques and the knicknacks and the things that were important to us, and she was the linchpin of our family, keeping us all together in our Dutchness while we made our way in Canada as Canadians.

She epitomized the sturdy and healthy determination which seems to characterize so many immigrant families, and they allow the Canadian way of life to touch but not overwhelm their essential Dutchness, and that way we added our part of our uniqueness to Canada.

7 WE NEVER HAD IT SO GOOD

7 WE NEVER HAD IT SO GOOD

Immigrants came to Canada because they wanted happiness and all it entails: a good job, perhaps their own small business, but few thought of getting rich. Those first few years were hell for many newcomers, but they possessed a resilience developed from their years of terrible war and the uncertainty of the years after. Gradually, they made their way.

They worked hard. Everyone had the European work ethic, and they were well aware that everything they would achieve was up to them, nobody else. That was the Canadian way. They liked it and were eventually counting their possessions: a house with a good down payment on it, a good secondhand car, a bank account. They were content that their kids were in school and doing well, that they were getting promotions at the factory or office. The blatant discrimination that had plagued the first arrivals was ending. They could afford to bring in parents and relatives from Europe now. More affluent and highly skilled immigrants from Europe were arriving, adding to the breakdown of barriers. Everything was looking up.

Newcomers thought that Canadians did not work hard enough, and cited themselves as examples of good workers. They did not think that Canadians loved their country enough, either, and said they loved it more.

Canada suited them just fine, and they made the most of it.

HOW TO BE A CAPITALIST

I'm not saying this because it was so obviously true, but just because a lot of people today might have forgotten just how it was. I mean, when we got off those ships in Montreal and Quebec we were, just about everyone of us, we were a bunch of capitalists.

I'm not sure we knew what the word meant. After all, it wasn't a well-worn European word, so we learned it later, but we were determined to get ahead, succeed, get a business, that kind of thing.

My wife and I were from Czechoslovakia, but I could talk about the Polish people, the Greeks. Ukrainians, I suppose, if there were that many. The Balts, people from those Baltic countries. The Jews, of course. We were the downtrodden. The unhappy. We'd all lost our homes and money and farms and relatives, and we decided we were not going to put up with this sort of bullshit any longer.

We were capitalists at heart. We didn't have money. We had to find jobs and places to live and, if we had kids, we had three, we had to get them into schools and we had to start looking out for Number One. Get a job. Save money. Get money any way you could, but get money. Invest it. Lend it to other people. Forget those damned banks. Lend it on a monthly basis. You know, buy low and sell high. Hah! Oh yeah, that kind of thing. Just get the show going.

Learn English. Study and go to night school, and you could do that. Take courses. Work two jobs a day. There was nothing wrong with that, as we saw it. Canadians thought that was terrible.

They'd say, "Hey, you're working in that factory in the daytime and you're pressing clothes, pants, skirts for that guy at night. You shouldn't be doing that. Some other people could use that night job, don't you know that?"

I'd say, "If some other guy wants to work to ten or eleven at night pressing clothes in that shop, then why doesn't he? I'm not taking a job away." I'd tell them, "We want to make enough money fast so my wife and I can buy that shop off this guy, and then we can both work from eight in the morning until six at night pressing pants and stuff and we'll be our own bosses. Then I won't have to work in the factory making clothes so the owner can make a lot of money and Eaton's can make a lot more by selling them high."

"What are you going to do when you've made money and bought the shop and made a lot of money?" That's what they'd ask me.

I'd say, "Then I'm going to buy that factory, and then when I've got a lot of money and a lot more, then I'm going to buy Eaton's."

They'd laugh, but they didn't know the terrible need we had to be our own bosses. None of this business of Czechoslovakia, a nice country, a fine place before the war, but then the war and the three years after it when it was terrible, and now, Canada.

Canada was our chance. In every little heart in every little landed immigrant, if he was smart at all, and so many were, he'd think this capitalism is for me. My own shop. My store. My little company. Mine, ours. And see, we did it!

This was Canada, oh, about 1950, and everybody had a chance to do this. So many of us did. We worked. God, Mother, Sacred Mother, we worked hard. You Canadians just don't know how hard. You will never know. Hey, you know what? You don't want to know.

IF CANADIANS WORKED HARD . . .

When the war ended about a million Yugoslavs had been killed, but a lot of that was political killing too, murdering, and then the Germans would go into a village when they got mad and they'd shoot thirty, forty people, or hang them from trees. And so, the patriots, us, we were blamed sometimes for making the Germans mad.

I thought when I got to Canada there would be people waiting, cheering, saying, "Oh, hey, here come the brave Yugoslavians, the Serbs, everyone who helped us win the war so much." In the camp I had taught myself a lot of English, and I told the officer in charge there would be a big welcome for us because we were with Tito and we beat the Germans in the mountains. He laughed. I remember him laughing, and he said, "Canadians never heard of you guys."

That was true, but I guess you knew that. We were nothing to them. Then they took us across to Vancouver to find my uncle. I found his name in the phone book and I made a telephone call, and his wife said he was away fishing and would be gone for three weeks. I said, "I am his nephew, all the way from Yugoslavia, and can I come and stay with you?" She said no, no I couldn't. I said, "What will I do?" She said to wait until her husband's boat came back. She said it was called the *High C*, and it would come in at the foot of Campbell Avenue. Then the bitch hung up. Oh, shit, I thought, she's doing that because she's English or something.

I didn't know what to do, and I only had about fifty cents in my

pocket. I was hungry and I went into a restaurant and bought a bun
and a cup of coffee and there I am, a big dumb kid and speaking this
funny English, and a guy sits down, and I ask him where Campbell
Avenue is. He talks back in Serb. My language. Right there on Hast-
ings Street, and he's saying things like, "How are the folks at home?
People still killing each other? What you doing here, kid?" I tell him
I've got my Uncle Josef out there somewhere on a fishboat and I've got
no money and my aunt won't let me stay with them.

He says, "Hey, kid, you're not in such a hell of a mess as you
think." This big guy, Veronek his name was, he is a deep-sea fisher-
man too, and he knows my uncle, and he says to come with him. And
away we go and he says, "You know, your uncle, he owns the boat.
He's not a poor man. He's a king to you, he's got so much money he
made in the war fishing for the companies."

We got on his boat and I start to learn fishing, and we're up off the
west coast, and then we go into the gulf, and when we come back he
said, "Kid, the crew like you and you're a tough one and a good workers, things like that, and how would you like to sign on, as I'm going
to be one short?" They're going trawling after the salmon are over,
and I say okay, fine with me. I'd made four hundred dollars that trip
for only three weeks, and I wasn't even a crew member, and could get
a share. He just gave it to me out of the boat share because I worked so
hard. I worked hard, but to me it was fun.

Then we met my uncle in a hotel there, and he's happy to see me,
but he can't have me over to his house to live. To visit. Not to live.
His wife thinks I'm a Bohunk or a DP. I know what these words mean.
Boy, did I learn a lot of English on the boat with that crew! I could
swear as good as them and I could swear in Serbian too, and that's a
good language to swear in.

That's how I got going in fishing. I've worked in it on and off a lot,
and I think it is the best life, and there ain't no better one when you're
high boat. Everybody thinks you're top shit, and you've got all this
money to spend. You can buy part of a hotel. I got part of two. Not
much, but as long as the boys keep drinking, the stuff rolls in. Not so
good now, though. This depression. I own part of a racehorse, and
you go out to the track and watch it, but the thing always loses. I got
my own boat. I've had five boats. You always want a better one. I
could go to Japan in this one. She would fetch a million dollars, easy.

I got everything by working. I always say, you work harder than the
next guy you win. You can't miss. A bit of bad luck comes, okay, so

work harder. This is a country that is set up for people who work hard. Canadians don't. They don't know how to work hard. They say, "Oh, I gotta work eight hours, so I'll take it easy, and that means I'll only be working five hours, and so I'll beat out the boss." That's the wrong way. If Canadians worked hard there would be a lot of rich Canadians, but they aren't there. But look around this city. You see a lot of rich immigrants. Look at those Germans. Look at some of those Italians. The Chinese, look at them little guys. They make all us immigrants look bad. You work hard and you think hard and you say, "This is the way I'm gonna get rich." You keep doing that and one day, maybe fifteen years, you count everything up and there you are, pretty goddamned rich. You can go back to the Old Country and walk into the tavern and say, "Hey, everybody, look at me, I'm rich!"

MRS. McRAE AND HER FIGURING WAYS

If you ever spent a summer in southern Alberta like I did at Claresholm taking pilot training under the Commonwealth training program, then as far as I was concerned you pretty well had your life planned out ahead of you. Alberta, here I come.

The Ontario government had some kind of scheme at that time, in 1948. They wanted immigrants, lots, from England and Scotland, and they would fly you out. Hey, I thought, this is better than paddling my own canoe across, as I had no money. I told my dad, "When I write, you send me everything you can afford and I'll pay you back. I'll be on to a good job by the time you get my letter, and that will just hold me over until things get better." He said he would. Remember, he said he would. I think he just said that because he was as glad to see me out of the country and to the colonies as my wife was. No reason, neither of them seemed to like me too much at that time.

Nothing went wrong. I signed on with Colonel Drew's immigration plan, got my papers, and there I was in April with a bunch of other larky lads and families, off to Toronto on some old kite that I think had flown The Hump in Burma. I thought I almost recognized the old thing, but it was a DC-6, not the old DC-3.

We were supposed to work in Ontario industry in some plant or other. We were supposed to have mechanic's skills and I had none. God, I had trouble winding my own watch. I didn't waste my time. When the bus dumped us off at the briefing point in Toronto, I was gone, just down the street with my duffel bag on my shoulder, and no-body yelled, "Hey, you! come back here!" I was away.

Calgary, I walked into the little pub in the old Paralyser Hotel, and I was right at home. Same old faces. Johnny the waiter, still there, limping around. A super-tall, red-haired guy named Yorke was still there, looking off into space, and it seemed he hadn't moved since that Saturday afternoon more than five years ago when I'd sat at his table and said so long just before I was off to fight a war. He looked at me and nodded and said, "Sit down, and where ya been? In jail?" I said, "No, been to London to see the Queen," and he chuckled and shoved one of his beer at me. That started a little party which seemed to go on for quite a bit, and I felt quite at home, and I thought, so far, so good.

So, let's see. Jobs weren't all that easy to get, so I did it the hard way. I mean, two weeks working on a furniture truck with people moving, it being around May first. Stacking groceries for a week in a new supermarket that was opening. Three weeks working at a riding stable until the guy with the steady job came back from hospital. A week cutting lawns for the city. A bit of heavy work, carrying shingles to the roofs of a line a mile long of houses some contractor was putting up. Oh, yeah, in between somewhere, joe-boy work on the midway at the Stampede, fourteen hours a day and I liked the life they led. Free and easy. But not enough to take a job with them hitting all the towns the rest of the summer. There were lots of jobs, but no good ones. Little ones, but you got your money at the end of the day or the week. Oh, about four bits an hour. In and around there. Enough to pay the room and cook a bit and eat out and survive a few hours in the Paralyser when it was over.

I had written my dad and asked for the two hundred pounds he'd promised me, but in his letters he just ignored me. I finally thought, to hell with it. Two hundred quid was worth about six hundred dollars then, and that was one awful lot of money, and I wanted to buy a sec-ondhand truck. A pickup, but a three-quarter ton. All these jobs I'd been doing, all for little guys, I'd noticed they were always hiring a truck to get something hauled on the job or taken to the dump. I thought, they think well of me and if I had wheels and a box, they'd hire me. I talked it up with them and one said, "Yes, all we want is someone reliable." They knew I was that. Through sweat and mud, guts and blood, that was me.

I was chummy with my landlady. An old Scottish widow. I had the upstairs of her wee house over on Fourteenth Southwest, and I did all the odd jobs for her for nothing. She'd give me the odd Sunday dinner. This Sunday in September we're sitting there and she asked, "Normie, what are ye going to do with your life? I'm worried."

I guess I was feeling down about money, and I told her about the truck and the jobs I could get and the money my old man hadn't sent me, and so on. Not having a girl or a steady job and that Alberta hadn't quite worked out the way I wanted to. I told her I guess I sort of blamed myself, not waking up one morning and saying, "Normie, this morning you're going to go and get a job at the Bay and wear a shirt and tie every day and say 'Sir' to your boss and become the president." I told her that and we both laughed. I can see us now, sitting at the table in her wee kitchen, she dragging on her cigarette. She was a fearful smoker, and those days nice old ladies did not smoke.

She said, "Normie, take tomorrow off. Don't go to where you're supposed to work. We'll go down to the bank. Right off smart. We'll see what can be done about keeping you away from the president's job at the Hudson's Bay Company. I never did like those people."

The rest, as they say, is history. I never became as big as Trimac or Greyhound or the big boys, but when I sold out I had thirty-seven trucks and about twenty-four rigs and eighty trailers, and I was a little guy, but it all started from that one '41 Dodge pickup. We went to the bank, first in the door at ten, and into the manager's office, and she said, "Mr. Ward, this is my favourite boarder, Normie, a good lad from Hove. And I'm going to lend him one thousand dollars to buy a truck, and you give him the money right now. Not tomorrow. Today. I'll be standing here until he gets it."

The manager's eyebrows gave one of those little hi-ho-here-we-go deals, but he said nothing, and he gave instructions to the teller, and out we marched with the money firmly in her bag after she'd counted every last dollar and counted them again. She took me to the Old Brown Kettle Tea Room for tea and then she got us a cab in front of the Paralyser, an outrageous expense, I thought. The bus went right by. As we pulled away she said, "No more of that place for you, Normie. You're in business and I'm your partner." I asked, "What place?" She pointed, "There. Good businessmen don't drink beer until ten o'clock." I remember laughing, and I said, "Okay, just a few on Saturday night when the work's all done."

In two days I found a truck and paid eight hundred dollars, all cash, and the truck was mine, free and clear, and all I owed was a thousand dollars to Mrs. McRae. Hey, that was more money than I'd ever seen before, let alone owed. I'd pay her sixty dollars a month, which she figured would be one-quarter of my earnings, and she had it all figured out. I'd get another truck and another, and she'd take my orders on the phone, and we'd call it Norm's Trucking Service. The old lady had it all worked out, and work out it did.

On the Thursday I went around to my old jobs, just to say I was in business, and I never got around that first day to seeing the rest. I'd gone out to the contractor and he hired me at $2.40 an hour, me and the truck. It was hauling away scrap to the dump, and I remember the first payday. I got nine hours in, working into the dark, and it was $21.60. And I had the next day's work lined up too, still hauling junk. I remember it was about eight at night when I walked in, and she asked how it went and I kind of hugged her and said we were on our way.

Jobs were easy. A little ad in the *Herald* would pull them in and she would take down the orders, getting one great big kick out of it, and I kept that truck going six days a week, ten hours a day sometimes. That first month, it was October of 1948, just five months after I came to Calgary, I had worked eighteen days and made $360. I was doing far better than Mrs. McRae and I had figured it out, sitting at the table in her kitchen. It was work, work, work, and I knew I'd soon have to get another truck. Either a big one or another small one and hire somebody.

In the spring I'd paid her off, every last cent and five per cent interest, and Norm's Trucking Service was on its way. I bought a smaller truck and hired a bright kid from Denmark to run it, and after the payments on the second truck, I was making about another $150 a month.

By 1951 I had seven trucks and my own company and an accountant and doing advertising and running out to Banff regularly on a licence and down to Lethbridge, through all those towns, and money was just coming in like crazy, you know. One night when I'd come back from a few hours Saturday night and felt like a little boasting, I cabled $250 to my old man and told him to buy Mom an electric water heater. That would show him I was doing just fine.

I wasn't driving by this time, you know, but I'd work with a new driver for a couple of days before I let him on the road. I'd start him with an easy one, an old-time customer, and introduce him around. I never hired Canadian lads. Just couldn't trust them to do a good job.

Always immigrants, right off the boat. I had English lads from Birmingham and Liverpool, tough as they come. Lads from Scotland. Dutch boys who spoke English enough to get by. I trusted them and they showed it in the work they did. I paid every Saturday night at five o'clock in good Canadian bills.

By '67, Expo year, I was hauling right through to Montreal on trip tickets. I couldn't buck the big guys and I didn't try. They didn't try and break me. They figured I was just honest competition and no worry to them. Then in 1974 I got tired of it all and sold out, in pieces, a route here and route there, five trucks, five tractors, ten trailers, that kind of thing.

I just can't tell you how it all happened, but I can say it in two words, hard work. And in two more words, less beer. The two don't work together too well.

Anybody could have done it. My wife says the stars were right for me, but the little star at the top of my Christmas tree every year, the one I look up and say thank you to, that star is guess who? Right! First time. It's Mrs. McRae. That dear sweet lady, sitting home in her wee kitchen knitting and listening to the radio, and along comes a young whippersnapper and one day he tells her he wants to buy an old truck and do something.

I HAVE DONE MY SOMETHINGS

If you look back, seeing nothing but hard work, and then you say, I own eight houses and I live in one and I rent out the other seven houses and I get about $4,800 a month rent from them and it comes in every month and when I came to this country I had only seven dollars in my pocket and a cardboard suitcase with clothes, then you can say I've done pretty good.

I didn't get those houses by sitting in this park, and feeding the rest of my lunch to these pigeons. No, damned right, no. I got them because I didn't sit in the park. Even on Sundays I didn't sit in the park.

I was working. I was working for some guy who wanted a rec room built in his house, or I'd even go out and dig gardens for people, or if it was raining, I'd go around to one of the houses I'd bought and I'd look for things to fix. I would spend my Sunday making money.

People say, "How can Old Man Kofoed just sit out here in the park on a day like this? Why doesn't he do something?" I know that's what they tell my wife. Well, I tell her to tell them that Old Man Kofoed has done all his somethings. From the day he got off the boat in Montreal, he has done his somethings.

In 1955 when I came to Vancouver I didn't have nothing, but I did something a lot of Canadians didn't do. I had two jobs. One from eight to six, and that was on the green chain, hard work, down on the river. Then I'd come home and eat, and I'd be at H. Y. Louie, the warehouse, until eleven or so, and I'd be unloading fruit off the box-cars. And that's the truth of it.

That's how we bought the first house and rented it. With the rent and what I could pay from my two jobs, we managed a second house and rented that and, by the third house, you know what I found out was happening. I think this is why guys become millionaires. They have found the secret too. You buy more and more, but you use other people's money, and inflation is working for you too.

You have to keep thinking all the time, being up on your toes, but you have to work hard too. Damn hard. Say that after me, damn hard work. Then one day, you look at your book and you find you have bought and fixed up nineteen houses in twenty-five years and you still have eight, and they are good ones. Good houses, well built. Not the junk you buy now. They are well looked after and they don't cause trouble because you've got good people in them and they are in good districts. Location, that is important.

So I've got seven houses and they make me about $4,800 a month, and that is with nothing against it. I could have made more. Oh, yes, I know that. But it was enough. I'll never have to worry about money, and when I'm gone my wife will be very well off, and then, after that, my two kids will have about a million and a quarter in real estate to fool with. You just had to work hard. No fooling around. Right from the moment you got off the boat, if you want to know the truth. You had an awful lot of people to beat, because that was the way it was with immigrants, and you had yourself to beat. Your own laziness and starting to think like Canadians who want the government to do everything for them. Even bury them when they die.

WORKING IN THE CARPET TRADE

Peter and Mary lived near us where we lived on Sherbourne Street when we first came to Toronto. This was in 1947, and we used to have good times together. My husband got a job, and we went to Harboard Collegiate at night to learn English, and so did Peter Stilovic and Mary. And after the class was over, we'd go back to the two rooms we had and we'd sit and practise our English. We'd say, "Nobody talks Croat. Everybody talks English. If you want the sugar, please say it in English."

Peter had a good education. He was a bookkeeper, but he was working in a place where they cleaned carpets. With this machine, you put in the powder and heated up the water and did the carpets. They do it today, but they have trucks now, going to people's houses. Peter was the first.

Peter said he wasn't going to work for nobody but him and Mary and their little baby, so do you know what that guy did? He could speak English pretty good by this time, and he went to the bank and he said his name was Still. Peter Still. He asked for two hundred dollars and they gave it to him. My husband signed his loan paper even though we didn't have any money, but Peter got the loan because he said he was named Still.

He got a little wagon and he went up and down streets and told the women he'd do their carpets for a dollar cheaper, maybe five dollars. He'd bought one of the old machines from the company he worked for, and they thought, "Oh, he'll go broke and we'll get the machine back." We thought, maybe, but maybe we'll get our bonus money of fifteen dollars, which he said he would pay us when he paid off the bank.

Well, you know that guy did it? He made lots of money. He got lots of customers because he knew the prices the company charged and he'd say to the woman, "Look, that company will charge you five dollars, and I'll charge you four dollars." She'd say no, so he would say three, and she'd say yes, feeling good she had cheated him down. He'd make good money anyway. He was a smart guy because he had an education and he spoke English and he could talk good. They thought, he looks like a DP but he can't be because his name is Still.

That's the way he did things, and he paid us the bonus. That's the way you could do it, see? You were smart, you had an education. You'd think, these people in Toronto don't like DPs but they like bargains, so he'd let the ladies think they were getting a bargain, and they'd forget that he might be a DP.

THEY CALLED ME PRETTY MANUEL

That was a good time for me. I was working on a Spanish ship called *The Countess* in English, a small freighter, and we would go from Spanish Morocco, French Morocco and Algiers over to Marseilles, and then to Belgium. I made lots of money, because I would buy cigarettes in these places on the black market and sell them to people in Marseilles, and back in Tunisia I would change the francs to American dollars.

Before that I had been on a freighter, and once we went into Montreal for six days, and I liked it very much, so I decided I would go to Canada to live and bring my parents over from Spain later. You just couldn't get a passport. You got a visa for every trip, so I thought it out. I paid a man in Marseilles a lot of money and he arranged the passport. A Spanish one. It was a fake, you see.

In Barcelona I got on a ship going to New York, and I jumped it, ran away, and because I could speak some English I told them in the United States I was going to visit Montreal. I had met a Spanish family there on that one trip and I gave their name. There were a lot of people on the bus, and they didn't check me. So I was in Canada, but I didn't want to go to Montreal to live, as there weren't many Spanish people there. I knew a lot of the people had gone to Toronto and that's where I went. By bus.

I could read English pretty good and I read an advertisement that the YMCA would help immigrants, and they sent me to a boarding house. A big old house, run by a Jewish lady.

Her husband asked for fourteen dollars a week ahead of time, and I paid him in the American dollars I had, and he asked me how I had them, and I said, oh, I just had them. He wanted to know if I had any more, and I said yes, and he said there was a store on Yonge Street where a Jewish man would change them for me. He said it would be bad for me if I went to the bank. They would ask, how could a person who hardly speaks English, how could I have so much in American money? I cashed them with this man. He did it for a lot. English money, French, Portuguese, I guess, and Spanish. What he did, I don't care.

This Jewish fellow, we got talking and he said, "Don't work where there are a lot of fellows from Europe. You won't learn much English that way." It was lunch time, and he'd made quite a bit of money on me, so he took me to lunch and we got along fine. He could speak all these languages, including mine, and he said he knew I was in the country the wrong way. He meant illegally. He said he'd get me a job, and when we went back to his store he phoned, and I got working with a cartage company his friend owned. The pay was ninety-two dollars a month, which wasn't much, but they were all English guys—I mean Canadian guys—in the storage warehouse. It is funny, but if you have to talk English all the time, you get it quickly, and I did it much better in about four months. Then I could talk mostly like I am talking now.

I was young. I was twenty-two. I liked girls, but I didn't know how I was going to see any. At the boarding house there were only men, so I went to dances, and the first few times they didn't know me. But it was pretty good after. These were dances where you paid to get in, ballrooms they called them. Then you danced.

I bought new clothes and soon I was having a fine time, all the girls, them calling me Pretty Manuel. I was a favourite, but I wasn't going to get married, and then I heard I could get a better job at Kirkland Lake where they wanted gold miners. I would come back in a year with a lot more money and buy a house. I worked there for a year and, boy, I was strong when I came out! It was shovelling rock and stuff at the 3400-foot level. You never saw any gold. It was just in the rock. That was a different kind of gold mining than I thought. But I stayed a year and didn't spend any, and when I came back to Toronto I had a lot.

Then I met this girl, Marge Maynard, at the ballroom. She worked for the telephone company, Ma Bell. I told her about the house I was going to buy and about myself, and she said I had better go to the immigration people. She said, "If you get in trouble or you get hurt and go to hospital, they will find out and it will be your head that is being pounded." So I went. Boy, I was afraid. They said come back in three weeks, and when I did, there were three men at the table in front of me and they asked what I had done, what was I doing, who I was seeing and so on. I said I worked at the General Electric plant out on Lansdowne at a good job and I think I said I was making $380 a month and I wanted to buy a house and I had a girl I wanted to marry, and they said, "Okay, we'll be in touch with you. If you move, let us know." One man said good luck to me as I left the room, and I thought that was a good sign.

It was, and six weeks later I went back and they said I could be a landed immigrant, and a year later, on July fourteenth on a Saturday afternoon, we got married, and I bought the house and we both worked. Everthing went fine. We've got two kids, both grown. One looks like me, dark, and the girl, like her, white. Good kids.

HE LIKED PEOPLE FROM HOLLAND

We went to Bremerhaven and got on the boat, an Italian boat that served Italian food, oh boy, and we came to Canada and, well, what shall I say? I think I maybe had about five thousand dollars' worth of jewels and rings and precious stones, and what do I do? I only had about a hundred dollars in Canadian money.

I thought, I will be honest. I asked a man at the Ford Hotel. That's where they sent us when we got to Toronto. I told him. He wrote me a name on a card and said to see this man. The address was on Spadina. It was an old street, I think, even then, and there were a lot of jewellers and buyers of gold on that street. I think most of them were Jewish. By the signs, anyway. It was a funny store. Dark and long and not wide. There was a young man at the counter, and I took out a woman's pendant, and it had diamonds and rubies in it. The young man looked at it and then called out a name. "Papa!" he said. An old man came out and took it and pushed the young man away, and he looked at it and said, "Ver did thizz piece come from?"

My English was not good at all, but I could tell him it was in my family a long, long time and I wanted to sell it.

He asked, "It is not stolen?"

I said no, and he spoke to the son, and the young man went to the phone, and I was afraid. I thought he might be getting the police, but no, in about two minutes another little old Jewish man in a long, dark coat came in, and they both looked at it, talking away.

Then the first, he said, "For this, we will give you $1,500. Cash. In five minutes. Say yes, say no, that's our offer. My brother and me, we will buy it together. It is too much for one man to buy." That's just about the way he said it.

I said, "Okay, give me the money." I didn't know what it was worth. Maybe they'd sell it for three thousand. But what could I do? I knew nobody. I knew nothing. I was a dumb Dutchman in a foreign city with a wife and kids in a hotel and maybe seventy dollars in my pocket, and they had to be fed.

I said yes, and I held out my hand like this, palm up, meaning I wanted the money. The other brother went out the door and I just sat down and waited and then the old man said, "Have you more like this?"

I said yes, more, all heirlooms from the family, old. And he told me when I wanted to sell, come to him. He'd give best prices. I could trust him.

That's how I started with that old man. I'm not telling you his name. That son of his might be embarrassed. He was the louse in that family. But that is another story. In the two years that I sold my stuff, I sold it all to this kind little man, and I don't think I was cheated out of a penny. He just liked me. He just liked people from Holland.

That is the way we got started. With that money we could buy a little farm, eighteen acres when the prices were low. It was on the way to Peterborough, and a house and some barns. Nothing much, but it cost me just two thousand dollars down on it because nobody wanted it, and we got some cows and just kept going. A bit. Slow. A bit more. Sell something else, buy three more cows. Farming. A dairy. Just like we do it in Holland. And just because of that little guy who was honest with me. Pretty good guy, that little man.

OH, WHAT A BUSINESS HEAD SHE WAS

In 1952 my sister and myself came from Bruges in Belgium to work as maids in a big home in Toronto.

When we got to Toronto there was nobody to meet us but the Travellers' Aid woman at the station who said, "Oh, they are probably at their cottage. This is a long weekend." She phoned, and nobody was home.

She phoned a hotel around the corner and they sent over a bellhop, and he brought our baggage back on a pushcart. It was the Strathcona Hotel. We thought it was heaven, and there we were bouncing on the bed and flushing the toilet and picking up the phone and hearing the man say, "Desk," and then we went down and ordered lunch, saying "omelette" and "lait" and giggling.

The next day we went back to the station, and the same lady was at the Travellers' Aid. She told the taxi to take us to this house in Rosedale, and when we got there it was a big one, and the woman said, fine, we would do, and said she would drive us back to the hotel in her big car. This was Mrs. Reynolds, whose husband came home from his business and he looked us over, and it was pretty good because he spoke a lot of French, the Canadian kind of French, but we understood him. We worked for Mrs. Reynolds for a year, and then we went to work for a company which Mr. Reynolds had a part of. It made sheets, pillowcases and things for the bathroom, and everything was done by hand and, you know, in Belgium we have the lace industry and we had worked in a shop there. That's how we knew how to do pretty things.

We lived in a room in a house and we had a little kitchen in it, just in a corner, and we saved our money, and when we visited the Reynoldses at the lake, we asked him what to do with our money. I said we had more than four thousand dollars, and he said, "How could you girls have so much money? Have you robbed a bank lately?" I said we had worked in Canada for a year at their house and for nearly two years at the shop, and we didn't spend any money for foolish things, and he said, "Let me think." Then he said, "Well, you can stoke a furnace because you did it at our place," and he said, "Let me think." And when we were going to catch the bus the next night to go back to Toronto after our little holiday, I asked him again and he said, "I'm thinking. Let me think. Phone me in a couple of days."

For two days Genienne and I were wondering, what is he thinking about? I phoned Mr. Reynolds, and he told us to come to his office, and he said, "You girls should run a boarding house. There are a lot of immigrants in Toronto who need a good place to stay and where they can eat. I have a friend who is in real estate and he has found two or three places where you can do this, and I want you to go and see him." That's what he said.

We were very surprised, although we knew what boarding houses were because the place we lived in, west of Spadina, there were places around that took in people.

On Saturday the friend took us around, and he said, "This one is good. Look at the brick, it will last half a century, fifty years," and he pointed out everything.

He said, "You will need a $3,500 payment down and the house is yours, and it will cost another $4,000 to buy it, to buy it completely. That is $7,700." And Genienne said, "We will give you $6,800." Oh, the little business head she was! And so we bought it, right off Jarvis where the CBC is, part of it, and we had that place until 1968 when we sold it for a big office building, and we made a lot of money just being boarding-house ladies.

I will tell you this. We were both married by this time and we each had an apartment in the house, tiny ones, but we still made a lot of money. I think you could say our husbands must have known this. They wanted to marry wealthy ladies. One was Greek, mine, and the other was Italian, Genienne's, and they weren't marrying poor ladies.

I KNOW YOU AND TOR ARE HONEST

There was no trouble emigrating from Norway, and this was in 1947, and we were able to sell a lot of our good things, practically everything, and that was the money we used to buy our trip on the boat. It was the *Gripsholm,* and we had to go to Bremerhaven in Germany to get it, and I thought, all these German people going to Canada? The passengers all seemed to be German and Austrian and a few Dutch and us, but Tor—that's my husband—said that Canada must be a good country if it would allow these enemies to go over there.

In Toronto my husband's cousin met us, and he said we would live with him. This was arranged by letter before. So there we were in this little town called Barrie, and I thought, so different from home. But it really wasn't if you had a job. That made it like home.

There were no jobs, you see. All the Canadian soldiers were getting any jobs that did come along, and they didn't have a hydroelectric plant that Tor could work for. It was all Ontario Hydro, and the stations were so far away. His cousin had fixed up his garage as a place we could sleep, and we went to the toilet in his house, and, why, you could say it was certainly different from our comfortable home in Bergen.

There were a lot of houses being built because no houses had been built in the war, and Tor went to the head of a firm and he said this. "If you give me a job, I will work for free." Tor told me the man almost fell over. That didn't happen in Canada. Tor told him he would work for free if he could learn how to be a carpenter and build houses, and the man said, "Sure. There's a hammer there, take it and start."

We had enough money to keep us going and to buy our share of the groceries for his cousin and wife, and so Tor worked for three months all that summer doing everything. He learned carpentry. Not good carpentry, but the carpentry you do to build a house, and he learned about plumbing and electricity, and then he was pretty good. My husband said it was time for the contractor to start to pay him, and the contractor laughed and said, "You stupid immigrants." He said he would have paid Tor right from the start, just a little, but he got Tor's work free. I would have been mad, but Tor told me, "I learned how to build a house and I learned about how Canadians do business. It is okay."

He got $1.10 an hour, and that was good because they worked ten hours a day, and by this time I was knitting and making quilts and I think I made about thirty dollars a month on them, good quilts. Norwegian ones, and when I'd paid for my cloth and things I had thirty dollars a month for us, and with Tor's $1.10 an hour we paid his cousin twenty-five dollars for the garage.

Then my husband got a job in a factory making doors and screens and windows, and in April he bought a lot and we built a house. They gave us lumber and bricks and flooring and shiplap and tarpaper on credit, and so we worked fourteen, twelve hours a day. When we had it half-finished, Tor sold it to a schoolteacher from Toronto who was coming to Barrie to teach in September, and he gave us a thousand dollars down. We paid five hundred to the wholesalers for the supplies. Tor bought two other lots for $250 each, and so we started what they now call a land bank.

That is the way it went. We didn't have a company yet. Just our bank account with the Bank of Montreal. We bought a lot, and Tor and I and a university student finished that house and started another small one, and in October we had sold the smaller one too, and we had money in the bank and no money we owed to anyone, and we also had the other lot we had bought. That winter we bought five more lots at, I think, one hundred dollars as a down payment, and that's how it went.

Lake Simcoe was right there, not far away, and people from Toronto wanted cottages, and they were easy because they didn't have so many fancy things, and in the next ten years we built a lot of those, maybe fifty or sixty. By now we had about ten men working for us and maybe another ten university students who would sleep and cook in the houses they were building, and they would work maybe fourteen hours a day. They made a lot of money to pay for their schooling. I did the books, and we had an office in the house we had.

It was hard work. Long hours. Nothing ever stopped us. If it rained there was something else the gang would do, and in the summer I'd bring them hot dogs and coffee if they wanted to work through until it got dark.

Then he had a heart attack. At fifty-eight he was finished, the doctor told him, and I said good. This was about 1960, and everybody had lots of money. People were always phoning and saying, "I've got a lot up at Muskoka or on the Bruce Peninsula and can you build it?" One day when Tor is in the hospital still and I'm in the office, a gentleman from Toronto comes in and is trying to get our company to build a huge house for him at Georgian Bay because we'd built him a good one at Stroud on the lake. I kept saying "No, too busy, my husband is sick," and he heard all these calls. Maybe five of them in one hour, people wanting us to work for them in the spring. Finally he said, "Will you sell me your company?" Without thinking I said yes.

I phoned Tor in the hospital and told him, and he said, "Okay, you go ahead. You know the books." Just that. I phoned our lawyer and we started working out a price, and when we took it to this Toronto millionaire, he said that was fine.

The lawyer, he just couldn't believe it, and he asked why the man hadn't dickered, tried to make us come down. The man said, "I know you and Tor are honest."

I don't know, but that's when I felt, maybe for the first time, that we had finally made it as Canadians and not strangers, because this businessman said that. It was a good feeling, and that was a long time ago and I am old and Tor has been dead eleven years, but it is still a good feeling.

WHAT'S A SUCCESS STORY?

My wife, Anna and I, we decided we would not have children until we got to America, not even if it took five years, and my father and my grandfather, they'd say to me, "Hey, Tony, haven't you got it anymore?" Things like that.

We wanted to go to America, the United States, because we wanted to have a better life than in Naples or Roma and we knew we could never do that. Old Italy was finished, I figured. And it was. Look at it today. Not much, I'd say. Nobody listens to what the Italians say anymore.

Then it was time to go to America, and that meant the United States where our children would be born and would be American citizens and get an American education and be doctors and lawyers and drive Lincoln Continentals.

Education was everything, big, the thing. Anybody with any sense knew that, and we'd see in the American movies we got after the war, those colleges and how they got those big jobs and all that. We saw so many of these movies we started to believe them, but that's a joke. I mean, we saw so many our English began to get much better.

But we couldn't go to the States. The quota that year was full and so was the one next year. If I had a house I could sell or some land so I could support her and myself for two years, that would have been fine. But they didn't want a bunch of poor immigrants. How do you like that, eh?

So we went to the Canadian people and they said "Sure, sure, come on in, get your medicals, get your documents, a letter from your mayor, the chief of police, the priest, and if you are okay with them, you're okay with us." This is how the immigration guy talked. He loved everybody. Maybe he'd met an Italian girl in Naples, I'll bet.

So we come in and I work hard in a fruit store, and Anna, she says, "Tony, we got no kids and maybe we aren't going to have any," and I say, "Maybe, but we'll keep trying," so she says she's going to work.

In Italy no woman works. She stays home and looks after her kids and the old people. Anna's got no kids and we need the money, so that blouse factory near Cabbagetown where we lived among all those tough guys, it is looking for seamstresses and she's a whiz, eh? I'm working in the fruit store on Jarvis, and she's working, and I'm learning the fruit business and in three years I get my own, on King Street West. Just a little place, but there's lots of Italians and other people from Europe around and I'm doing fine, working long hours, but you gotta. Anna quits the factory where she's a supervisor over all the other girls and just works two days a week, and she worked in the fruit store, Tony's store, my place.

Then comes the first, and we give them Italian names first and then an English name, like Dana and Jordan and Eric and Joanne—for Paul Newman's pretty and smart wife—and that's it. I say to Maria, "Close the factory, no more kids. Four is enough."

All our life we worked to get those kids through school and university. I'd say, "Emilio"—that's Dana—"you got to get that scholarship or I'll kill you." Things like that. The same to Jordan, that's Gino I'm talking to. I say, "You get that bursary. Tell them your old man's just a poor fruit peddler." Stuff like that, eh?

They make out fine. All of them. The girl is a big shot's secretary. Emilio, an engineer in Edmonton. The same with Eric—that's Mario—he's a teacher here in Toronto, and they all are shooting up the old ladder, eh? That's right. The Italian success story right here in Toronto.

BEWARE A RELATIVE WITH A RESTAURANT

It was for the kids. Sure. Anybody who came to this country in the Fifties will tell you that. For the kids. The Old Country was no place to live.

Greece! Look at it. Not now, not now, but then. The Germans get kicked out and then there are the Communists and all their killing of our people. Greek people killing Greek people. It is hard to believe—now, I mean. What happened. There's this valley, okay? Across it is one village and they are for the government. So they fight. That's crazy, see. They don't even know why they are fighting.

I say to my Maria, "We are leaving this village." We go to Athens. Hard. Very hard. No work, and what you call tension. Suspicion. You can't live in a place like that. It is not happy.

We come to Toronto. This is in 1951. Fighting is over, but people still hate each other. Whose side was he on? Like that. We come to Toronto. My cousin has a restaurant. Not like Greek restaurants now, all fancy. Hell! Just a café, booths and tables, and it closed at six o'clock because it was downtown. It was a business, okay? My cousin John, he is doing well. He thinks, Zun—that's me—and my wife, he'll bring us over on the boat and we'll work for him.

Listen, mister. I think I should tell you it is not a good idea to work for a relative if you owe him money. Most of the money for my wife and me and my four kids, he pays it. So we owe him a lot of money. Naw! I don't hate the guy. He's my wife's cousin. Not a bad guy. But he made us work three years in his café, this restaurant, to pay for the boat. That was a long time. He paid us almost nothing. Really nothing. Like, you know, peanuts. The house, we had two rooms on the top over there by Chinatown. Kensington. You know, Baldwin Street. Lots of immigrants. We get the food home from the café. We eat there. I'm a cook. She washes dishes. Kids go to school and after they come and help clean up. Home to the house. It is no fun. No chance to go to night school and learn English. No chance in the kitchen. You see, how can you learn English when every guy doesn't speak English?

Kids did okay. They learned, and they taught Maria and me a lot.

Not enough, but these kids would come home and say, "Poppa, I got some new words for you." What good to me? Hah! I know what they mean, but I can't put them into talk. I don't talk any good now. Everybody asks, "He's a foreigner, isn't he? Greek? Well, sure, he could be." I don't even have a nationality. Not Greek. Someday I'm gonna go to the court and be a Canadian. My wife too. She wants to. I think my kids are Canadians. They been here long enough, but I got to find out about that and tell them. I think they think they are Canadians. The boy is forty, works for Metro. The girl is married. Montreal.

Then this cousin says, "Okay, you've paid off the fare." I think it was $1,200. Now he says I got to start paying rent in his house. "Okay," I said, "then you got to give Maria and me a raise." No raise, he can't pay. He says, "I can't afford it. Look at those empty tables. No customers." I said, "Okay, cousin, you can stick the job up the ass and you can stick Maria's job up your ass, and the kids too." Not the kids up his ass. I mean their jobs.

He laughs and pounds my shoulder and says, "Good for you, Zun. You gonna do fine. Get out on your own, because I got another couple with kids from home coming over next month. They take over from you."

We have a couple of bottles of wine and talk it over, and he says it this way. He will phone this friend of his in Hamilton who has this big restaurant. Maybe we can go there and I can be the cook, one of them, and Maria a waitress. She done a lot of that in my cousin's place and she's real good.

You notice I don't use my cousin's name. If I did and he read this he'd say, "Zun, you talk too much." Then he'd have guys talk to me and I wouldn't be in such good shape. I'm sixty-nine now. Too old for hurts now.

We go to Hamilton. I work on the stoves and Maria works as a waitress, and this Italian guy, a nice guy, he shows me everything about how to run a restaurant. Books. Books. What people steal. I know some about that. So does Maria. This thing, public relations. That is the easy part. Maria is the best at it there is. People love her. We learn all this for two more years and then we go back to this cousin and I say, "Lend me some money." Not family any more. Business. We get five thousand dollars. Just like that. How much you want? Got a location? What you gonna be, Italian or Greek? You know what you're doing? Like that. Then he says, "Okay, five thousand, but you got to be far away from me. No more competition. So, there we go out on St. Clair East when it isn't like it is now, but getting like that, and by God, we work hard. Nobody works harder. Fifteen, sixteen hours a day, six days a week. That was nothing. The kids work hard, every chance. Family business, just like at home.

We make it. It is hard, but Canada gets richer and people learn how to spend money, and we're part of the neighbourhood and we make it just fine.

NO FANCY THINGS WITH ITALIAN NAMES

People think that when people from the Old Country came to Toronto or Canada, that every one of them wanted to make a restaurant. Sell spaghetti. To me, spaghetti is pasta, but pasta is not spaghetti. All those funny sauces and all the other funny things that go with it.

We had a café, outside of Rome on the highway north, and when they put in the big highway we were off to the side. No business. Nobody along that road any more. Everybody lost business and quit, and that's when we decided to bring everybody to Canada, and we came to Toronto. Everybody said, "There is lots of Italians there."

We had some money, but how many lira I can't tell you. My husband Pasquale, he always looked after the wallet. He said to me, "Sara, we'll start a café for all these Italians here," but that's when I said, "No, we won't. We'll start a café for Canadians, because every one of these Italians are as poor as we are. You look around, who has the money?" It was the Canadians. They had it.

I was right. I usually am in things like when you are thinking of people. I told him, "We start an Italian restaurant around here and only Italians will come. Canadians will see it is full of Italians all yelling at each other and they won't come again. Italians, those people, they'll order a meal and they'll argue with you about the sauce, or not enough cheese, too much of it, and where do you buy your olive oil? This is not the kind we had at home, they would say. Argue. Somebody gets mad. More yelling, and there's the Canadians saying this is a crazy place. Besides, you know yourself, they would order a meal and then sit around all night saying how much better Italy was than this country, and so on. Bad for business. And all that Italian gossip, talk, chatter, gabbing." I didn't think I could stand it. I had enough of it just with the truckdrivers in our place in Rome.

Canadians will come in and order a meal and eat it and then they'll get up and thank you, pay you and go, and you'll have enough time to clean up and have a table ready for the next customers.

Pasquale, he says, "How can you have an Italian café and keep out the Italians?" And I said, "Goofy, we won't give them Italian food. We will be a Canadian restaurant, and if they want bacon and eggs at dinner, then you'll make them bacon and eggs, and if they want fried chicken for breakfast, then you'll make it. We got to do business, not hear a bunch of guys arguing about Italian movie actresses."

That's why we started our ordinary restaurant, and this was in 1952, and we asked a few people who had restaurants around, but not close as being in business against them. We'd ask, what do people eat? Oh, they like steak and they like roast beef and they like liver and onions, and if you put fish on the card you are wasting your time.

One guy said, "They want potatoes. Don't try rice with these people." Another said, "These people in Toronto think jello and ice cream is dessert, and I said, "What about minestrone soup?" I made it wonderful. He says, "They don't know what it is. Give them carrots and beans and peas and don't ask me about broccoli and things like that. They don't have that kind of stuff around here." And he said again, "Rice may be better, but they want potatoes and they want them mashed."

You think I am running down, making fun. I'm not. Canadians were good people and good to us, for us. We just said, okay, just as it is. The way they want it. I'm right, no big Italian show. No showing off. No fancy things with Italian names.

We did fine. It was long and not wide, just near where the Chelsea is now, and it was Canadian, Toronto, right from the start. Good food, and clean. The youngest boy as busboy and my daughter and me, waitresses. A long counter, and I think it was eighteen seats. Booths over there, and everything clean, clean and more clean, and we served breakfast, seven to ten. Then lunch. And at four o'clock we served dinner—roast beef, steaks, always fried, and tomato soup. I'd put a double squirt of my own tomato sauce in it and a spoon of vinegar and some more peas, and that was in each bowl, and that sold and, my gosh, did that ever sell! They loved it.

We had that restaurant for about eight years, I guess, and we did good, so good that sometimes we'd wonder if we could do better with some Italian food. That was Pasquale talking. "Momma, let's try this or that." I'd say, "No, goofy, no," and then he'd laugh and say, "Okay, Momma, when in Roma do as the Romans do," and that worked. We didn't try and be fancy. It was a business, and to make a business work, you gotta have business. So we kept it that way, all the time.

I DON'T WANT TO OWN A RESTAURANT

I said no, working for yourself, that's fine if you can do it, but you get the headaches too. Staff! You don't know, you'll never know the headaches of help in a restaurant. They cheat, lie, they steal you crazy, and in some places they just about own the cash register and, mama mia, I know guys who own restaurants who could write a book about restaurant stealing.

I never stole. I didn't have to. Work fourteen hours a day, know all your customers, know their kids, joke with them and make them feel special. They'll ask for your station, where your six or eight tables are, and they'll tip. You can get rich on tipping.

When I'd get a thousand dollars, I'd send it to my uncle. He was the mayor of our town once. He's a lawyer in Italy. I'd write, here's a thousand dollars and I want you to buy me land or a house or a little farm, but buy me cheap. I said, for this you get one-quarter of it. I'm making him a partner and because he's a blood relative, there's no cheating. I send money back all the time, and he writes letters saying he bought this little farm. I know the one. This is about '62 I start sending money back. First about five thousand dollars, my savings. That is one hell of a lot of money in Italy then. You wouldn't believe how much. Every two months, three, I'd send money, two thousand, more than that. All at once. Nothing stays in Canada, except to have a little suite, and that comes out of my salary. The rest is tips.

I make a trip to Italy, to Rome, and then take the train to my town, and my uncle says to me, "Tony, you're the richest man around here." He drives me around and he says, "That is yours, and that, and those little farms. That villa, why don't you buy it and come back to Italy to live and get a nice girl and have a lot of kids? You're not getting younger."

I say, "Maybe, but you keep on buying for me," and that's when land was so low. You can't think how low it was, but it began to get higher, and that was good for me. I was getting the rise in the price of land and the rents which my uncle was collecting, and buying more land, and it just went on.

Listen, I don't have a big restaurant now and try and get the *Globe and Mail* and the *Star* to come and write about my place. I am not a big big shot. I don't go on CHIN and speak to the Italian community. No yacht. I got my little house, my Canadian wife, my little place at the lake, but I'm still a waiter. Still a waiter. Still picking up tips, still with a smile, still making with the jokes, and I got none of these headaches, no lease expiring so you have to move or pay double the damned rent. I got none of those stupid things. I got no staff problem. I got a good boss, and when I leave it is because I'm gonna fire myself. I'll quit. In Italy I'm I guess what you'd call a rich man. I got my partner—he's old now but he's sharp, you see, and the guy is honest. The blood is there. In Canada everybody says, "Oh, how can he still be a waiter? Why ain't he got his own place?"

I know where my own place is—right here. And when I want to, maybe I'll go home and be a big shot in Italy.

I'm gonna ask you to ask me a question. Ask me how I got this way, this rich way. I'm telling you, I got it because I knew how to be a god-damned good waiter and not be a businessman who wants his own restaurant.

NONE OF US MADE A FORTUNE

No, we don't have much money. We know other Danish people, although I can't say we're like the Italianos or the Greeks who stick together and have these street festivals and eat food from their homeland and make a big fuss of it. There are quite a few Scandinavians in town, up the valley, over on the island. There are organizations, but we don't stick together much. None of our neighbours are us. They are everything.

The guy on the right is a Hungarian, came over after the revolution and has a few stories to tell. I go fishing with a Ukraine chap, a real squarehead, but I love him and he'd give you the shirt off his back. He can tell you about those Russians, believe me. There is a Limey just down the street, a teacher. Others. A couple of Chinese families. I work with a lot of immigrants, but we're getting old. I'm fifty-five. Can't hit the ball like I used to. My floor job is what I like. You bet.

No, none of us made a fortune, but how many people born here did? Ah, sure, I know. You hear stories. This German guy started a little machine shop, and how he's got a hundred-foot yacht. Or this Greek with five restaurants. Any guy with more than one restaurant needs to have his eyes tested and his head examined. That would be five times more trouble than I'd need. Guys like me who started out in the woods, we never made it. You seem to stick with the job, and when things were going so good, that was the best job I could think of. Lots of good money and fresh air.

I'm comfortable. Elsa has her little job. She's always had it. She pays her own income tax and I don't know how much she makes at the bakery shop, just eighteen hours a week, but it's her money and that's fine.

WE WANTED FREEDOM, NOT RICHES

No, I can't think of a single person that became a millionaire in Canada, although, well, you read about them in the papers or magazines sometimes.

I think those people would be millionaires if they hadn't left Holland or Germany or Austria, maybe Yugoslavia, Denmark, Norway. They were just that way. They were born to become millionaires.

I know hundreds of people who came to this country without a penny except the few dollars they were allowed to come with. That was dumb, see. You come to Canada and you don't speak the language and you have no money, just maybe a few dollars, and they expect you to be a success, and how could you?

You can't speak English, and it takes a few years to speak it, and so you work at poor jobs like my wife and I did. You work hard, but you're always working for some other guy, some English guy, because you still can't find a good enough job to let you save up enough money to start a business. Even if you had had a business or knew a business in the Old Country, you still couldn't get going.

I think one mistake I made was sticking with people who were what you call the Slav races. Russian and Ukrainian and those, and you worked for them. I should have said, I'm not going to speak another word of Polish again. I'm only going to work and have fun with Canadians and that way, maybe I'd have got a break.

Sure, look at me. We've got a house and a camper. No money on the mortgage. That's paid off. I get along with my neighbours and I'm in the union and I got a good job. Two kids, and one is a nurse and the boy is in accounting, and that kid, I had to talk him out of changing his name to English. I said, "Be proud of your language and remember, a hell of a lot of good and brave men died fighting for your language. Be proud of it."

He says to me, "Okay, Pop, okay, I'll do it for you," but I know that he's talking of going with his girl to Calgary to work when he finishes his course at university, and I got this feeling that when he goes there he's going to apply for a job, and he'll be using an English name.

That's the way it goes with some of our kids. They think having vic on the end pegs them as a Bohunk. Nothing wrong with Bohunks. People may not like the name, but a lot of us did a lot of awfully hard work and helped this country. The railways, the mines, the bush. Helped this country grow strong, and they didn't mind a Bohunk name.

No, none of my friends is a millionaire. I don't even know what one is. Is that a guy who's got a million dollars? Or does it mean somebody who is worth a million, like in a house and cars and a business and things like that? Sure is a big difference.

When we came in 1948 nobody wanted to be a millionaire. We wanted to get away from all the killing and Communism and no food and all that went with it. We wanted freedom to have what we have now, this house and the camper and boat and saying, "Mama, let's take a week off and go down to Reno and play the slots."

That may not sound much to you, but that's pretty well the way it all worked out, and we've got no complaints. None. That kid, maybe, because when I die that name dies too, if that kid starts calling himself Danny Smith or Jones or Brown.

WE'LL NEVER HAVE A MILLION

Oh, sure, you can hear of fifty of these immigrant guys and they are millionaires, maybe more. There is this guy, he owns two seine boats, and there's a million right there. Another guy owns four hotels. Sure, that's true. All these stories.

But that's not us. Look at this house. Look at those two across the street. Those two guys, they came from Europe. One from Italy, the house with the red all around it. He likes that. I don't, but it is his house. The other house, a guy from Yugoslavia. He works for the city.

Drives a truck. My two cousins, they come from the Ukraine like me, and you don't see them living in big houses, and they don't have no big boats. We got small houses and nice wives and nice kids and quiet lives. We don't have a million, and we won't.

I say this. I have worked in Ontario, when I came to Canada, and on the prairies and now in Vancouver. That is thirty-six years. The first four years, when I work in those other places, I just work. I work for poor pay, sixty cents an hour, five dollars a day. I am learning English. I am having fun too, because I am a young guy. You see.

When I come to Vancouver I don't have any money. Oh, I would be in the Regent Hotel one day where a lot of Yugoslavian and Ukrainian guys used to go and a guy, George Bukikowski, he says to me, "You come with me. Put your money in with me and we go fishing." I say no. I don't know about fishing. I got no money anyway. He finds somebody else, and they make a lot and they get a company and he changes his name to a Canadian one and he is a millionaire, I guess. I walk in there one Saturday afternoon a long time later, and he is there. In that beer parlour, and he is a millionaire. He says to me, "Hey, I will buy you beer all afternoon if you will admit you were wrong in not coming with me."

I say to this George guy, this rich guy, I tell him no, I won't admit it. I say I didn't have no money and I wouldn't borrow it if I could have, and I tell him, "George, I was not made to be a businessman. You got to lie and cheat your workers and you got to cheat the government and you got to bribe people to get things and you got to lie to yourself every damn day." That is what I tell him. He laughs and says he will buy me beer all afternoon because I am a good guy, and he says I am also right because I am honest. All these things I tell him, he says they are the truth.

I don't think people like me, I don't think we are good at business. I think we are like most Canadian guys. No good at it. We try, some of us, not me, but they go out of business because they are too honest. They can't look some government guy in face and say black is red, black is white. We know black is black.

That's why not many guys from the Old Country who came over here made it much. First, no English good enough for a long time. Another thing, so many had it so hard with the Russians, the Germans, maybe both, that all they wanted was a place to be free. Live in peace. You know, have a good wife, some kids, a house and a garden. A job, and you got paid every two weeks and you worked hard and you drank a little beer. Played some cards. Maybe went fishing a couple of times. You just didn't want a big time in life. Like my youngest kid says, I didn't want to ring the big bell. That kind of got it right.

A GOOD LIFE, BUT NO FORTUNE

Looking back and considering what most of them had, which was sweet bugger all, I'd say, most of them did well.

I'm not talking about those of us who came from Britain, no, not at all. That gave us a good three- or four-year jump in opportunities over the poor bastards who came to this country with no English.

For reasons too complicated to explain, this company I was working for asked me to supervise a large bunch of Displaced Persons across the Atlantic and then get them to where they were going in Canada. Now remember, this was 1947, and Brits like me, we could have flown over in, oh, maybe eighteen hours, but these poor buggers, there they were, maybe eight days on the Atlantic. That's what our old tub took. And then, off at Montreal, a hot summer, and there they are in their heavy clothes, right off the shelves of the storeroom in whatever camp they came from, and out into the din and the glare of Canada.

No money. No language. No nothing, except the luggage they had and some even had their worldly goods. Hah! I wonder if you could even call them that? But these goods, in pillowcases or canvas bags, anything.

I won't say I considered it disgraceful then, but looking back I guess it was. I got them to Toronto, and thank God for the Salvation Army and the churches, because they moved in and picked them up. All I had had to do was count noses every morning and figure out the complaints and see that they hadn't lost their bloody name tags.

Now, the Sally Ann lads and lassies and the churches and a couple of people from the Ontario government had to take over, sort them out, figure what to do with them, figure out if they really were what the papers said they were, and get on with the job of making them Canucks.

That's when I scuttled out. I'd worked for this company, a travel company in a way, and they told me I could have free passage to Toronto if I got these blokes across the briny. It was a chance to save a few dollars, and I did. That's where my job ended.

Oh, I did well. Nothing too hard for an artful dodger like myself, but in the years that have gone by, about forty now, I'd say, I've thought about those people from time to time. Not those same people. I didn't even know who they were when I had them in charge. Just faces and tags, you know.

But you read in the paper. Say, like there is Gretzky. Maybe his parents were DPs. I don't know, but just an example. Or some of our other fine young athletes. The tough names to pronounce. Or the writers or the engineers you read about, or architects. They all seem to be young now. The ones I'm talking about, they often have foreign names.

Their parents, a lot must have come from the Old Country. They all must have done well. Not rich. No. None of us get rich in this country being honest, but you don't hear of these people being wards of the state, the country, that kind of thing.

My idea is that they came in, looked around, talked it over, man and wife, if you will. Buckled down, took any work, any work, and slowly, just like the rest of us—me included— built up a modest little life and fortune, very modest, and now here we are, one big happy family fighting like hell among ourselves and leading a very good life. Bitching and screaming about this and that, and knowing we'd never have it so good in any other country in the world you can name.

8 BECOMING CANADIANS

8 BECOMING CANADIANS

I know one thing now. The hundreds of thousands of immigrants who came to Canada love this country. In fact, some of them think that those of us who are native-born do not love it enough.

True, many immigrants still keep hold of a few ties to their homeland, such as the languages some speak at home, the special foods they eat and the celebration of their national days and festivals. It is their way of keeping alive the memory of other times and places: their roots. But Canada is their home. It has become all they had hoped it would when they were crossing the Atlantic, dreaming and wondering about the unknown land ahead.

Deep in their hearts, there is the sure knowledge and strong feeling that Canada has been good to them, so very good. They also know how hard they worked, the hardships they faced, the despair they knew at times; and they know they have earned the right to be Canadians.

I understand a lot more about Canada now than I did when I started this. I should. I had some very good teachers.

NOW I AM A CANADIAN

I knew the day I got my first pay cheque, that is the day I said, "I am a Canadian."

It was that way because my wife and I didn't take out our naturalization papers until seven years later, but that day when I went home and showed her the cheque, that's when I said we were Canadian.

She said go out and cash it, and we went and got the money from the bank, and we bought a feast: pork chops and spinach and ice cream. We had a feast and that was a good time, and we invited our neighbours to come in for beer. They were from Germany too. Klaus had been an instrument maker and he was working in a warehouse, and I was a master baker as you called it in Canada, but the only thing I could get was janitor work. Cleaning.

My pay cheque for those two weeks was forty-two dollars and I worked ten hours a day. That is for five and a half days. If you work it out on paper, that comes to about forty cents an hour. We didn't mind. My wife worked too, but that was different.

I had been with the Afrika Corps, and when we were captured in Tunisia I was sent to Lethbridge. It was a good camp if you minded your own business. It was the best thing to do so. There were Nazis in that camp who thought the British would be beaten and then they would help to take over Canada. Three were hanged by the Canadian government, do you remember?

Then they asked, who wanted to go work on a Canadian farm, and my hand shot up, and so we went for the harvest around Medicine Hat, and the police didn't say anything when two of the boys sneaked into town and had a good time. That's when the rest of us started to go, a few at a time. I liked Canada, and when we were sent home I had some friends there, but Germans weren't allowed to come back into Canada until, oh, about 1952.

I came in 1954 with Anna. I saw this place as somewhere a man and wife could make a good kind of living. We would work hard and have a good life and have a car. I thought the biggest car in North America would be nice.

In 1952 I convinced Anna we should go to Canada. She said, if Canada, why not the United States? "No, Anna," I said, "you go where you know people, and you will like Canadians." She was just thinking, you see, if the wages in Canada were good, then the United

States being much bigger, those wages would be better. She was a farm girl at heart.

We got on a boat and then on a train and then four days going to Calgary, and I phoned. I had told this farmer I was coming, and he said to come down. That was in June. I worked for him, and Anna, oh, she was going to be the fine lady and not work. I said everybody works in Canada. Man and wife. That way they save for the house. She worked in Coaldale.

There were a lot of foreigners then, and Anna spoke Ukrainian and Polish too, so then she got on as a checker in the canning plant, and her money, my money on the farm, every week we put a lot in the bank. In November I told Mr. Barter, "Sir, we are going to Calgary now, and thank you very much because you have helped us." That is why we worked on the farm, to get enough money to go and live in Calgary until we got jobs.

It was in November we went, and I got a job. I just asked myself, what kind of job can I do so I will learn this city and get to know people, and in the paper was an advertisement for a cleaner.

I went and the boss said if I would work very hard, I would have the job. If I didn't keep going, you know, keep up as he said, I would lose it. The driver and I would travel around cleaning offices and places like that after five o'clock, and when you finished your route, your job was done. We could do it in ten hours, so that was until three in the morning, and I would go home on my bicycle and sleep. I'd get up with my wife at eight and she went to work, washing dishes. Then at one o'clock I would go to the school for immigrants, and at four it would be over, and then to the truck again. That was our life until spring.

The pay was only thirty-eight cents an hour at first, but that was fine. I was learning the job, and soon it became sixty cents when I took over the truck by myself. That was two months later, when I knew the job and the routes, and then I had my own helper. A Dutch fellow. We got along okay. No talk of the war, though.

I didn't stay with the cleaning company too long. It was just a job to have while I learned English better, and the other things they taught at the school. When I was ready I got a nice job where I had to work awfully hard. Good pay.

I wish I knew the date of that first cheque. It was what is called a red-letter day. Just about forty bucks. That is nothing now. That is just such a tiny bit, but then that was a lot of money. It was my first pay cheque, with my name on it, and the bank clerk didn't look at me. She just took it, looked at the back, gave me the money. I liked that. I thought, now I am a Canadian.

KITIMAT—WHERE IT BEGAN FOR SO MANY

It was an eye opener, I'll tell you, up there in Kitimat. In the early days there were nineteen ethnic groups there. Everybody pulled together at the same strength, at the same time, and very rarely did you hear a snide remark, an ethnic slur against someone. It was very nice.

It was a good place for a new Canadian to start his life in this country, I'll tell you that. I think thousands of people who are successful now thank Alcan for hiring them, for taking them in when they looked for jobs in Europe and told them they would have a job if they could get to Canada.

We were carving out a new frontier, a new town. By God, I can show you pictures of swamp and bush, mountains, hills, and that is where the city of Kitimat is today. It was exciting. Very much.

No, there was no cultural life in the early years, but there was something else. Remember, these weren't labourers, a lot of them. We worked as labourers, but a lot of us were doctors, engineers, accountants, and there were teachers and professors from Europe and people like that. They were well educated, and many had come from big cities and they were cultural people. But first, you know we had to make our way in Canada, and not many of us spoke English at first. And another thing, when we went there, I don't think any of us had any money.

No, there were no blocks. Germans didn't go with Germans. Italians didn't go with Italians. We were one large group, and not like in Vancouver and other cities where Italians would be taken in by the church and their societies and their clubs, and they would know nothing about other ethnic people and nothing about Canadians. This was all one big family and it was good that way. Everybody was jolly. You'd have a card game and there would be an Englishman, a Canadian, a French-Canadian—and they are jolly people, I like them. And there would be a German and an Italian and a Portuguese and maybe a Spaniard, and we'd all get along together. We'd help each other.

After a while, people would make their money and say, maybe in two or three years, they would have quite a bit and they'd leave to go south and start a business or get a better job or bring their fiancée over from Portugal or Greece, and then they'd live in a big city like Vancouver.

You'd meet someone from another part of the camp and you'd think, oh, I like him, and he'd become your friend, and that's the way it happened. When he finally went to Vancouver, and he might be Polish or Greek, and then you'd move and you'd look him up or vice versa and you'd have a friend. We helped each other. It was good.

Everybody who was in that camp, and I guess there were thousands over the first ten years, they all wanted to improve themselves and learn English and make good in this country. Kitimat in the early days was like a big school for all the immigrants. It was a very good place to be. It was a place where you got your start, you see.

THAT FIRST CANADIAN CHRISTMAS

What I liked best about Canada was, there were no class distinctions.

We came to Hamilton in 1949 and my husband, he could speak English and he got a job in the big steel mill, and we could rent a little house, and it was too small but, by figuring, my husband and I and our three children, we made a happy home of this house.

I couldn't speak English the first year, but I would smile a lot at our neighbours, and my husband would read out the English in the *Spectator* and put it into Ukrainian, and this was the way I was learning. The two children in school, they were learning too. That was good. Children learn fast.

On Christmas Eve we were all alone, feeling sorry for ourselves. Not for being away from Europe and the camps. Just lonely because we didn't have anybody to spend our kind of Christmas with. We were having a little party. This was on January sixth, which you know is our Christmas Eve. We sang our Ukrainian carol, which in English is "God Eternal," and then we ate pampushky and kutja and kolach and kraplyky, which is borscht to you.

Then we were getting ready to go to bed and we heard this sound. It was coming up the walk of our little house. My husband peeped out and he didn't know what to think. He said, "It is people coming here and there is a man playing the bagpipes."

My husband, Ivan Yeremy—he is dead now—he opened the door and the piper came in and about ten people followed him, and the piper, he walked around our little living room, and the children were shrieking, and I think it was joy. This was a circus to them. The other people came in and the place, oh, it was so full you couldn't have got a mouse in, not one. When the piper stopped, a man began speaking to us in our own language. He said these people were from around and, as this was the Ukrainian Christmas Eve, they had decided they would celebrate with us. This is what they did.

Oh, and I was sad too. I didn't have enough food for half of them and there was no more wine in the house, but we did as best we were able to. My husband gave a little thank-you talk in English, and then I gave a few sentences in our language. The neighbour translated it and that was enough, I think. We had thanked them for a wonderful welcome to Canada. Then they left, and the women hugged me, and we went to bed feeling very, very happy to be Canadians. And after that it wasn't hard to live in that neighbourhood. Everybody, all the people, they were so friendly. I hope that it was the same for all the other people who came to this wonderful country when we did.

I say I hope it was, but I don't know.

THEY'RE THAT ENGLISH COUPLE

I think the day I really started becoming a Canadian was when I stopped saying, "Oh, yes, but you know, we don't do it that way in England."

That just antagonized some Canadians so much. I could see their faces going blank as if they were thinking, another Limey thinks she is too good for us, doesn't she? All her fine airs.

You know, I didn't have fine airs, and I was just being helpful, suggesting that maybe there was a better way to do these little things, but I never thought for a minute, a single minute, that I was antagonizing everyone. I thought I was being helpful. Hateful, maybe that's the word.

But I did realize it after a while, and I stopped doing it, and that was fine, but there was one thing I wished my neighbours had stopped doing, and that was referring to us as "that English couple who moved into the old Robinson house down the street."

They were saying that ten years after we moved onto Clifton Street, and we had been Canadian citizens for four years. It made me so mad.

I'VE GOT MY CITIZENSHIP PAPERS

We moved to Kitchener because my husband was a chemical engineer and he was hired by Goodyear to work in the lab of the rubber plant, and we started looking for a house.

The real estate company sent us around with a man who was a nice man, but he'd show us a house and he'd say that a lot of German people lived around it. He'd say we were close to downtown and I could walk into a shop downtown and be waited on in German. He'd say there were social clubs and churches we could go to where the people spoke German and were nice people.

This was in Kitchener, Ontario, and not Essen in Germany. This was in 1963, and we may have had a German name, Kroeller, and we may still have had a German accent, which we did, a little, but he was saying these things to us in English and we were talking back to him in English.

I thought, this never happened in Toronto or Oshawa where we had lived before and when, like in Toronto, we had just been off the boat from Hamburg. Why is he saying these things to us now when we'd been in Canada for ten years? I don't know.

Canadians like him, maybe he thought he'd sell us a house quicker if he thought we wanted to be around German people. We didn't. We wanted to be in a nice district and if there were German-speaking people, okay, they wanted a nice neighbourhood too.

It was so stupid. These Canadians never seemed to say, these people are not Germans, they are Canadians. I wanted to say, I'm not German and I've got my citizenship papers to prove I'm a Canadian.

We wanted to be Canadians, but some people didn't want us to be.

I'VE BEEN WORKING ON THE RAILROAD

When I got to Canada I was with a lot of other Yugoslavians. Mostly from Slovenia. That was good. I was born in Kranj. I knew how to work with these fellows, and on the boat I was put in charge of them because I knew English too. I was the interpreter and sort of boss.

We signed papers saying we would work on the railroad for a year. That was okay, I told the guys. This meant they would get to know Canada by travelling and be paid and fed too. I thought the word *railroad* meant we would travel. We worked on the line east of Fort William, Port Arthur. I think the pay was $5.40 a day for pick and shovel. They took off a dollar a day, and that was for food and your laundry and for your medical health insurance, so we could make about $120 a month, but that was for hard work and no fooling around. They watched us all the time. They didn't think we would run away. They just wanted us to work all the time. That was the CPR for you. Very tough guys.

In a year I had saved about a thousand dollars because I didn't go to town once and I had a job the last six months as a kind of subforeman, and when the year was passed, I went to the timekeeper and I said, "I want to go."

He said, "Why do you want to leave, Franz? You're a good man. I was planning to make you one of the foremen soon."

I said, "Well, Mr. Shipton, I have done my work and the CPR has got their work out of me, and we are even now, so can I please have my pay?" He said okay, but I should stay, and then he asked where did I want the pass made out to? I didn't know about any pass. What was this pass business? He said everyone who quit after doing his year got a free pass on the railroad, to anywhere. So where did I want to go?

I told him I don't know anything about Canada. That is why I am leaving, to learn. I want to see another part of this big country and not just the sixty miles of track I know now.

He said okay, and he wrote me a pass to Revelstoke, and he said, "You'll find some people from Yugoslavia there to drink wine with and we've got a big roundhouse there, track gangs, so you will be able to get a job."

That's how I chose Revelstoke. That bookkeeper chose it for me. I liked it. The mountains, good place to stretch your arms, take a big breath, and I stayed there for four years. A good place to learn how to be a Canadian.

THE CANADIAN METHOD—PERSEVERE

My husband was a draughtsman, and as soon as we got settled in—and that's a Canadian term for you, settled in—after we found a place to stay, off he trotted with his portfolio. I expect he thought he'd just walk in the first door and the managing director would rush out of his office and say, "Mr. Barling, we've been waiting years for you. Come right in and start to work. We certainly need your English training and expertise and wisdom."

Oh, no, it didn't happen that way. Frank walked many a weary mile those first few days and came back to our little room with its little hot plate and bed and dresser and the loo down the hall and he would wonder: what about the immigration people in London? Where were all the jobs they had said were there in Toronto for the asking?

You see—and I'm sure many of those who came from the Old Country around 1950 will say the same—we were told that Canada was a land of milk and honey and there were jobs for everyone. Well, there may have been, but not for draughtsmen. Labourers, yes. Men to work in laundries and brick yards and washing dishes, I suppose, but Frank considered himself a professional, and he was. What he didn't realize was that a draughtsman in London was different than one in Toronto. In the Old Country he knew a great deal more than just drawing lines with a T-square.

I believe it was eighteen firms he saw in that first week, and every one of them gave him a short interview but no job, and we didn't have much money, and the British government had devalued the pound. That meant the little store of mad money, you might say, that we had in England was cut by a third. So a bit of a blow. He was very downcast, and I said we'd forget our troubles and cares and take the train Saturday morning to Niagara Falls. The little room on Sherbourne Street was surely getting us down, so off we went.

We couldn't afford it, but we stayed at the Isaac Brock and had a lovely dinner and saw the falls like the tourists we were. On the way back to Toronto I told him, "Now, Frank, you go back to every one of those firms, in the order you saw them, and you try again. Show them you have character. Show them you can be determined."

The next day off he goes with another clean shirt and in his three-piece English suit, and he came in the door at noon, and he had a job. The first shop he visited, this time they gave him an application form to fill out, which they hadn't done before, and the second, they said they'd keep an eye out for him, and the third, the manager said, "Oh, yes, I liked your drawings, but we didn't have anything last week, but we do have an opening now. When can you start?" Wasn't that lovely? My thinking, maybe Canadians want to look a person over and they expect him to be persistent.

The wage was $150 a month, which we thought was jolly good, but it paid only once a month, and by the time our first pay cheque was cashed, we were so broke. Coming to Canada just stretched us to the limit, and we just made it to the end of the month.

With a wage coming in, our first move was to get out of that room, and Frank, with little old me by his side, went to the Bank of Commerce on Yonge Street, and we asked for a loan. We didn't have much to offer except our sincerity, I would suggest, but the bank manager just asked a few questions and there we had it, one thousand good Canadian dollars at six per cent and a note that said we'd pay fifty dollars a month. My, that certainly wasn't like England where you'd have to bring your rich maiden aunt in from Brighton to cosign for you. Just a few questions and a form to fill in, and a smile and a handshake from that very nice man, and we were on our way to find an apartment and buy furniture.

The apartment was no problem. The want ads in the *Star* and *Telegram* had many ads, and it was pick and choose, and the one we picked—I sensed from the ad it would be nice—was in an old house on Sheppard. It had the kitchen overlooking a little lawn and garden, and the sun was streaming through the window, and I said to myself, this is where we'll settle down and learn to be Canadians.

By this time I realized we had a lot to learn. Just being English wasn't going to get us on the road to riches and happiness. We'd have to get out and dig and work hard and forget that we were English in the sense that we thought we were better than Canadians, which we weren't. It was a whole new world opening up for us. We were both under thirty, and that is a good time to start a new life.

NOTHING COULD STOP US

There were plenty of things to do, and you can understand that. We had to get a certificate that we were law-abiding. We had medical checks and interviews with immigration people who were very good, very nice, and they told us we were the kind of people they wanted. It was all very pleasant talking to them, and I've had people say they made too much of Canada, telling them a person would be rich in ten years, but that didn't happen to us. They just said, work hard, don't make fun of Canada and Canadians, obey the law, these kind of things, and we would be okay.

We signed the papers to bring us in, and about eight months later we were on a ship from Bremerhaven along with a lot of other emigrants, and we took the train to Toronto. I remember the first thing I did on the train was buy a Toronto paper which a young boy was selling. All the advertisements for jobs and the pages of Eaton's with all the clothing, and I thought, well, it wasn't a dream. There really is a paper like this showing things they want to sell.

We got jobs in two or three days. They weren't good jobs, but we didn't expect everyone to bow down to us and say, here, please take this good job. I worked washing dishes for twelve hours a day, and Jan got a job in a clothing factory, and it wasn't much like teaching, but we didn't mind. We loved it. We got a room with a hot plate, and we'd buy a big steak and some tomatoes and ice cream, and we'd eat like kings and queens.

We had no trouble. The jobs were just to start us out, and we went to night school and got better jobs, and that is about it. It took us five years to get our own house, one of those boxes, but by then we had become Canadians, and from then on it seemed that nothing could stop us from getting ahead. We were very happy.

THE BEST DAMNED COUNTRY

Coming to Canada was the biggest mistake of my life, but I didn't like Denmark. I was young and couldn't do much about it, so I came to Canada, and I hated it. I hated it for twenty years.

Then in 1970 my wife said, "Per, if you hate Calgary so much, why do we stay here? I'll go back with you, and if you want to stay, then we'll work out something."

So next year we went back, and I didn't like the country at all, and I didn't like the socialism and, quite frankly, I didn't like the people or my own relatives. We came home, and when we got back to our house in Calgary we sat down for a few drinks to relax, and my wife said, "Per, why do you never hear of Canadians emigrating to Denmark or Germany or France or Britain? Why does everybody come the other way, to Canada? Canada is the promised land and the other countries, they may be rich and the people are doing very well, but why did all those people ask us so many questions about Canada? What it was like? How we made out and how we like it, and so on."

That's my wife talking, and I remember my answer, and I told her, "Canada is the best damned country in the world and Calgary is the best damned city in Canada, and I've just spent about five thousand dollars to find that out!"

THE ARTIST AND HIS '53 AUSTIN

I remember George Heti well. He was Hungarian, a small little guy, always smiling, always helpful, a real good guy to have around the office.

After the Hungarian revolution they came to Vancouver as refugees, maybe three or four thousand of them. Firms and companies in the city were asked by the Red Cross to hire them. George was hired by the *Sun*. Their token Hungarian Freedom Fighter, you might say.

He worked in the darkroom, developing prints and working on the colour process, but he really was an artist. The *Sun* job was the only one he could fit into at that time. His English was quite good, and I used to have lunch with him in the cafeteria and one day, about a year or so after he joined the *Sun*, I asked him about this. I said he was far more qualified than for the job he was doing, and he said yes, but he was doing jobs on the side. I asked him what they were and he said he would show me after work. About 3 P.M.

George had bought a car. Why is it that every immigrant's grand passion is to buy a big car as soon as he can? Anyway, George hadn't gone that far, but he had bought a small one. A 1953 Austin. Something like that. They were just starting to fill up the West End with apartment towers then, and George stopped in front of one of them.

We went into the lobby and, my God, there was this fountain which was a masterpiece. I've never seen anything like it since. It was intricately laid with many kinds of stone, but the overall effect was blue, and it was in extremely good taste. It was a masterpiece.

He grinned at me and said, "Nice?" I said, "Yer damn tootin' it is," and I meant it.

I cannot remember how George got this commission. For all I know he might have done it for free, as an example of his work, so he could bring others to it and perhaps earn other commissions. But it was something you'd expect to see in Paris or New York. Certainly not in Vancouver.

That's one story about George. The second happened that same afternoon. As soon as I got in the car and George had navigated about four blocks, I knew I was sitting beside one of the world's worst drivers. He had absolutely no co-ordination. No depth perception. I'm sure he was colour-blind, but of course after looking at that fountain I knew he couldn't be. And he was so delighted with his car. The Heti family's first Canadian possession, I guess. The status symbol.

I should have said no, but after seeing his fountain he offered to drive me home. I lived out in Point Grey, and so it meant going over the Burrard Bridge. George got us to the bridge, and it was hairy. To hell with stop signs. To hell with stoplights. I thought he must have been smoking paprika cigarettes. But on the bridge he did fine because there was no traffic. Oh yeah! There was a big tractor-trailer truck in our lane and George caught up to it and hung right in under it, and we must have been going twenty-five miles an hour.

I said, "George, there's a stoplight at the end of this bridge and this guy might have to stop suddenly." "Okay," he said, "okay."

And the big truck did stop, without much warning, although we couldn't see his signal lights because by now we were hanging right in under the end of his box. I yelled and George slammed on the brakes, and there we were, one-eighth of an inch from smashing the front end of his car all to hell.

I yelled something like, "George, you could have killed us!"

He threw his hands up off the wheel, smiled at me and said, "No matter. Have insurance."

What do you do with a guy like that? No wonder they went out and tried to fight Russian tanks with gasoline bombs, no wonder if they had quiet, smiling and artistic guys like George Heti.

THEY HAD FIRE IN THEIR EYES

Those were the days. We were getting our fair share of immigrants into Calgary in those days, around 1955 or so. A lot of English
and Scots, but the ones you looked for were the Dutch and Germans.
The Dutch had been coming in for a few years and the Germans for
only about two, but both were getting flush, getting good jobs and
moving into houses.

I worked on this lot on Centre. A good location, and the owner did
a lot of advertising in the *Herald* on Friday. That brought them in on
Saturday. You could see them. Spot them, I mean. They all looked
the same. Usually momma and poppa and three kids. It seemed to me
the Dutch had bigger families of kids than the Germans, but no matter. Here they would come. Now listen.

These people had fire in their eyes. They had saved and saved and
saved and they wanted a car. It meant something to them. Nobody in
the history of their family had ever owned a goddamned car. Now they
were making good money, or so they thought. They had a few bucks
in the bank. Maybe five hundred dollars. Who cares? We didn't want
their goddamned money. We wanted to hang paper around their
necks until they tripped on it. Pay one hundred dollars down on this
lovely car, this masterfully designed and beautifully built 1949 Chev,
which was a piece of shit anyway, and you'll only have to pay a little a
month for a few months. Yeah, seventy-five dollars a month until the
sun grows dim.

You could sell them anything. There were actually 1939 Nashes,
and not a bad car by the way, but a lot of prewar stuff going for next to
nothing because GM and Ford were going full blast and had been since
1948. So you hit them hard with a big car. You know, so much down,
so little, and surely, Mr. Dutchie, you can afford seventy-five dollars a
month? Look at the pleasure it will give your family! And so on. You
owe it to yourself. Look how hard you work. Think what your folks in
Amsterdam will think of you when you send them a picture of you
standing beside this beautiful shiny car. And so on, and so on. Blah!
Blah! I hate myself sometimes when I think of it.

Yep! They wanted a car. It gnawed at them. They all wanted it for
different reasons, and I know the big one, the one that they didn't
know about. Not having a car, and you're an immigrant, see. Owning
a big and shiny and nearly new car meant you had arrived. You were
now a Canadian. Nobody was gonna say "DP" to you anymore.

ASSESSMENT OF CANADIANS

There was a cemetery for Canadian soldiers at Bergen op Zoom, and in the spring our family and other neighbours and people from the town, we'd go to this cemetery and put flowers on the graves. My mother looked after maybe a dozen graves, and we'd go there in the fall too, as my mother said, to say good-by to them for the winter.

When I told my parents I wanted to go to the United States and see New York City and live there, she got mad and she said, "You will go to Canada. They are our friends. The Canadians liberated us from the Nazis and they gave a home to Juliana during the war, and you will go to Canada, because there you will find friends. You will go there or you don't go. We won't sign any papers if you don't."

The way it was, the parents didn't have to sign papers, but I went to Canada anyway, and I'm glad I did. This was in 1952. I could speak good English in a Dutch way and I had two years working for a shoemaker, although I found Canadians didn't use shoemakers. They just threw the old shoes away. Just like that.

I had a new suit and cap and a suitcase full of clothes when I got on the train with my ticket to Montreal, and there were a lot of other people on the boat going to Canada, and everybody said they were going to Toronto, but they were all travelling in bunches. Like a family. The government was paying their way and they would pay back later. I've often wondered, did they ever pay it back?

I got to Toronto, and because I spoke English pretty good and wasn't afraid to ask questions, I just asked where there was a hotel, and the woman at the traveller's booth, she said to try the Victoria Hotel. It was just around the corner, on Yonge Street, and I went there and I got a room for a week for six dollars. The first night I talked to a man in the washroom and he said, "Go to the Strathcona Hotel and ask questions there because a lot of men who work on the railroad stay there. They will know about jobs."

I went to the Strathcona Hotel and asked guys who were sitting in the little lobby and they said, sure, the CPR would hire me.

I told them I came from Bergen op Zoom and we had looked after the graves of Canadian soldiers after the war. They said, "Look, kid, we don't know anything about that place and we don't know anything about the war. Just go over to Union Station and ask where you can get a job." And they were right.

It was the springtime and they were making up the gangs to go out through Ontario and fix bridges and repair track.

Everywhere I went it was the same. People in Canada didn't want to talk about the war. One man at the hotel told me Canada really wasn't in the war. They sent a lot of guys overseas and then they came back, but the civilians in Canada, they didn't know there was a war on except for what they read in the *Star,* and everybody had a good time in the war. They don't know about this place in Holland I came from, and he knew and I knew the Canadians liberated Amsterdam, but nobody else knows. He said to forget it.

Looking back over those years, I can see that he was right, but I remember at the time I was very surprised and I guess I was shocked. It was when I got to know Canadians much better that I understood that they weren't a very loyal people. They didn't care very much about their country, and most of them would like to live in the United States and not pay all these high taxes we have.

I am a Canadian now, but sometimes I wonder why I am. Canadians are not a proud people. I think it is because they are all so, well, everyone is so busy making money and trying to be on top of their neighbours and they don't go to church enough, or they don't have a little church of their own in their hearts. They are too greedy, and that makes people very unsatisfactory. Besides, they watch television too much and believe like simple children. They believe too much of what they see.

I could not go back to Holland now, and I don't want to go to the United States, but I wish there was a place in the world like Canada but not filled with people like Canadians, and I would be happy to go there. They have no feeling of being real people, a good nation.

WE ARE THE BEST CANADIANS

My parents brought me to Canada when I was seven. The other children in school, and for some reason I don't know, they picked on my brother and me. They'd call us dumb DPs and dirty names, and I think today it was because this was just after the war and they got confused between "Dutch" for us and "Deutsch" which is German but has kind of the same pronunciation.

That was when I decided . . . No, when I had children I thought, they are Canadian because they were born in this country and their father is Canadian, but there is their Dutch heritage. They should have part of that. Be a Canadian but be proud of your Dutch part of you.

We speak the Dutch language at home when we are alone, and we do that because it gives them another language besides the French they take in school. Dutch also gives you the basics in high and low German, and the more languages you have, then that is good.

I teach them Dutch history and literature and love of fine things and Dutch cooking, but when they walk out the door to school they are little Canadians, so they have both worlds, and that is good.

I teach them thriftiness. That doesn't mean I want them to be cheap. No, no, no. Thriftiness is a very good thing. It will make them better Canadians and better people. I can't remember what it was like when I was growing up, but I can't believe today how much Canadians waste, throw away. Oh, I've used this dress three times. I'll give it to the Goodwill. Oh, dear me, we've had this old car for three years and I'm tired of riding in it, so let's buy a new one. So they spend another $7,000 and they haven't got it. And around here the high school students take a lunch to school and throw it in the wastepaper basket and buy a Pepsi and potato chips.

You can say that it is true that I never really knew anything about Holland because it was the war and I was a little girl, but there is something inside me. I think it is Dutch, and it tells me things shouldn't be wasted. That's true, you know.

I teach them to love their country. I tell them Canada is the most wonderful country in the world. I think children should salute the flag and sing "O Canada" every morning in school. Sing it loud. Sing it with a free heart. Sing it as if you are saying, this is the flag of the most wonderful country in the world. I teach my children this, and I can do it by telling them to look around this city and then watch the television and see the misery and poor in the world.

You know what one boy of ten or eleven told me? I asked him about this when I was fixing up a cut he'd got playing on our swing, and I am always talking about this. He said, "Kids are supposed to have fun in school and not spend their time learning things they don't have to. What weirdo's gonna listen if you're going around singing "O Canada" all the time?"

What I'm trying to say is this. I see a lot of people and I talk to them. Maybe I'll make a lot of people pretty mad, but I think the best Canadians you have today are the ones who weren't born in this country. They came over. They didn't speak much English, maybe none. They worked so hard. Oh, so hard, on little farms, at poor pay in a factory, but now they are happy and they have money and good homes, and they know that this is what they did. It was in Canada, and they couldn't do it any other place. Not even in the States. Just right here in Canada.

People like me, like others, we may have had funny names to you people, but we are the best Canadians this country has.

JUDGE WILSON WISHED US WELL

The day we became Canadians it was sunny and warm and my wife and I dressed up in our finery and we went to the courthouse and into the big courtroom and there were all the people there— Polish, Russians, Portuguese, Dutch, Norwegians, Chinese and a lot of others, and it was all very solemn in that big courtroom.

When the judge came in we all stood up and came to the front. The judge was named Mr. Wilson and he was an important judge, and we went through the ceremony, taking the oath and swearing to be good Canadians, and everybody answering that they would be, and then the judge talked to us. Not like a judge but like a friend, and he told us about Canada and what it meant to him and what he hoped it would mean to us, all of us from different countries. He was a very kindly and great man, and he spoke to us beautifully and with great feeling, and then it was over and we were Canadians. He shook our hands and wished us well, and I remember a Portuguese woman was crying and she kissed his hand. That made me choke up with tears too.

Then everybody was talking and laughing and I felt so good. I had never felt like that before. There would never be a day like it.

When it was all over the people who were our sponsors, the Kryschuks, who were our neighbours, they took us across the street to the Cavalier Grill in the Georgia Hotel and we had a huge lunch and we laughed and talked, and it was the most wonderful day of our lives.

ON THAT NOVEMBER DAY I WILL BE THERE

I love this country. I just love it. This has always been my home as far as I am concerned. My kids are born here. I am a Canadian, not just a fellow who came out from Holland and became a Canadian.

I remember how it was during the war. I know what happened to the Dutch people at the hands of the Germans. I was there in Amsterdam that morning in 1945 when the Canadian regiments marched into the The Dam and there was the big ceremony and at last we were free.

I am not a member of the Canadian Legion as a veteran. I was too young to fight for the Dutch army, and when I would say to my father after the war that I wished I could have fought, he said to me, "You are lucky you were too young. You would not be talking like that now."

So, on Remembrance Day, every November eleventh, no matter where I am, what I am doing, I go down to the Cenotaph for the memorial service. I do it for the hundreds and hundreds of Canadian boys who died freeing Holland and for the way they were so good to us, helping us whenever they could. I stand there with the people and I think of those days, and I say thank God for the Canadians, thank God for this country, thank God for deciding that I would come to Canada.

I have done well in this country. I have never been on unemployment insurance and I have never been without a job, never in my life, and, on that November day—and I don't care how many Canadians don't show up—I will be there.